PRAISE FOR *THE LAYPERSON'S LIBRARY*

"There are so many books about the Bible and theology out there, how is a person supposed to figure out what to include in their personal library? Buying and reading a book involves time and money so you don't want to make a bad decision. That is what makes Robert Yost's *Layperson's Library* so helpful. I find it amazing that Yost not only evaluates commentaries, but so many other resources that are helpful to Bible readers. I recommend this guide to everyone who wants to build a library to assist them in understanding of the faith."

—Tremper Longman III, Distinguished Scholar and Professor Emeritus of Biblical Studies, Westmont College

"*The Layperson's Library* is a friendly guided tour around a wise Christian teacher's study, as he picks volumes off the shelf and explains why they are useful. It introduces key books needed for personal development and ministry, and it offers the serendipity of encountering the unexpected gem. Robert Yost's knowledge, humor, and love of reading shine through, and make this book the ideal companion for the pilgrim who wants to read and grow."

—John W. Taylor, Professor of New Testament, Gateway Seminary

"This book is so much more than a collection of reference material. It is a treasure trove of wisdom that will be a game changer for students of the Bible. *The Layperson's Library* should be a fundamental addition to the library of every church, pastor, teacher, or Bible student."

—George Gasperson, Lead Pastor, Christ Community Church, Winter Haven, Florida

"Robert Yost's excellent resource, *The Layperson's Library*, is an outstanding follow-up to his earlier similar volume for pastors. As a personal compiler of bibliographies on Bible and theology for many years, I can highly recommend both of these works to students of Scripture. Yost very successfully accomplishes his stated purpose in this latest volume of assisting 'laypersons in making wise choices in purchasing books for the study of the Bible.' Every serious student of the Bible should own this book."

—ROBERT B. SHELLEY, SEARCH MINISTRIES OF CENTRAL PA; ADJUNCT PROFESSOR, LANCASTER BIBLE COLLEGE & SEMINARY

"Robert Yost has put together a well-organized collection of biblical and theological resources for the layperson. The collection provides an excellent survey and guide to help navigate the complex landscape of the literature available. This is an essential book for someone just beginning or looking to expand their own library and resources."

—RYAN A. BRANDT, ASSOCIATE PROFESSOR OF CHRISTIAN HISTORY AND THEOLOGY, GRAND CANYON THEOLOGICAL SEMINARY AND GRAND CANYON UNIVERSITY, AND MANAGING EDITOR, *JOURNAL OF BIBLICAL AND THEOLOGICAL STUDIES*

"Time and money are limited, but it would appear that the production of books is not. With so many Bible resources and commentaries on the market, where should a layperson begin to get quality information? I can think of no better starting point than Robert Yost's welcome and timely volume."

—MATTHEW AKERS, ASSOCIATE DEAN OF GRADUATE PROGRAMS, MID-AMERICAN BAPTIST THEOLOGICAL SEMINARY

"Dr. Robert Yost, or 'Dr. Bob' as he is affectionately known in the congregation I pastor, is generous in offering his gifts of teaching and study to the service of the local church. Teaching Bible studies to laypeople in multiple denominations has given him a unique understanding of the Bible study needs of the laity. I commend this work to laity seeking to go deeper in their study of Scripture and theology, as well as pastors seeking for their congregations to go deeper in their own personal study. Thank you for offering this labor of love for the edification of all believers in the body of Christ."

—DAVID T. AVERILL, SENIOR PASTOR, ST. JOHN'S UNITED METHODIST CHURCH, WINTER HAVEN, FLORIDA

"'Of making many books there is no end,' said the preacher (Eccl 12:12). But for finding the right book, *The Layperson's Library* is a great place to start. Dr. Yost has given the serious Bible student a valuable tool for finding the best resources available. Highly recommended!

—BRUCE SINCLAIR, LECTURER IN BIBLICAL STUDIES, AFRICA REFORMATION THEOLOGICAL SEMINARY, KAMPALA, UGANDA

"If you are looking for just the right source to help you in your theological studies or for help in preparing a Sunday school lesson, you will be well-served to consult Dr. Robert Yost's new book, *The Layperson's Library*. I strongly recommend his judgments and annotations on every book. This book is immensely helpful to interested laymen as well as clergy."

—SHARON WILLIAMSON, RETIRED HIGH SCHOOL ENGLISH TEACHER; ADJUNCT FACULTY, CHARLOTTE CHRISTIAN COLLEGE

"It is an honor to endorse Dr. Yost's book, *The Layperson's Library*, for it will prove to be a valuable asset to the English-speaking church as a handy reference for Bible study. Having served as a colleague in ministry and academics with Dr. Yost for many years, I am glad that this book will share his wealth of wisdom into biblical resources with the entire Christian community. It should become the first book pulled from the shelf to aid every worker 'to handle accurately the word of truth' (2 Tim 2:15)."

—Stephen Stout, Adjunct Professor of Biblical Studies, Charlotte Christian College and Theological Seminary

"If you're looking for that trustworthy and reader-friendly Bible study resource, check out Yost's wide-ranging recommendations. You'll find both newer and older books to guide your desire to know God more and live in light of his word. Not only information about commentaries, Bible handbooks, and works on many Christian doctrines, but also suggestions on prayer, daily devotions, biographies, and Christian fiction. Search through titles representing a wide variety of interests and needs."

—Klaus Issler, Emeritus Professor of Educational Studies & Theology, Talbot School of Theology, Biola University

The Layperson's Library

The Layperson's Library

ESSENTIAL BIBLE STUDY TOOLS
FOR THE MAN AND WOMAN IN THE PEW

Robert A. Yost

foreword by Jeff Winter

WIPF & STOCK · Eugene, Oregon

THE LAYPERSON'S LIBRARY
Essential Bible Study Tools for the Man and Woman in the Pew

Copyright © 2021 Robert A. Yost. All rights reserved. Except for brief quotations in critical publications or reviews, no part of this book may be reproduced in any manner without prior written permission from the publisher. Write: Permissions, Wipf and Stock Publishers, 199 W. 8th Ave., Suite 3, Eugene, OR 97401.

Wipf & Stock
An Imprint of Wipf and Stock Publishers
199 W. 8th Ave., Suite 3
Eugene, OR 97401

www.wipfandstock.com

PAPERBACK ISBN: 978-1-7252-8126-4
HARDCOVER ISBN: 978-1-7252-8127-1
EBOOK ISBN: 978-1-7252-8128-8

12/29/20

To my three wonderful sons, Micah Samuel Yost,
Matthew Joseph Yost, and Nathan Andrew Yost,
who are themselves laymen who are involved in their
respective local churches. My prayer is that they would
fall in love with the study of Scripture and that this book
would be a guide towards that end and that they would
familiarize themselves with many of the books I describe. . .
and actually read some of them.

Contents

Foreword by Jeff Winter — xiii
Preface — xv
Acknowledgments — xvii
Abbreviations — xix
List of Contributors — xxi

1. Introduction — 1
2. General Reference Works — 10
3. Commentaries — 45
4. Devotional Literature — 149
5. Theological Topics and Church History — 235

Bibliography — 285
Author Index — 287

Foreword

You probably don't think it's a big deal that you can turn over, burp, or feed yourself. But it's a big deal when your child or grandchild does those things for the very first time. I remember when our oldest child was feeding himself Cheerios. He had been studying his hand for months, flexing those little fingers, eventually grabbing available targets like noses and glasses. But now, he's sitting in his highchair with Cheerios on a tray. He's reaching for one of those O's by wrapping his fingers around it, then putting it in his mouth all by himself. He smiles delighting in what he just accomplished. Mom and Dad were so proud of him.

I think all grownups know that it's a big accomplishment to be able to finally feed yourself. My wife and I knew that this was the beginning of lots of times our son will do that in his life. He moved from needing someone else to feed him to being able to feed himself. Interesting enough, God desires all His children to be able to feed themselves.

As a pastor for almost forty years I have found that many Christians depend too much on getting fed intellectually and spiritually by someone else. Many believers live only on the nourishment given to them by their pastor, small group leader, or someone they listen to on Christian radio or TV. The Lord's goal for His children is for them to mature and grow up in their faith. Sadly, many Christians grow older but never grow up. They remain stuck in spiritual infancy. That is why *The Layperson's Library* is such a profitable and useful book. Using this detailed bibliography will help a Christian grow up in their faith.

So often I've had members of my congregation ask me questions like, "Pastor, can you recommend a book on angels, Islam, or how can I interpret the Bible for myself? They may ask what is a good devotional book, Bible atlas, or commentary on the Book of Revelation? If they have *The Layperson's Library*, a member doesn't have to ask me any questions. Within minutes they can find several books that will help them in their research of a particular topic. They will discover biblical and thoughtful books written by such persons as John Bunyan, R.C. Sproul, John Piper, John Calvin, Josh McDowell, Donald Grey Barnhouse, Charles Colson, N.T. Wright, C.S. Lewis, J.I. Packer, Norman Geisler, Lee Strobel and many others. They will encounter pertinent topics such as Apologetics, the Atonement, Baptism, Christian Biographies, Arminianism and Calvinism, Church History, Cults and other Religions, Devotions, End Times, Grace, Genesis—Revelation, Holy Spirit, Prophecy, Theology and the Sovereignty of God. Each book listed in *The Layperson's Library* will include a brief description of its content.

The author of *The Layperson's Library*, Dr Robert Yost, is a faithful member of the church I serve in Haines City, FL. He teaches one of our adult Bible classes. A graduate of the University of Maryland (B.S., M.A.), Capital Bible Seminary (Th.M.), Trinity Theological Seminary (Ph.D.) and Carolina Graduate School of Divinity (D. Min.). He is an Emeritus Vice President of Academic Affairs at Charlotte Christian College and Theological Seminary where he is presently a Research Professor. Dr. Yost is a biblical scholar who has a passion to help the members of the church I serve and Christians everywhere learn how to feed themselves.

Spiritual growth is not automatic. A Christ-follower must decide to grow, make an effort to grow, and persist in growing. This book will greatly help the growth process of all Christians who desire to go deeper and wider in their faith.

Dr. Jeffrey Winter
Senior Pastor
First Presbyterian Church, Haines City, FL

Preface

This book is an annotated bibliography of Bible study resources. My intended audience is laypersons, who make up the vast majority of the people who inhabit our churches. My inspiration was the book, *The Minister's Library*, by Cyril Barber, which was first published in 1974 and was a great help to multitudes of pastors and seminary students a generation ago. In 2017 I published a work in a similar vein, *The Pastor's Library: An Annotated Bibliography of Biblical and Theological Resources for Ministry*. Although I knew that countless laypersons were involved in personal Bible study, it never occurred to me that they could benefit from a similar resource that would not be so specialized. Some in my Sunday school class at First Presbyterian Church in Haines City, FL helped me see the light. Hence this book.

The annotations in this work cover four broad areas: General Reference Works, Commentaries, Devotional Works, and Theological Topics and Church History. Many of the annotations have been written by folks who are more knowledgeable than I am in certain fields. Some of the contributors are themselves laypersons who know what they want and need better than I do.

A final note: the evaluations contained herein reflect opinions that are highly subjective and are not meant to be the final word on the subject. They simply express one person's opinion. This book is meant to be a resource to guide the thoughtful student in the right direction.

Acknowledgments

It is unlikely that anyone ever writes a book in isolation from other people. I certainly did not. There are a host of people who deserve my heartfelt gratitude for their assistance to me during the process of writing this book.

First and foremost, to my wonderful wife, Tessie, who endured numerous lonely evenings and late dinners over the past two years while I toiled away on this project. Many times, she would come in and ask me to stand up and stretch my legs lest I develop blood clots, which have threatened my health several times in the past. She is my dream girl, my best friend, and I could accomplish nothing without her support.

To my three friends and colleagues at Charlotte Christian College and Theological Seminary: Garry Baldwin, Bill Fleming, and Ted Wright. Your expertise in the many areas in which I am largely ignorant was necessary and so much appreciated. Thank you for your thoughtful annotations and input into this project.

Two of my dear friends from my adult Sunday School class at First Presbyterian Church in Haines City, FL, Dennis LeRoy and Linda Van-Hook, were not only gracious contributors to this book, but also readers and editors. Oftentimes, they helped me to word something a bit better or with a less harsh tone. They also saw many of my errors that were made in the earlier drafts. Denny and Linda, I love and appreciate you both.

My dear cousin from Dallas, TX, Pam Buckroyd, was an extremely helpful editor. Her returned chapters were covered in red. I often wondered how I could have written something so full of mistakes. She saw things that I did not see even after repeated readings. Pam, this book is so much better for your contribution.

My dear friend, colleague, and mentor, Sharon Williamson, read parts of the manuscript and offered helpful suggestions. She was for many years a high school English teacher and college professor who saw many errors that I did not. Sharon, for your long friendship and assistance, I give my humble thanks.

Finally, to my good friend and former neighbor, Dan Moore, who provided computer assistance on more than one occasion. When I lost Chapter 5, I was in panic mode. It appeared that months of hard work was down the drain. Thank you for showing a near computer illiterate how to recover lost files. Were it not for you, I would torn my last remaining threads of hair out in frustration. You are much appreciated.

Abbreviations

BIBLE VERSIONS

ASV	American Standard Version
AV	Authorized Version
ESV	English Standard Version
KJV	King James Version
LXX	Septuagint
NT	New Testament
NASB	New American Stand Bible
NIV	New International Version
OT	Old Testament
RSV	Revised Standard Version
TEV	Today's English Version

COMMENTARY SERIES

AOTC	Apollos Old Testament Commentary
BNTC	Black's New Testament Commentaries
BST	The Bible Speaks Today
BTCB	Brazos Theological Commentary on the Bible

CBC	Cambridge Bible Commentary on the NEB
CBSC	Cambridge Bible for Schools and Colleges
CC	The Communicator's Commentary
EBC	The Expositor's Bible Commentary
IVPNTC	IVP New Testament Commentary
NAC	New American Commentary
NIBC	New International Bible Commentary
NICNT	New International Commentary on the New Testament
NICOT	New International Commentary on the Old Testament
NIGTC	New International Greek Testament Commentary
NIVAC	New International Version Application Commentary
OTS	Opening the Scriptures
Paideia	Paideia
PNTC	Pillar New Testament Commentary
TNTC	Tyndale New Testament Commentaries
TOTC	Tyndale Old Testament Commentaries

MISCELLANEOUS

ECPA	Evangelical Christian Publishers Association
ETS	Evangelical Theological Society
OP	Out of print

List of Contributors

David W. Baker: Professor of Old Testament, Ashland Theological Seminary
    Doctor of Philosophy, University of London

Garry Baldwin: Pastor, Midwood Baptist Church, Charlotte, NC; Faculty, Charlotte Christian College and Theological Seminary
    Doctor of Ministry, Carolina Graduate School of Divinity

William Brafford: Retired Assistant U.S. Attorney for Western North Carolina
    B.S., University of North Carolina; J.D., University of North Carolina

Bill Fleming: Head of Department of Pastoral Studies, Charlotte Christian College and Theological Seminary
    Doctor of Ministry, Gordon-Conwell Theological Seminary

Daniel Juster: Director of *Tikkun America*
    Doctor of Theology, New Covenant International Seminary

Dennis LeRoy: Retired U.S. Navy Reserve Commander
    B.S., U.S. Naval Academy; M.A., Naval Postgraduate School

Linda VanHook: Retired Registered Nurse
    B.S. in Nursing, University of North Carolina at Charlotte; M.A. in Theological Studies, Reformed Theological Seminary in Orlando

Stephen Waterhouse: Senior Pastor, Westcliff Bible Church, Amarillo, TX
    Doctor of Ministry, Dallas Theological Seminary

Barbara Woodruff: Retired Professor of Criminology and Sociology, Penn State University
    Ph.D. in Sociology, Penn State University

Ted Wright: Faculty, Charlotte Christian College and Theological Seminary
    Founder and Executive Director, Epic Archaeology
    Master of Arts, Southern Evangelical Seminary

1

Introduction

When George Orwell's *1984* was published in 1949, he envisioned a world in which people were going to burn books. Likewise, American writer, Ray Bradbury, in his novel, *Fahrenheit 451*, describes a futuristic society in which books are outlawed and "firemen" burn those that are found. Aldous Huxley in his *Brave New World* envisioned a world in which there was no need to ban books because people would not want to read them anyway. More than anything, Christ-followers are people of the Book, the Bible, and ought to be readers not only of the Holy Scriptures, but also sacred works. This book is about books that would be of assistance to Christians who love to study the Bible. Because I am a bibliophile (a lover of books), writing this book is a natural progression for me.

When *The Pastor's Library: An Annotated Bibliography of Biblical and Theological Resources for Ministry* finally made it into print after four long years of research and writing in 2017, I took a deep breath, sat back, and anticipated a well-deserved rest. However, some well-meaning folks in both my adult Sunday School class at First Presbyterian Church in Haines City, FL and my Monday adult Bible study class at St. John's United Methodist Church in Winter Haven, FL had other plans for me. One of the students in my Sunday School class first broached the subject by asking me why I hadn't written a similar work for a lay audience. I asked myself why, indeed, that idea had never entered my mind. I immediately jumped into the project. Since that initial seed thought germinated about two years ago, I have been pursuing this project with great enthusiasm.

Students and friends from all over the Northern hemisphere have been asking me about its status and ensuring that there is a great interest in Bible study tools among laypersons. Hence, the title of this work: *The Layperson's Library: Essential Bible Study Tools for the Man and Woman in the Pew*. It is written in the style and format of *The Pastor's Library*, but with a lay audience in mind.

The main purpose of this book is to assist Christians, primarily laypersons, in making wise choices in purchasing books for the study of the Bible. The basic underlying assumption is that there are a great many in the church who are interested in the serious study of God's Word. This book, then, is geared both towards those laypersons who simply want to know more about the Bible and those who are inclined toward more serious study. It would also be useful to pastors, particularly those without seminary training, and students, particularly those who are undergraduates.

The reader will also notice that I have included sections on Christian Biography and Memoir and Christian Fiction. These were later additions to this work.

USE OF THIS GUIDE

A few preliminary comments are in order that this bibliography may be utilized judiciously. All works selected for inclusion include a bibliographic entry. It may be brief or it may be more detailed. But every book has at least something about it mentioned. The reader will also notice a code to the left of many of the authors' names. A coding system provides guidelines as to the most important works in a particular field. These codes appear in bold face to the left of the author's name in each bibliographic reference. They are as follows:

- * Recommended. My personal recommendation. You can't go wrong with this book.
- + A recognized classic in the field.
- ! A work for the more advanced or motivated student.

It will be noticed that some annotations include quotations followed by the author's last name in parentheses. An attempt has been made to incorporate the comments of some of the leading writers who have previously evaluated those books under consideration. In many instances, these authors echo my evaluation of a particular work. In other cases, their evaluations are supplemental or they may disagree with mine. These evaluations are from some of the books in the Bibliography by authors such as Spurgeon, Rosscup, Barber, Longman, Evans, or Carson. They receive attribution by having their names in parentheses after the quotation along with the page number where the quotation can be found.[1] In any event, all evaluations are subjective and simply reflect a particular writer's opinion

With respect to commentaries, every effort has been made to identify the eschatological perspective of the author at the end of the annotation with respect to books that deal with prophetic themes (e.g., Revelation, Matthew, Ezekiel, Isaiah, etc.). These are so designated as Premillennial, Amillennial, Postmillennial and the like. Dispensational writers are also so designated if at all possible. If a work is written from a certain theological perspective, that is also so designated whenever possible (e.g. Reformed, Arminian).

I have also enlisted the assistance of friends who are themselves laypersons as well as colleagues from my institution and other institutions of higher learning who are specialists in a particular field. Obviously, no one is qualified to evaluate resources in every field covered in this guide. These annotations were often solicited of friends and colleagues when a book under consideration for inclusion was out of my specialty area or when I wanted to enhance the quality of this work. Their contributions appear in quotation marks and their names appear in **bold face** in parentheses after each quotation (e.g., **Fleming, Baldwin, Wright, Stout, Mounce** and the like). Their names as well as a brief biographical sketch with the credentials of each can be found on the page titled List of Contributors. I would like to thank such persons for their contributions to this work. It could not have been completed without their generous assistance. Someone once told me that I was like Tom Sawyer enlisting help to whitewash the fence. They did all the work and I claim authorship.

A WORD ABOUT THE TITLE

First of all, I must admit that I do not like the words "layperson," "layman," "laity," and the like. Plus, I am not entirely happy with the title

---

1. An exception to this rule would be if the quotation comes from one of Cyril Barber's three supplemental works.

of this book. Indeed, my wife told me that she wasn't too keen about it. The word "laity" comes from the Greek word, *laos,* meaning "people." The term "lay people" is found twice in 2 Chronicles 35 where they are distinct from the Levites, the clergy of the Old Testament. Historically, the terms were used of those who were not ordained to the Gospel ministry (in other words, clergy). These words have particular significance in the Roman Catholic and Eastern Orthodox Churches. "The duty of the laity is to be taught, to obey, and to make financial contribution" in those churches, according to Geoffrey Bromiley (*Evangelical Dictionary of Theology,* 617). Protestant churches have found these terms to be convenient, albeit misguided, to distinguish between those ordained to the Gospel ministry and those who have not been. I even have a book in my library titled *A Layman's Guide to Christian Terms* by Ellen C. Shannon.

The New Testament makes it very clear that there is no distinction between ministers and laypersons. We are all ministers. We are all priests. This has often been called "the priesthood of believers." Thus, the Apostle Peter describes Christ-followers as "a holy priesthood offering spiritual sacrifices to God through Jesus Christ" (1 Pet. 2:5; NIV). The Apostle Paul exhorts believers "in view of God's mercy, to offer your bodies as living sacrifices, holy and pleasing to God—this is your spiritual act of worship" (Rom. 12:1; NIV). Therefore, if we want to be technical and accurate, the term "layperson" is not a very good one because it reflects a distinction that in the New Testament does not exist. Which means that my title is not a very good one. But for practical purposes, I needed to make a distinction between pastors and biblical scholars in a general sense and those who are not. Hence, *The Layperson's Library.* Of course, there are many pastors who are not biblical scholars, sad to say, and there are many laypersons who are. The bottom line is, no matter whether the term is technically accurate or not, in the twenty-first century, there should be no lack of understanding when the term "layperson" is used in conversation or print.

Secondly, although the subtitle of this work is *Essential Bible Study Tools for the Man and Woman in the Pew,* it could be effectively argued that many of the titles included are not "essential" for Bible study. For example, is it feasible that the average reader of this book will need all twelve of the multi-volume commentary sets on the entire Bible or is it possible that he/she could actually read through them even with a life span of 969 years such as that of Methuselah? Or does the average reader actually require seven individual commentaries on the book of Exodus or another seven on the Ten Commandments? I think not. Not to mention the eight commentaries on the two books of Samuel. So, in a sense, the subtitle is misleading in that all of these books are not "essential" to Bible study.

What I have attempted to accomplish in this book is to provide the reader with suggested titles for building a good library as a foundation for study of the Bible. Few would purchase every title recommended, but some might be tempted. This book is intended to serve as a guide for the acquisition of good Christian books. So please do not allow the title or its subtitle to mislead you into thinking that you need to acquire every book listed. Use this book judiciously and prayerfully.

A WORD ABOUT CLASSICS AND OUT-OF-PRINT WORKS

A classic is a work that has stood the test of time. Its ideas have been judged against the great body of collective Christian thought over the centuries and it is widely regarded as timeless and universal. It was Mark Twain who said that a classic is a book which people praise, but don't read. It is a sad reality that many today fail to mine the vast repository of the past. They read the current books, but not the timeless ones.

This book contains many classic works because I hold them in such high esteem. A book like this would be incomplete without including works such as *The Pilgrim's Progress*, *The Imitation of Christ* or Alexander Whyte's *Bible Characters*. Of course, there are modern classics such as Dallas Willard's *The Divine Conspiracy* (1997) or Roland Bainton's *Here I Stand: A Life of Martin Luther* (1950).

Many of the books listed in this guide are now sadly out of print. My decision to include this work or that was not predicated on their availability today. It is an unfortunate truth that many excellent books are no longer being published today. That is not to say that some publisher won't pick up the title and thankfully reprint it, but meanwhile you may need to do a little digging to find some books. Speaking as one who has haunted used bookstores over the past half century, I can say confidently that much of the joy in locating used books is in the search. Don't forget to check in your church library. Thankfully, in recent years it has become much easier to locate used books online. Some helpful online booksellers are:

Abebooks.com

Alibris.com

Amazon.com

Biblio.com

Bookfinder.com

eBay.com

fetchbookinfo.com

Also, keep in mind that many older titles can be found in digital form for free.

There are also numerous secondhand bookstores scattered across the United States. A listing of Christian bookstores can easily be found by Googling "Cramer's Corner Bookstore." Dr. Cramer keeps a list of such bookstores current. Some other reliable used bookstores are:

Archives Books

John Wipf

(626) 797-4756

archivesbooks.com

Kregel Used Books

525 Eastern Avenue Northeast

Grand Rapids, MI 49503

(616) 459-9444

www.kregel.com

Noah's Ark Book Attic

31 S. Trade St.

Tryon, NC 28782

(828) 859-5141

https://www.noahsarkbookattic.com

Zondervan

3900 Sparks Dr. SE

Grand Rapids, MI 49546

(800) 226-1122

www.harpercollinschristian.com/zondervan/

Baker

6030 East Fulton Road

Ada, MI 49301

(800) 877-2665

www.bakerbookhouse.com

Bright Light Books

161 East State Rd. 436

Fern Park, FL 32730

(407) 622-6657

www.brightlightbooks.com

FOR FURTHER STUDY

For more advanced students or those who want to take their Bible study to the next level, the following books will provide invaluable information beyond the scope of this one.

For those who love old commentaries, particularly those of the Puritans, one should not overlook Charles H. Spurgeon's *Commenting & Commentaries,* which was originally published in 1876 and lacks the product of over 140 years of research. Spurgeon was an Elizabethan Baptist pastor in London who has been considered arguably the greatest preacher the English language has ever produced. Anything he wrote is worth consulting.

I am particularly partial to my own 2017 book, *The Pastor's Library: An Annotated Bibliography of Biblical and Theological Resources for Ministry.* I wrote it primarily with pastors and seminary students in mind who need a reliable guide to building a ministerial library for the pastorate, the mission field, or teaching in a Christian college. However, my inspiration was Cyril J. Barber's *The Minister's Library* published in 1974. Three supplements were published in 1976, 1978, and 1980. Although nothing published in the past forty years is included in Barber's book or his supplements, his work is still extremely valuable and much more comprehensive than my book. It is worth consulting.

For those interested primarily in commentaries, three books are noteworthy. The first is James Rosscup's *Commentaries for Biblical Expositors*. First published in 1966, it was revised in 1983, 1993, and 2004. The comments on each book are often detailed and quite helpful. *Old Testament Commentary Survey* by Tremper Longman III, originally published in 1991 is now in its fifth and final edition which came out in 2013. There are no more revisions planned according to the author who is now happily retired. In the same vein as Longman's book is D. A. Carson's *New Testament Survey* now in its seventh edition. Begun in 1986, the last edition came out in 2013. Both Longman and Carson's books are extremely helpful particularly for those looking for individual commentaries on a particular book of the Bible. They also happen to be two of the top evangelical scholars in the world in their respective fields.

Two fine books which are a bit more comprehensive in scope than those of Longman and Carson are David R. Bauer's *Essential Bible Study Tools for Ministry* (2014) and John F. Evans' *A Guide to Biblical Commentaries and Reference Works* (10th edition, 2016). Bauer's book is extremely well-done and includes such helpful topics as history of the Bible and English Bible, biblical history and geography, biblical archaeology, concordances, Bible dictionaries, and biblical ethics to mention just a few. Evans' book is a massive work, though perhaps not as broad in scope as that of Bauer, but it is more conservative and evangelical, which counts a lot in my estimation. Evans' work on commentaries is staggering. He obviously knows the field very well. It is in its 10th edition and he is, at this time, planning an 11th edition. No work on commentaries is nearly as complete as this.

Other books worth consulting are Mark Lau Branson's *The Reader's Guide to the Best Evangelical Books* (1982), Frederick W. Danker's *Multipurpose Tools for Bible Study* (revised and expanded, 1993), John Glynn's *Commentary & Reference Survey: A Comprehensive Guide to Biblical and Theological Resources* (10th edition, 2007), and David M. Scholer's *A Basic Bibliographic Guide for New Testament Exegesis* (1973).

For those undertaking the exciting venture of studying the Bible, there is a cornucopia of resources available. The student can go as far as his or her energy, time, and resources allow. The opportunities are almost limitless. It is my hope that this book will assist you in your journey.

2

General Reference Works

BIBLE ARCHAEOLOGY

The science of archaeology has made important contributions to the study of the Bible. It is difficult to conceive making sense of much of the biblical story before the advent of archaeology. Biblical archaeology seeks to unravel the past by digging up the material remains and has tended to corroborate the biblical materials. It has been rightly said that with each shovelful of dirt that the archaeologist uncovers in the Holy Land, another critic is silenced. You might believe that Bible archaeology is as dry as dust, but it provides us with another tool to help understand the Scriptures. The following books are helpful. Some may be a bit dated and not abreast of the latest archaeological discoveries, but they should provide a fascinating and informative read nonetheless.

*Bruce, F. F. *Abraham and David: Places They Knew.* Nashville: Thomas Nelson, 1984.

> A beautifully photographed and illustrated guide to the places with which Abraham and David were familiar by perhaps the foremost evangelical New Testament scholar of the twentieth century. This book draws upon information from the Bible, early church histories, and archaeological findings to trace Abraham's journey from Ur to where he was entombed at the

cave of Machpelah. In like fashion, Bruce also follows David's rise from his birth in Bethlehem through his exile in the wilderness of Judah to his becoming king over all Israel.

*Holden, Joseph M., and Norman Geisler. *The Popular Handbook of Archaeology and the Bible: Discoveries that Confirm the Reliability of Scripture.* Eugene: Harvest House, 2013.

A fascinating book by two Christian apologists that examines some of the latest archaeological finds and their significance in confirming the reliability of Scripture.

!+*Kenyon, Kathleen M. *Archaeology in the Holy Land.* Fifth edition. Nashville: Thomas Nelson, 1985.

A classic, written by one of the foremost archaeologists of her generation. It is a fascinating resource that draws heavily upon the author's 1961–67 excavations of Jerusalem, which are important in understanding the fall of the Israelite kingdoms. This revision, completed just prior to Kenyon's death in 1978, outlines her discoveries at different sites and her interpretation of the data. At over forty years of age, this book is now somewhat dated, but Kenyon's work was stellar and brilliant. Well worth reading for the truly motivated!

*Negev, Avraham, and Shimon Gibson, eds. *Archaeological Encyclopedia of the Holy Land.* Revised and updated edition. New York: Continuum, 2001.

A priceless resource!

*Price, Randall. *The Stones Cry Out: What Archaeology Reveals About the Truth of the Bible.* Eugene: Harvest House, 1997.

Examines archaeological discoveries in the Holy Land and how they confirm the message of the Bible.

*Price, Randall, and H. Wayne House. *Zondervan Handbook of Biblical Archaeology.* Grand Rapids: Zondervan, 2017.

> An indispensable resource for laypersons, pastors, students, and Sunday School teachers.

Thompson, J. A. *The Bible and Archaeology.* Grand Rapids: Eerdmans, 1972.

> An older standard work on the subject.

Unger, Merrill F. *Archaeology and the New Testament.* Grand Rapids: Zondervan, 1962.

> Covers the range of New Testament archaeology, but at almost sixty years of age is rather dated.

———. *Archaeology and the Old Testament.* Grand Rapids: Zondervan, 1954.

> A companion volume to the author's *Archaeology and the New Testament.* Even more dated than the author's New Testament volume. "Informative, fascinating, and perhaps the best book written on the subject" (Barber, 90).

BIBLE ATLASES

The Bible atlas is a helpful tool that in a sense is a more specialized extension of the Bible dictionary. It focuses on Bible history and geography. Often in Bible study, it is useful to see the relationship between cities, rivers, seas, mountains, and the like. A good atlas can also assist the Bible student to understand how the geography of an area can change over hundreds or thousands of years. For example, The Jerusalem of Jesus' time is much different than the Jerusalem of today. Palestine has also changed in many ways. Cities are no longer there. New cities have been built. Territories have changed, for example, since the time of Joshua and his distribution of the land to the twelve tribes. But a good atlas is much more than just a collection of maps. The historical material is invaluable too.

There are at least five reasons why you need a Bible atlas if you want to study the Bible. (1) It enables you to visualize where biblical events took place. (2) It reminds you that the events actually occurred in real times and places and weren't just fairy tales or stories. (3) It reminds you that the stories of the Bible occurred before there was a Europe or United States and that the events are not rooted in Western culture. (4) It reminds you that the geography of the biblical events influences how you interpret each passage of Scripture. (5) It assists you in understanding the Bible's overarching story, its timeline. Otherwise, the Bible may appear to be simply a random collection of nice little stories which have no overall connection or theme. For many Christians, the stories and events of the Bible are like a large jigsaw puzzle whose pieces have no discernible relationship to one another. A good atlas can allow you to see the big picture.

*Aharoni, Yohanan, Michael Avi-Yonah, Anson F. Rainey, Ze'ev Safrai, and R. Steven Notley. *The Carta Bible Atlas*. 5th ed. Jerusalem: Carta Jerusalem, 2011.

> An Israeli Jewish work that was previously titled *The Macmillan Bible Atlas*. This fifth edition is completely revised and expanded from the previous edition. However, the 1977 edition that I have in my library is perfectly serviceable for most uses. This is an excellent resource that is carefully done and shows great detail. One of the most comprehensive atlases available.

*Beck, John A., ed. *The Baker Book of Bible Charts, Maps, and Time Lines*. Grand Rapids: Baker, 2016.

> A beautifully illustrated and extremely helpful work that is a compendium of information on a variety of biblical topics not just limited to maps. You will find yourself coming back to it again and again, and will find it difficult to put down. Its charts, maps, and time lines draw the reader in. Highly recommended!

*Beitzel, Barry J. *The New Moody Atlas of the Bible*. Chicago: Moody, 2009.

> Integrates the geography of Bible lands with biblical teaching. Winner of the ECPA's 2010 Christian Book Award in the Bible Reference & Study category.

*Brisco, Thomas V. *Holman Bible Atlas: A Complete Guide to the Expansive Geography of Biblical History.* Nashville: Holman Reference, 2014.

> Not the most complete or comprehensive atlas available, but perfectly fine for a lay readership. "Well-formatted and informed synthesis of maps, illustration, and historical and geographical discussions" (Bauer, 22) When it first was published in 1998, it was the winner of the ECPA's 2000 Gold Medallion Book Award Winner in the Reference Works/Commentaries category.

*Lawrence, Paul. *The IVP Atlas of Bible History.* Downers Grove: IVP Academic, 2006.

> Using a narrative approach, this fine resource helps to draw the reader into the Bible's history, geography, and archaeology. Numerous maps, photographs, drawings, and reconstructions. Readable and user-friendly. Winner of the ECPA's 2007 Christian Book Award in the Bible Reference & Study category.

*Littell, Franklin H. *The Macmillan Atlas History of Christianity.* New York: Macmillan, 1976.

> Portrays aspects of the history of Christianity that can be shown on maps.

*Pfeiffer, Charles F., ed. *Baker's Bible Atlas.* Revised edition. Grand Rapids: Baker, 2003.

> A helpful, easy-to-use work that is particularly suited for laypersons. First published in 1961, it has been revised several times and retains its usefulness. "An important work incorporating a geographical gazetteer to assist the reader in identifying Biblical places with present-day name" (Barber, 72).

*_____, and Howard F. Vos. *The Wycliffe Historical Geography of Bible Lands.* Chicago: Moody Press, 1967.

> Not an atlas, but an examination of the ten areas of the Near East and Mediterranean world: Mesopotamia, Egypt,

Palestine, Phoenicia, Syria, Biblical Iran, Cyprus, Asia Minor, Greece, and Italy. A fascinating blend of historical, geographical, biblical, and archaeological information making for a valuable reference tool.

BIBLE CONCORDANCES

A good concordance can be one of the most valuable tools for Bible study. Next to a good study Bible, a concordance may be the most important resource for Bible study. A concordance is a versatile tool that will enable its users to accomplish several tasks. First, it will enable the student to do word studies to determine the precise meaning of a word or phrase by examining the different passages where it occurs. Second, it will show which Hebrew and Greek words are translated by the same English word. It is not necessary to be able to read Hebrew or Greek to understand how this can be helpful. Third, it will allow the student to trace the development of an idea or theme throughout the entire Bible. When making your choice to purchase a concordance, make certain that it is an exhaustive concordance, which will list every occurrence of every word in the Bible.

+Cruden, Alexander. *Cruden's Complete Concordance to the Old and New Testaments.* London: Midwinter, 1738; Reprint, Peabody, MA: Hendrickson, 1988.

> Although Cruden's concordance was not the first one in English, it quickly replaced its predecessors when it first appeared in 1737. Spurgeon claimed that it never left his side when he was doing Bible study. Cruden's famous work has now been replaced dozens of times over by more up-to-date and serviceable concordances, but it is still used today and has enriched generations of God's people.

*Kohlenberger, John III. *The NIV Exhaustive Bible Concordance.* Third edition. Grand Rapids: Zondervan Academic, 2015.

> The only concordance based on the NIV that provides a complete index of every appearance of every word. There is an alphabetical listing of every word in the Bible with book/

chapter/verse references. Contains dictionary indexes that define every Hebrew, Aramaic, and Greek word in the Bible, including frequency counts for each word, both in the original languages and in English. It uses a unique numbering system developed by Goodrick and Kohlenberger that seeks to replace and improve upon the old Strong's numbering system.

*Mounce, William D. *The Crossway Comprehensive Concordance of the Holy Bible: English Standard Version*. Wheaton: Crossway, 2002.

Compiled by a renowned New Testament scholar and a member of the ESV translation team, this concordance provides a complete listing of every one of the roughly 14,000 words that appear in the ESV (with the exception of common words such as "a," "in," "he," and the like), more than 300,000 concordance entries. Contains the verse segment for each citation to give the reader a clue to be able to identify the Bible passage being sought.

*Strong, James. *The New Strong's Exhaustive Concordance*. Expanded. Nashville: Thomas Nelson, 2010.

Originally published in 1890, this exhaustive work indexed every word in the *King James Version*. This allows users to find words where they appear in the Bible. An invaluable feature of the original work is that it keyed English words to the 8674 Hebrew root words and 5624 Greek root words found in the Bible. This edition is greatly expanded and includes the best of *Vine's Complete Expository Dictionary of Old and New Testament Words*. For well over a century, this was the most widely-used concordance to the KJV. "This work is of the utmost value, particularly when working from the English text" (Barber, 48).

Young, Robert. *Analytical Concordance to the Bible*. Reprint, Peabody, MA: Hendrickson, 1984.

First published in 1879, this concordance was designed specifically for those who want to be able to see at a glance the way Hebrew and Greek words were used. "Ideal for word studies!" (Barber, 48)

BIBLE CONCORDANCES: TOPICAL

A topical concordance can also be of utmost value for students of the Bible. A topical concordance differs from a standard concordance in that it indexes Bible verses under alphabetized subjects, doctrines, and themes. For example, the student studying the subject of "idolatry" would find dozens of verses relating to that one theme. Particularly valuable for teachers and preachers. Indispensable!

Holman Topical Concordance. Philadelphia: A. J. Holman, 1973.

> A serviceable tool perfect for most purposes. Now the *Holman Concise Topical Concordance.*

*Kohlenberger, John R, III. *Zondervan NIV Nave's Topical Bible.* Reprint, Grand Rapids: Zondervan, 1999.

> A complete revision and expansion of Nave's famous topical Bible that was published in 1907. "The most complete topical concordance to the Bible in existence. Invaluable for locating all biblical passages pertaining to a given topic" (Bauer, 31).

BIBLE DICTIONARIES AND ENCYCLOPEDIAS

Bible dictionaries and encyclopedias are two of the most practical and useful reference works available for biblical studies. They contain articles and definitions for thousands of names and words found on the pages of Scripture. No believer's library should without one or the other or both. A Bible dictionary is usually one-volume, whereas the Bible encyclopedia is multi-volume. Choosing from the following volumes and sets, one can hardly go wrong.

*Brand, Chad, and Eric Mitchell, eds. *Holman Illustrated Bible Dictionary.* Nashville: Holman Reference, 2015.

> At 1,800 pages with over 6,500 articles, this volume is a helpful resource for laity and Bible teachers.

*Douglas, J. D., Merrill C. Tenney, and Moises Silva, eds. *Zondervan Illustrated Bible Dictionary.* Premier Reference Series. Grand Rapids: Zondervan, 2011.

> A condensed version of the *Zondervan Pictorial Encyclopedia of the Bible.*

*Freedman, David Noel, ed. *Eerdmans Dictionary of the Bible.* Grand Rapids: Eerdmans, 2000.

> An excellent single-volume dictionary containing approximately 5,000 articles. Winner of *Christianity Today's* 2001 Award of Merit for Biblical Studies.

*Longman, Tremper III, ed. *The Baker Illustrated Bible Dictionary.* Grand Rapids: Baker, 2013.

> At 1,792 pages, this helpful resource contains over 5,000 articles and over 400 full-color illustrations. It is thoroughly evangelical and covers theological topics, biblical words, biblical imagery, and historical topics.

*Tenney, Merrill C. *Zondervan Pictorial Encyclopedia of the Bible.* 5 vols. Grand Rapids: Zondervan, 1975.

> This five-volume set has had a treasured place in my personal library for the past 40+ years. It is a gorgeous resource well-organized, beautifully illustrated, and thoroughly evangelical. For my purposes, the set is quite serviceable and gets a lot of use. Has been replaced by *The Zondervan Encyclopedia of the Bible.*

Unger, Merrill F., and R. K. Harrison. *The New Unger's Bible Dictionary.* Chicago: Moody, 2007.

> Originally published in 1957, this has been one of the best single-volume Bible dictionaries available. The author was a professor of Old Testament at Dallas Theological Seminary.

*Vine, W. E., Merrill F. Unger, and William White, Jr. *Vine's Complete Expository Dictionary of Old and New Testament Words.* 3rd ed. Nashville: Thomas Nelson, 1996.

> Originally published in 1963 and and at that time including only the New Testament, this dictionary is most useful for those who lack a knowledge of the original languages and would like to know the rich nuances of the biblical languages.

Youngblood, Ronald F. *Nelson's Illustrated Bible Dictionary.* New and enhanced edition. Nashville: Thomas Nelson, 2014.

> At 1,280 pages, this resource contains more than 7,000 entries and 500 full-color photographs, maps, and pronunciation guides.

BIBLE HANDBOOKS

A Bible handbook is a hybrid, something of a condensed combination of a Bible dictionary and a one-volume commentary. It seeks to combine some of the advantages that Bible dictionaries and commentaries have in one handy volume. Unfortunately, because of the brevity of the information included in a Bible handbook, it cannot replace the more detailed treatments of topics found in a Bible dictionary and its biblical interpretation is much more condensed than that which a commentary offers. Having said that, there are several handbooks that are very good and will prove quite helpful to the layperson. There is not a weak offering in the bunch.

*Alexander, Pat and David. *Zondervan Handbook to the Bible*. Revised and expanded edition. Grand Rapids: Zondervan, 1999.

> A beautifully illustrated work that, at 815 pages, is a goldmine of information. User friendly and easily-accessible.

Halley, Henry H. *Halley's Bible Handbook*. Revised and expanded edition. Grand Rapids: Zondervan, 2014.

> This 25th classic edition of this old standby is completely revised, updated, and expanded. Over eighty years after its initial publication, this resource continues to inform Bible readers about the cultural, religious, and geographic settings surrounding the writing of Scripture.

*Hays, Daniel, and J. Scott Duvall. *The Baker Illustrated Bible Handbook*. Grand Rapids: Baker, 2011.

> This beautiful volume, edited by two professors of biblical studies at Quachita Baptist University in Arkadelphia, AR, contains a compendium of information in its 1100+ pages. It offers 112 up-to-date articles by leading evangelical scholars along with over 500 color photos and illustrations as well as eighty maps and charts.

+*Mears, Henrietta. *What the Bible Is All About*. Rev. ed. Ventura, CA: Regal Books, 1983.

> "This is a 'must-have' Bible handbook for every believer's library. Henrietta Mears, the innovative Director of Christian Education at First Presbyterian Church of Hollywood, CA, was founder of the National Sunday School Association and considered one of the foremost proponents of Sunday School programs for all age groups. Under her direction, the Sunday School program at First Presbyterian grew from 400 students to 6500. In 1933 she founded Gospel Light, which to this day remains a leader in publishing Sunday School and ministry curriculum. This book, first published in 1952 and a perennial religious best seller, has influenced thousands of readers including Billy Graham, Bill Bright (Campus Crusade), Jim

Rayburn (Young Life), and Louis H. Evans, Jr. (former pastor of National Presbyterian Church, Washington, D.C). An excellent supplement to Bible reading, it includes previews of each book of the Bible as well as helpful overviews of the entire Bible. Containing selected Scripture readings for each week, this book is both practical for personal Bible study as well as an excellent resource for group study" (**VanHook**).

Unger, Merrill F. *The New Unger's Bible Handbook*. Revised by Gary N. Larson. Chicago: Moody, 1984.

This edition is a fully revised treatment of the 1966 work by Unger. A beautiful, easy-to-use volume that is full of useful information. Of the 1966 edition Barber wrote, "The best work of its kind from the conservative viewpoint" (Barber, 47).

BIBLE MANNERS AND CUSTOMS

Oftentimes reading about life in the days of the Bible is almost like reading about life on Mars. The manners and customs of those times are incomprehensible to us. When reading the Bible, it is helpful to remember that there is a gulf of thousands of years and that the culture of the Bible is Eastern, not Western. One of the joys of Bible study is reconstructing the manners and customs of those ancient peoples. Many passages of Scripture that are difficult for a Westerner to understand are readily explained by a basic knowledge of the customs of that day. What did people wear? What did they eat? How did they mourn? How did they dispense justice? What were the family and legal customs? How did they vary from period to period throughout Israel's history? The following books are indispensable resources in gaining a basic understanding of the biblical world.

!*Matthews, Victor H. *The Cultural World of the Bible: An Illustrated Guide to Manners and Customs*. Fourth edition. Grand Rapids: Baker Academic, 2015.

First published in 1988, this revised and updated edition continues to offer students of the Bible a reliable guide to the manners and customs of the biblical world. Divided into five periods in Israel's history: Ancestral Period, Exodus-Settlement Period, Monarchic Period, Exile and Return, and Intertestamental and New Testament Periods. Highly recommended!

*Wight, Fred H. *Manners and Customs of Bible Lands.* Chicago: Moody, 1953.

A rather dated, but still helpful, resource for the Bible student.

BIBLE STUDY METHODS

See Biblical Interpretation (Hermeneutics) in Chapter 5.

BIBLE VERSIONS

Today Bible readers have more choices than at any time in history. When I was growing up in the fifties and sixties, the only readily available choices for Protestants were the King James Version and the Revised Standard Version, or perhaps the American Standard Version (ASV) or the New American Standard Bible (NASB). Recent decades have seen a proliferation of new Bible translations. It has been estimated that there are as many as fifty different English versions of the Bible. Yet all translations are not created equal. There are several questions that need to be asked by the reader in order to evaluate a particular translation. But before we try to answer those questions, we might ask ourselves why people need a reliable translation in the first place.

One reason why most people need a reliable translation is that the Bible wasn't originally written in the English language. It may be a shock to some people, but Jesus, Peter, and Paul and the rest of the Apostles did not speak Elizabethan English. The Old Testament was written primarily in Hebrew with small sections in Aramaic, a Semitic cognate language. The New Testament was written in Koine Greek, which was the common Greek of the day, not the refined Greek of the classical literature of the Greek Empire. Therefore, the English translations that we are reading are translations of the original language. It is good to keep in mind that not all Bible translations are of equal quality. Another thing to remember is that the English language changes over time. If, for example, you were to attempt to read a copy of Chaucer's *The Canterbury Tales* in its original Middle English, you would find it virtually unreadable. The changes in the English language over the roughly 600 years since its publication are astronomical. Likewise, the modern reader who attempts to read the *King James Version* (published 1611) would find it as difficult as reading Shakespeare's plays. They were both written in what is now known as Elizabethan English. There are many changes that have taken place in the language over hundreds of years, from spelling, to grammar, to syntax, to phraseology. Thus, the need for up-to-date translations for each generation of Bible readers.

Which brings us back to the questions that need to be asked in order to evaluate a particular translation. First of all, what determines what is a good translation of the Bible? Is it faithful to the original languages or to something else? What does it actually mean to be faithful to the original languages? Are we talking about faithfulness in form or faithfulness in meaning? There are three major theories used today with respect to the translation of the Bible: (1) Formal Correspondence (word-for-word), (2) Paraphrase, and (3) Dynamic Equivalence. Keep in mind that all English translations are somewhere along the line on the translation spectrum withFormal Correspondence at one end and Paraphrase at the other.

Formal Correspondence (Word for Word). This is the older and more traditional approach to Bible translation. It is sometimes called formal equivalence. A translator adhering to this philosophy of translation tends to render the text in a literal fashion, translating a Greek or Hebrew word with an English word, hence word-for-word. Examples of translation using this method would be the *King James Version* (KJV), *American Standard Version* of 1901 (ASV), the *Revised Standard Version* (RSV), the *New American Standard Bible* (NASB), and the *English Standard Version* (ESV). One advantage of this approach is that it minimizes the possibility that the translator might insert his own interpretations into the translation. The disadvantage is that the translator might adhere so closely to the original text that it produces a translation that can be so stiff, wooden, and awkward that it is virtually unreadable and lacks the normal flow of the English language.

Paraphrase. This translation technique is at the opposite end of the spectrum from formal correspondence. Translators adhering to this philosophy of Bible translation exercise considerable freedom in their renderings of the text into English. Their goal is to make the reading of the Bible even easier. Such translators are often not overly concerned with details. Paraphrases can be notoriously unreliable as they introduce considerable interpretation into the translation. They should not be used for serious Bible study. Examples of the use of paraphrase are *The Living Bible* and *The Message*.

Dynamic Equivalence. This is a newer philosophy of Bible translation that lies somewhere along the spectrum between Formal Correspondence and Paraphrase. The main advantage of Dynamic Equivalence is that it usually produces a translation that is easily readable and more understandable. It has more of the normal flow of language and is less awkward than Formal Correspondence. The big disadvantage is that occasionally the translator inserts his own ideas into the text and the result is "what he thinks it means" rather than this is "what it actually says." Examples of translations that employ the theory of Dynamic Equivalence are the *New International Version* (NIV), *New Living Translation* (NLT), *Today's English Version (Good News for Modern Man)*, and the *New English Bible* (NEB).

A couple of books helpful in making sense of the many Bible translations are David Dewey's *A User's Guide to Bible Translations: Making the Most of Different Versions* (Downers Grove: IVP, 2004) and Alan S. Duthrie's *How To Choose Your Bible Wisely* (2nd ed., Carlisle, UK: Peternoster, 1995).

Following are some of the English Bible translations that you may encounter and a brief description of each:

American Standard Version (1901). This translation began as an attempt to revise the *King James Version*. It was a favorite in seminaries because of its accuracy and adherence to the original Hebrew and Greek texts, but it lacked readability and was quite stilted in its phraseology. It used the Formal Correspondence theory of translation.

Douay-Rheims Bible. The DRB is a translation of the Bible into English, not from Hebrew, Aramaic, and Greek manuscripts, but rather from the Latin Vulgate for the Roman Catholic Church. The New Testament was published in Reims, France, in 1582 and the Old Testament in 1609 and 1610 in two volumes by the University of Douai. Because of difficulties with readability, this translation was replaced in the mid-eighteenth century by a revision largely based on the *King James Version* by bishop Richard Challoner.

**English Standard Version*. This translation, published in 2001 by Crossway, is a revision of the 1971 edition of the *Revised Standard Version*.

There have been several minor revisions since that initial publication, but nothing of great substance. It uses the Formal Correspondence theory of translation and is my choice of an English version for those preferring that philosophy of translation.

Geneva Bible. This was the primary Bible of sixteenth century English Protestants and preceded the *King James Version* by fifty-one years. Copies of it were taken over to the New World on the Mayflower. Although it is rarely used today, it is important historically. It used the Formal Correspondence theory of translation.

Holman Christian Standard Bible (HCSB). This translation, by a team of international scholars all committed to a belief in biblical inerrancy, was initiated by the Southern Baptist Convention and its publishing arm Lifeway Christian Resources in 1984 and was completed in 2004. A second edition was published in 2010 with few significant changes from the original. It uses a mixture of the Formal Correspondence and Dynamic Equivalence theories of translation.

King James Version. The KJV, published in 1611, is also known as the *Authorized Version* (AV) since it was authorized or commissioned by King James I of England. It was the most popular English version of the Bible for hundreds of years and is still popular in some circles today. It is unsurpassed in the beauty and majesty of its phraseology, but sadly out of date with respect to philology. Its defects, which are obvious today, were not the responsibility of the translators, but were rather the result of an inferior text and a primitive understanding of the original languages. It used the Formal Correspondence theory of translation.

The Living Bible. This translation first published in 1971 is not technically a translation at all, but a paraphrase. Kenneth Taylor wanted to produce a Bible that even children could understand. He used the *American Standard Version* (1901) as his starting point. This version became a huge best seller in the 1970s mainly because it was comprehensible to those with weak reading skills and/or a poor background in the study of the Bible. Because Taylor exercised considerable freedom with the text and did not even use a base of Hebrew and Greek, he took numerous liberties in his attempts to paraphrase. He sometimes incorporated a high degree of interpretation into his final product. This is not the version you want to use for careful Bible Study.

**The Message.* This paraphrase by well-respected Presbyterian pastor and Bible scholar, Eugene Peterson, is a very creative attempt to render the Bible into modern idiomatic American English. It was published in sections over a nine-year period beginning in 1993. Unlike most paraphrases, Peterson translated directly from the Hebrew and Greek texts. In some places he uses contemporary slang and some of his renderings are a bit beyond the pale. In spite of this, if you feel the need to use a paraphrase, this is my choice. Winner of *Christianity Today's* 2003 Book Award for Biblical Studies.

New American Standard Bible. This translation was an attempt to revive the ASV (1901) with an new rendering of the original texts based on the same principles of translation and wording as its predecessor. Very faithful to the original texts, but very wooden and awkward in places. Some scholars felt that this attempt was not a significant improvement over the ASV. It used the Formal Correspondence theory of translation.

**New International Version* (NIV). This is perhaps the most popular translation of the Bible into English used today. It was first published in 1978 and has been updated twice, in 1984 and 2011. The 2011 update has been somewhat controversial because of its use of the gender-neutral language. It uses a mixture of the Formal Correspondence and Dynamic Equivalence theories of translation. This is my English version of choice for devotional reading, but I use the 1978 edition and suggest you do the same.

New King James Version. The NKJV is a conservative revision of the KJV first published in 1982. The aim of the translator of this Bible was to update certain features of the KJV such as grammar and vocabulary, while preserving the literary grandeur of the original. This version has been widely used by those who realize that the KJV is outdated, but who do not want to jettison its positive features. It uses the Formal Correspondence theory of translation.

New Living Translation (NLT). This translation is an attempt to render the Bible into modern English. It began ostensibly as an attempt to revise *The Living Bible,* but evolved into an actual translation using Hebrew and Greek texts. The NLT was first published in 1996, followed by second and third editions in 2004 and 2007. It uses the Dynamic Equivalence theory of translation.

Revised Standard Version. This 1952 translation was published by the National Council of Churches and was itself a revision of the *American Standard Version* (1901). It attempted to replace the KJV as the best "all-purpose" English version, but received resistance from conservatives because of some questionable renderings. A basically accurate and reliable translation that retains much of the KJV's linguistic beauty. It used the Formal Correspondence theory of translation.

BIBLICAL HISTORY

It is important to know something about biblical history if only to be able to place persons and events into some kind of context. Once upon a time when I taught English in an inner-city high school, I was disheartened to learn that many of my students were unable to place the Revolutionary War and the American Civil War in the correct centuries. Those students had learned about both wars to be sure, but they had no sense of historical context. In a similar fashion, many Christ-followers, who attend worship services on a weekly basis and may even attend Sunday School, have little concept of the historical context of many biblical persons and events. For example, they may know something about Abraham, but they have no idea when he lived, whether it was 2200 B.C. or 1000 B.C. They may have heard (or not have heard) about Judah's Babylonian captivity, but could not provide the date when it began, its duration, and the reasons why God decreed it. In any case, any of the following books will give the reader a wealth of information that would be helpful to know.

!*Arnold, Bill T., and Brent A. Strawn, eds. *The World around the Old Testament: The People.*

> An indispensable resource! If you ever wanted to know who the Hittites were, or the Assyrians, this is the book for you. In thirteen chapters, written by different authorities in the field, the reader is taken from the Amorites to Phoenicia and the Phoenicians to Greece and the Greeks. Fascinating reading!

!+*Bright, John. *A History of Israel.* Fourth edition. Louisville: Westminster John Knox, 2000.

> For over fifty years, this book has been unsurpassed and the critically-acclaimed work on the subject. Evangelicals be warned: Some of Bright's views such as on the date of the Exodus and the unity of the book of Isaiah are questionable. However, that does not negate the value of this classic.

+*Bruce, F. F. *New Testament History.* New York: Doubleday, 1969.

> A standard work on the subject by a towering figure in New Testament studies of the twentieth century. My textbook in seminary. "A well-documented, brilliantly written, generally conservative history which covers the entire NT era and will remain a standard for many years" (Barber, 137). Barber's words have proved prophetic.

!+*Josephus, Flavius. *The Works of Flavius Josephus.* 4 vols. Translated by William Whiston. Reprint, Grand Rapids: Baker, 1974.

> Josephus was a first-century Jewish historian who was born in Jerusalem and fought against the Romans. His *Works* include *The Wars of the Jews* and *Antiquities of the Jews.* Although not always considered accurate as an historian, Josephus provides useful information about individuals, groups, customs, and the geography of first-century Palestine. He also aids in understanding the Old Testament and Jewish history. I initially considered including these volumes, but then rejected the idea because I wondered how many laypeople would actually be interested in reading his works. However, I was talking with a member of my Sunday school class last evening and she told me that she was engrossed in *Antiquities of the Jews.* I decided to reverse course and included it. It is sad that many pastors and scholars never read Josephus and mine his riches. Perhaps this review will encourage some of the laity to do so.

*Kaiser, Walter C., Jr., and Paul D. Wegner. *A History of Israel: From the Bronze Age through the Jewish Wars.* Revised edition. Nashville: B & H Academic, 2017.

> A comprehensive introduction to the history of ancient Israel up until the events just prior to the New Testament era. Kaiser is one of the foremost evangelical Old Testament scholars of the past fifty years and Wegner is professor of Old Testament studies at Gateway Seminary in Ontario, CA.

*Wood Leon J. *A Survey of Israel's History.* Revised by David O'Brien. Grand Rapids: Zondervan, 1986.

> First published in 1970, this selective history has served the needs of a generation of undergraduate students. I read it while a student in seminary and again many years later. Strongly evangelical, this book is ideal for a lay audience.

BIBLICAL LANGUAGES

The vast majority of laypersons who study the Bible will have no more than a passing acquaintance with the biblical languages: Hebrew, Aramaic, and Greek. However, the reality is that the Bible was not written in King James English, which may come as a shock to some. Most laypersons will not want to invest the many years of study required to become proficient in one or both of the biblical languages. If a layperson decides to study a biblical language, it is usually Greek, but I have known some who have undertaken the study of Hebrew. Few laypersons that I know want to learn Hebrew or Greek or to become scholars in either discipline. However, they do want to understand the Bible better, particularly the New Testament. They want to understand what certain Greek words mean. They also want to be able to use the Bible software that is available to them. The following, particularly the Mounce book, will assist towards that goal.

*Mounce, William D. *Greek for the Rest of Us: The Essentials of Biblical Greek.* 2nd ed. Grand Rapids: Zondervan, 2013.

> When I was a seminary student, I taught an intermediate Greek class for laypersons at my church (Wallace Memorial Presbyterian Church in Hyattsville, MD). That year those three very motivated saints read 1, 2, and 3 John and 1 Corinthians in Greek and were an inspiration to me. They shamed those who were studying for the ministry who complained that "the Greek language was too hard!" This course for beginners in the study of New Testament Greek is not meant to replace the author's *Basics of Biblical Greek,* but is designed more as a "crash course" on the essentials of the language. The subtitle

of the first edition read "Using Greek Tools without Mastering Biblical Greek." This approach is more for those who do not plan to go on to the next level, but are content to know just a little bit of the language and be able to use some of the basic tools. With today's de-emphasis on biblical languages and the fact that some seminary programs do not require them at all, this volume is desperately needed not just for laypersons, but also some pastors. After all, a little bit of Greek is better than no Greek at all.

*Robertson, Archibald Thomas. *Word Pictures in the New Testament*. 6 vols. Nashville: Broadman, 1930–33.

A work of impeccable scholarship by a master Greek grammarian, this set is essentially a verse-by-verse commentary on the English text of the New Testament in which Robertson points out those word pictures and nuances in the Greek that are often lost in the translation. Greek words are transliterated so this work can be used by a very broad audience.

Vine, W. E. *Vine's Expository Dictionary of Old and New Testament Words*. Reprint, Nashville: Thomas Nelson, 2003.

This useful work is for those who have no knowledge of Hebrew or Greek, but who want to know what certain words in the Bible mean. Thousands of biblical words are listed in alphabetical order in English for each testament. Each entry gives a definition of the word and how it is used, an English transliteration, and key occurrences in Scripture. An old standby.

STUDY BIBLES

The world of study Bibles is an embarrassment of riches for the believer. There is a multiplicity of offerings ranging from and including *The Chronological Study Bible*, the *NKJV Study Bible*, *NIV Essentials Study Bible*, the *Old Scofield Study Bible*. With dozens of study Bibles in print today, finding one that fits you can be a daunting task.

A study Bible is a special edition of the Bible that is designed for the serious student. It contains such features as a concordance that indicates where key words are found in the Bible, maps and charts illustrating Palestine and the ancient world during biblical times, timelines, photographs, study notes and articles, word studies, photographs, charts, book introductions and outlines, and cross references.

King James Version

The New Scofield Reference Bible.

> The original *Scofield Reference Bible* is featured in Petersen and Petersen's *100 Christian Books That Changed the Century.* This book did more than any other to popularize dispensationalism at the beginning of the twentieth century and was hugely influential in the fundamentalist movement. This Bible, first published in 1909 and revised in 1917, was my first and I remember marveling at the copious notes at the bottom of many pages. This thorough revision uses a slightly modernized text of the *King James Version* and mutes some of Scofield's theology. Note: Most dispensational scholars today do not hold to the old Scofield system, but rather what is usually referred to as "progressive dispensationalism."

The Ryrie KJV Study Bible. Edited by Charles Ryrie. Chicago: Moody, 2008.

> This study Bible edited by the late distinguished professor at Dallas Theological Seminary carried the torch handed to it by *The New Scofield Reference Bible.* Published in numerous translations, this study Bible contains over 10,000 of Ryrie's notes and continues to popularize a more updated form of Scofield's dispensationalism. Also available in the NASB (*New American Standard Bible*).

New International Version (NIV)

Archaeological Study Bible NIV. Edited by Walter C. Kaiser, Jr. Grand Rapids: Zondervan, 2005.

Winner of the ECPA's 2007 Christian Book Award for Bibles.

Life Principles Study Bible. Edited by Charles F. Stanley. Nashville: Thomas Nelson. 2017.

"Includes 30 Life Principles articles with an index and Scripture references. In each Life Principle are included 'What the Bible says about,' 'Answers to Life's Questions' and 'Life Examples.' Life Lessons in each book explain key Bible passages with references to specific Scriptures. Book introductions and maps include an overview of book, theme of book, author, time and structure of book. Life principles that play an important role in each specific book are outlined at the beginning of each book and include specific Scripture references within that book. God's promises highlight more than 300 of the Lord's promises and are meant to encourage, strengthen and fill people with hope. Recommendations of how to study God's Holy Word are included in the main introduction and encourage keeping a notebook and pen to copy notes and questions as they may arise. Other suggestions for Bible study include using other dictionaries and commentaries" (**Woodruff**).

The MacArthur Study Bible. Edited by John MacArthur. Nashville: Thomas Nelson, 2013.

Winner of the EPCA's 2014 Christian Book Award in the Bibles category.

NIV Cultural Backgrounds Study Bible. Edited by Craig S. Keener and John H. Walton. Grand Rapids: Zondervan, 2017.

Winner of the ECPA's 2017 Christian Book Award in the Bibles category.

NIV Life Application Study Bible. Third ed. Carol Stream, IL: Tyndale, 2019.

This Bible helps readers apply the principles of God's Word to their daily lives. "The LASB has become the number one bestselling study Bible. The third edition has been updated and expanded to include, among other features, over 10,000 study notes, comprehensive introductions and overviews of each book of the Bible, numerous color maps, an expansive index and dictionary/concordance, as well as an extensive cross reference system. There is also a very helpful Christian Workers Resource section which covers the topics of how to witness to an unbeliever, how to follow-up with a new believer, and even how to prepare a Bible study or devotional. A feature that is unique to the LASB is the over one hundred profiles of people in the Bible. Each profile includes not only information about the individual, but also his or her strengths and sometimes weaknesses, as well as applicable lessons gleaned from that person's life. What also makes the LASB different from other study Bibles are the study notes. In addition to the information and explanations concerning the passages studied, the LASB expands the study notes to include how the text is relevant not only to the original audience, but also in our world and lives today. The notes enhance personal study and the application of Scripture, but can also be used in Bible studies and small groups as the basis for study and discussion. The LASB is in single column format. The new edition is available in both the NIV and NLT in personal size, standard size, and large print" **(VanHook)**.

New International Version First-Century Study Bible. Edited by Kent Dobson. Grand Rapids: Zondervan, 2014.

"Extensive book introductions and outlines for each book includes author and date of writing, theological theme and message, literary features and outlines. 'Day in the Life Articles' describe daily life of people in Bible times. Word studies illuminate Hebrew words and explore their meanings. 'Addressing the Text Articles' delve deeper into passages of

Scripture. Extensive study notes expound on the Scripture and incorporate writing from early church writers, rabbis and extra-biblical sources. Extensive maps and charts illuminate Old Testament chronology and New Testament chronology. The 'Between the Old and New Testaments' article contains maps and charts. Explores Scriptures in their Jewish and Early Christian Context" (**Woodruff**). Winner of the ECPA's 2015 Christian Book Award in the Bibles category.

NIV Study Bible. Edited by Kenneth L. Barker. Revised edition. Grand Rapids: Zondervan, 2002.

This landmark study Bible, first published in 1985, was and still is a remarkable achievement. It is an extremely helpful and user-friendly edition, which is my study Bible of choice and the one that I use on a daily basis. It's one aim is to help the reader better understand the Bible. Forty-four evangelical scholars, from across the broad spectrum of evangelicalism and committed to the authority of Scripture produced this magnificent edition under the direction of Old Testament scholar Kenneth Barker. If you would like to gain a deeper understanding of the Bible, you cannot go wrong with this study Bible

NIV Zondervan Study Bible. Edited by D. A. Carson. Grand Rapids: Zondervan, 2015.

At almost 2900 pages including index and maps, this is a huge volume, probably not one that you would use to take to church. At the same time, it is a monumental achievement and contribution to those interested in serious study of the Bible. The general editor is D. A. Carson, a highly respected New Testament scholar who taught for many years at the Trinity Evangelical Divinity School in Deerfield, IL. This is a top-notch tool and highly recommended!

English Standard Version (ESV)

*ESV Archaeology Study Bible. Wheaton: Crossway, 2018.

> "Archaeology is one of the disciplines that sheds light on the historical nature of the Scriptures; it reveals the setting and background in which the story of the Bible occurs" (from the Introduction). Because the events of the Bible did not occur in a vacuum, archaeology provides some of the pieces of the puzzle that provide us the historical background to the Scriptures. The editorial team of this excellent study Bible was committed to classical evangelical orthodoxy and the authority of Scripture. A trustworthy guide to the Bible and its historical background as illuminated through the science of archaeology. Winner of the ECPA's 2019 Bible of the Year.

*ESV Student Study Bible. Edited by Jeremy Royal Howard and Ed Blum. Wheaton, IL: Crossway, 2011.

> Adapted from the *ESV Study Bible* and geared towards students. Winner of the ECPA's 2012 Christian Book Award for Bibles.

*ESV Study Bible. Wheaton, IL: Crossway, 2008.

> This excellent offering is the product of a team of ninety-three evangelical Christian scholars headed by an editorial team including Wayne Grudem, J. I. Packer, C. John Collins, and Thomas R. Schreiner. These are some of the biggest names in the evangelical scholarly world and their inclusion here speaks of the quality of this work. At over 2750 pages in length, it is a massive edition full of useful information that is easy-to-use. If you prefer more of a literal translation that utilizes a Formal Correspondence theory of translation, the ESV is your Bible and the *ESV Study Bible* is your best choice! Winner of the Evangelical Christian Publishers Association Christian Book of the Year award in 2009.

ESV Systematic Theology Study Bible. Wheaton, IL: Crossway, 2017.

This study Bible endeavors to integrate theology with the Word of God organizing, Christian theology systematically, and relating it to the daily lives of believers. This book includes introductions explaining how and what each Bible book contributes to the discipline of systematic theology. It also includes 424 sidebars which connect important doctrines to specific passages of Scripture along with twenty-eight articles explaining the major doctrines of the Christian faith. There are two indexes that provide assistance with locating sidebars. An impressive contribution!

!**The Reformation Study Bible.* Orlando: Reformation Trust, 2015.

"An excellent resource for those interested in a scholarly study Bible with a definite Reformed theology perspective. In addition to the late R. C. Sproul, general editor, over seventy-five biblical scholars from around the world contributed to the theological notes and commentary, as well as over 100 topical articles. As with other study Bibles, there are comprehensive book introductions, multiple color maps and an extensive concordance. It is the extra material provided in the Reformation Study Bible that makes it distinctive from other study Bibles. The topical material written by a variety of Reformed scholars include articles on topics such as Apologetics, the Bible in Church History, Canonicity, Creeds, and Confessions, the Inerrancy of Holy Scripture, Old Testament Textual Criticism, the Preaching of the Reformation, and the Reformation and Worship. In addition to the topical articles, it includes historical creeds and confessions: The Apostles Creed, The Nicene Creed, the Chalcedonian Definition of the Faith, the Thirty-Nine Articles, The Heidelberg Catechism, The Belgic Confession, The Canons of Dort, The Westminster Confession of Faith with its Larger and Shorter Catechisms, and the 1689 London Baptist Confession of Faith. With over 2,500 pages, this Bible is large and heavy, though there is a condensed version available. It is single-column formatted and uses the ESV.

It provides a valuable foundation for the understanding of Scripture and Reformed Theology" **(VanHook)**.

New Living Translation (NLT)

Chronological Life Application Study Bible, NLT. Carol Stream, IL: Tyndale House, 2012.

> Winner of the ECPA's 2013 Christian Book Award for Bibles.

*NLT Study Bible. Carol Stream, IL: Tyndale House, 2008.

> Uses the second edition of the New Living Translation. Laypersons who use it regularly sing its praises. In my experience, I have found it to be user-friendly, informative, and generally quite helpful.

The Swindoll Study Bible. Carol Stream, IL: Tyndale, 2017.

> "The book's introduction answers key questions: Who wrote the book? Where are we? Why is the book so important? What is the main idea and how do I apply this? Prayer moments offer brief heartfelt prayers adapted from the end of sermons asking God to help us live out the truths of his Word. Practical Application articles explain important passages through stories, illustrations, and specific application points. People Profiles provide lessons from the lives of key biblical figures. Living Insights includes over 1600 study notes throughout Scripture and highlights of important passages. There are Holy Land Tour itineraries of six different tour experiences, each including a map of the routes along with Scripture references and page numbers for the tour stops on that route. Included is *The Swindoll Study Bible* App (IOS and Android), which contains all of the content of the print edition alongside search, note taking, bookmarking, and sharing functions" (Woodruff).

Christian Standard Bible (CSB)

CSB Study Bible. Nashville: Holman, 2017.

> The list of contributors for this impressive edition reads like a "Who's Who" of the evangelical scholarly world from Eugene H. Merrill of Dallas Theological Seminary, Iain M. Duguid of Westminster Theological Seminary, and Walter Kaiser, Jr. of Gordon-Conwell Theological Seminary in the Old Testament, to Charles L. Quarles of Southeastern Baptist Theological Seminary, Andreas J. Köstenberger of Southeastern Baptist Theological Seminary, and Stanley E. Porter of McMaster Divinity College in the New Testament. Such luminaries as George H. Guthrie of Union University, Daniel I. Block of Wheaton College, Gary Habermas of Liberty University, and Craig A. Blaising of Southwestern Baptist Theological Seminary contribute essays on topics from "How to Read and Study the Bible" to "What Really Happened to the Apostles?" This study Bible is an impressive contribution to the field.

Other Study Bibles

The Apologetics Study Bible

> Uses the *Christian Standard Bible* (CSB).

The Jeremiah Study Bible

The MacArthur Study Bible

> Winner of the ECPA's 1998 Gold Medallion Book Award in the Bibles category.

The New Inductive Study Bible

> Uses the updated *New American Standard Bible.*

New Oxford Annotated Bible with Apocrypha

> Uses the *New Revised Standard Version* (NRSV).

The Study Bible for Women

COMPUTER BIBLE STUDY RESOURCES

It is not an overstatement to say that the use of computers has revolutionized the field of biblical studies. The past few decades have seen a revolution in the way that Bible study is done. The Internet gives students, pastors, and scholars access to reams of data that were unheard of just a generation ago. Entire books and commentary sets, not to mention journal and magazine articles, can now be found online. Software enables scholars to complete studies, that previously would have taken them hours, in just minutes. Likewise, exponential changes in computer technology and software programs have occurred at a dizzying pace. This revolution has trickled down to the non-specialists who also enjoy studying the Bible. It has gotten where some of us from a bygone age are having difficulty just keeping up with the technology. Personally, although I have a Logos subscription and have been trained in its use, I much prefer the feel of picking up an actual book. My way may be slower, but it just feels better. Of course, were I thirty years younger, I likely would prefer using a Kindle to picking up a dusty tome. It is all a matter of preference.

There are two basic types of computer resources available today: Bible Study Software which usually does not come free and Bible Study Websites which are free to access.

Bible Study Software

There are some excellent software programs available that many have found to be most useful. The following Bible study programs are some of the most popular in use today. All of them operate across different platforms. Thus, they can be said to be cross-platform or multi-platform. Probably the top two Bible study software programs are Accordance and Logos. Both have strong capabilities for the original languages (if that is of interest to you) and have a high percentage of overlap in those capabilities. My opinion is that these programs will be of primary interest to the serious Bible student or scholar, but not to the average layperson

!Accordance

> This software was originally written for Mac, but now can be used by Windows users, too. It is quite impressive in its operation, extremely fast, and has many dazzling features. It tends to seek a middle ground between BibleWorks (which ceased operations in 2018, but was extremely popular) and Logos. I saw a demonstration back in 2015 on how to do Greek exegesis and came away properly impressed and dazzled. The website has a store where one can purchase Academic Bundles ranging in price from about $400 to $1,000, numerous Add-On Bundles for varying prices, as well as add-ons for English, Greek, and Hebrew studies and international languages. Although this program does not cost as much as Logos, it is still not inexpensive. But it does offer the best of both worlds for the serious student and can streamline your study. If finances are a consideration, this program offers a lot of bang for your buck and is much less expensive than Logos.

!Logos Bible Software

> This is the software that I own and have used the most. It has excellent original language capabilities as well as a huge library of resources. Eight standard base packages are offered (Starter, Bronze, Silver, Gold, Platinum, Diamond, Portfolio, and Collector's Edition). Base packages are the starting point for using Logos to study the Bible. They can be quite pricey. They range from the Starter which has a library of 315+ resources and is listed at $249.99 to Collector's Edition which has a library of approximately 9,818 books and lists for over $10,000.00. Resources are equipped with tags and hyperlinks to expand the capability of your research. In addition to a large library of books, there are also topical guides and online courses available. For the biblical scholar or pastor, Logos can be a veritable gold mine, but for the average layperson, cost would be a huge inhibiting factor. However, I was assured by a Logos representative that the average customers for the Collector's Edition are laypersons who are serious about Bible study. "The downside of Logos could be that it seems slower, is

more difficult to customize, and there is a long learning-curve with its more complex interface" (Evans, 40).

Other Bible Study Software
Other popular programs include e-Sword; Theophilos has been discontinued.

Bible Study Websites

There are numerous Bible study resources available online that Christians can access simply by using their computers. Some are good, some not so good. Most of these are absolutely free. Listed below are some of the most helpful. When choosing a website, please beware of sites that have a theological axe to grind or are heavily biased.

BibleGateway.com

> This is one of the premier, if not the best, websites available. It offers more than 180 different versions of the Bible in more than seventy languages ranging from English, Spanish, and German to Amharic, Swahili, and Cherokee. There are at least sixty English versions available along with twenty Spanish and five German. It also offers parallel translations so that the differences can be seen at a glance. There are also Bible reading plans available in addition to commentaries, dictionary and encyclopedia entries, and audio Bibles. Their BibleGateway app is available for iOS, Android, and Kindle Fire. An eleven-lecture series on Knowing Scripture by R. C. Sproul is worth viewing again and again. If you can have access to only one Bible study website, this is the one I would choose. User-friendly.

BibleHub.com

> This website features topical, Greek, and Hebrew study tools along with concordances, commentaries, dictionaries, encyclopedias, sermons, and devotionals. Their mission is summarized as follows: (1) Increase the visibility and accessibility of the Scriptures online. (2) Provide free access to Bible study

tools in many languages. (3) Promote the Gospel of Christ through the learning, study, and application of God's Word.

BiblicalTraining.org

According to their website, there are two forces that drive BiblicalTraining. One is "that every Christian should be educated and equipped for the fullest use of their spiritual gifts in serving others for Christ's sake." The second is "that Christian education up to seminary standard should be available free to anyone who can work a computer." They offer three levels of classes. The first level is called "Foundations: Classes for all Christians." The second level is called "Academy: University-level classes." The third level is called "Institute: Graduate-level classes." BiblicalTraining's faculty reads like a who's who of the American evangelical academy with professors such as G. K. Beale, Craig Blomberg, Darrell Bock, Gerald Bray, Bryan Chapell, Duane Garrett, Timothy George, Wayne Grudem, George Guthrie, Paul House, Craig Keener, I. Howard Marshall (Scotland), Douglas Moo, Bill Mounce, John Piper, Thomas Schreiner, Mark Strauss, Douglas Stuart, Frank Theilman, Miles Van Pelt, Daniel Wallace, Bruce Waltke, Bruce Ware, and Ben Witherington. Wow! That is a world-class faculty. Although the classes themselves are free, certificates of completion may be earned for a nominal charge.

BlueLetterBible.org

This website is easy-to-use and offers tutorial videos that demonstrate how to navigate their Bible study tools. This site is excellent for those preparing Bible study lessons as well as those doing personal Bible study. It boasts Bible commentaries (both text and audio/video), Bible reference tools such as encyclopedias/dictionaries, maps/images, Hebrew/Greek grammars, a harmony of the Gospels, charts and outlines, timelines, and introductions to the Bible. There are also theological resources which include cult resources, mission resources, and creeds, catechisms, and confessions. Their free BLBi (Bible Institute) offers a wide array of Bible courses including Biblical

Worldview I and II, Counseling God's Way, Growing in the Grace of God, History and Authenticity of the Bible. The Attributes of God, The Doctrine of Christ (Christology) and The Doctrine of Salvation (Soteriology).

GloBIBLE (globible.com)

A free app available for iOS and Android devices, this site is no longer available in the desktop platform because of budget cuts. This site is easy to use. One can find many resources linked to each verse by simply tapping on a passage which allows the user to explore media and study resources. It gathers study content from a variety of sources such as churches, publishers, pastors, and contributing ministries. Each verse has linked to it HD videos, pictures, sermons, commentaries, maps, virtual tours, etc. Translations available for free are the ESV, ASV, KJV, and CSB; available for purchase are the NIV, The Message, NLT, and the NKJV.

GotQuestions.org

"A website and available app that has answers to over 6,600 Bible, theological, biblical and church history questions, as well as other categories of interest. At the end of each article, there are recommended resources and links to related topics. The articles are very interesting, well-written, and resourced. The GotQuestions Ministry that provides the website describes itself as 'Christian, Protestant, evangelical, theologically conservative, and nondenominational.' In addition to the many categories and articles immediately available on the website, questions can be submitted and a return response given by email within 2–7 days. On the website is a link to the GQKidz site where children's questions are answered and games and activities are available. There is also a link to 412Teens.org which answers questions of most concern to that age group. A link to a free online Bible study is also provided. GotQuestions.org has been a valuable and reliable online resource since 2002" **(VanHook).**

Ligonier.org

"Ligonier ministries was founded by the late R. C. Sproul in 1971. Ordained in the Presbyterian Church in America, Sproul is considered to be one of the leading proponents of Reformed theology in our time. The website has an extensive treasury of resources for both individual and group study, particularly for those adherents of the Reformed faith. The site includes daily audio and video presentations as well as each day's devotional from *Tabletalk* magazine. Sproul's popular radio broadcast, Renewing Your Mind, is also accessible through the website. Also, hundreds of Sproul's sermons, preached while he was pastor of Saint Andrew Chapel in Sanford, FL, are available, and are listed by scriptural and topical categories. There is a link to a variety of blogs from Sproul and other theologians answering questions that have been asked through the years. A teacher index is provided in which over 100 biblical scholars are listed alphabetically. Each scholar is linked to either videos, many from past Ligonier conferences, or articles that have been written by that individual. Ligonier Connect is a link that has over 100 interactive courses for both individual and group study. Many of these study courses are offered free of charge. There are many other resources to explore on the website including the capability to live chat with a trained ministry partner from Ligonier" **(VanHook).**

3

Commentaries

Commentaries are immensely helpful tools for Bible study. They are particularly helpful for anyone seeking assistance in interpreting verses, the argument of a book, or a book's historical background. They can also be helpful in applying the Bible to today's world. There are literally tens of thousands of commentaries available ranging in quality from excellent to mediocre to poor. It is important to be able to distinguish the type of commentary needed. The average layperson will likely not need an exegetical commentary that examines in detail the Hebrew and Greek in which the Bible was originally written. Plus, many laypersons will be satisfied to have a one or two volume commentary on the entire Bible and find that sufficient for the level of study desired. Others will want to consult more detailed works on individual books of the Bible.

ENTIRE BIBLE

Multi-volume commentaries by different authors tend to be of uneven quality and should be considered and purchased individually.

Believers Church Bible Commentary. Edited by Douglas B. Miller and Loren L. Johns. Harrisonburg, VA: Herald Press, 1986–Present.

> A cooperative project in process of several denominations in the Anabaptist tradition. Currently thirty-four volumes are available with eleven more planned with a tentative

completion date of 2023. "This series covering the entire Bible is directed toward pastors and Sunday school teachers. Writers represent church communities drawing upon evangelicalism, Anabaptism, and piety, such as the Brethren Church, Brethren in Christ, Church of the Brethren, Mennonite Brethren, and Mennonites. In addition to explanatory notes upon the text itself, a section looks at 'The Text in Biblical Context,' how themes are developed further in Scripture, and also at 'The Text in the Life of the Church,' showing the history of interpretation and application of the passage throughout church history and within various theological traditions" (Baker).

The Bible Exposition Commentary Warren W. Wiersbe. 6 vols. Colorado Springs: David C. Cook, 2008–10.

This set is a compilation of the author's popular *Be* series, which are available separately in forty-nine volumes. The focus of each commentary is on practical Christian living and not technical scholarly details, which makes this set ideal for laypeople. The volumes of the *Be* series offer brief, easy-to-read treatments of each book of the Bible by a master preacher and Bible teacher. Wiersbe was formerly the pastor of Moody Church in Chicago and the speaker on the Back to the Bible radio broadcast. His writing is always practical and engaging. Particularly helpful are the study questions at the back of each chapter. Dispensational.

The Bible Speaks Today Edited by J. A. Motyer and J. R. W. Stott. Downers Grove, IL: IVP Academic, 1968–1983.

This series is devotional in nature. According to Stott, the goal of each volume is to relate the message of the Bible accurately to contemporary life in an easy-to-read format. It succeeds in those goals admirably. At present fifty-five volumes are available. "The series is readable, accurate, and relevant" (Longman, 9).

+*_Calvin's Commentaries._ John Calvin, 22 vols. Reprint ed., Grand Rapids: Baker, 1974.

> This magnificent set is the result of the Calvin Translation Society in the nineteenth century. Calvin, of course wrote these wonderful commentaries in the sixteenth century well before the advent of higher critical views and modern linguistic studies. But this set is worth its weight in gold. Calvin was known as the "prince of expositors," and his work paved the way for later commentators. Preachers will draw a wealth of insight from Calvin's lucid comments. I cannot recommend his work highly enough. It can often be found second hand. Please note that not all of the books of the Bible are covered here. Judges through Job in the Old Testament and 2–3 John and Revelation in the New Testament are missing. "The more you read him, the more you'll appreciate his nuanced comments and rich theological insights" (Evans, 47). Reformed.

Clarke's Commentary. Adam Clarke. 6 vols. Reprint, New York: Abingdon-Cokesbury, n.d.

> This famous commentary took forty years to complete and was a primary Methodist resource for about two centuries. Clarke, who lived from 1762–1832 was a noted British Methodist theologian and scholar. Available in a one volume condensed version edited by Ralph Earle (Baker, 1967). Arminian.

!*_The Expositor's Bible Commentary._ Edited by Tremper Longman III and David E. Garland. 13 vols. Revised edition. Grand Rapids: Zondervan, 2012.

> This highly regarded set is a completely revised and updated treatment of the 1992 set that was edited by Frank E. Gaebelein. This edition includes the work of fifty-six contributors, of whom thirty are new. If you want to purchase one set of mid-level commentaries on the entire Bible, this one is probably your best bet.

+*_Matthew Henry's Commentary on the Whole Bible._ Matthew Henry. 6 vols. Reprint, Old Tappan, NJ: Revell, n.d.

> Originally published in 1708–10, this helpful set continues to be reprinted. Henry tends to be wordy which makes for tedious reading at times, but his spiritual insights are superb. This commentary set has blessed numerous generations of preachers and laypersons over the past 200+ years. The essence of Henry's work can be purchased in a one-volume abridgement that usually stays in print. "Matthew Henry lived at a time when little emphasis was placed on the history and geography of the Holy Land. However, he was skilled in applying the truths of Scripture to the needs of those to whom he preached . . . May still be consulted with real profit today" (Barber, 46). "Shrewd, practical comments" (Carson, 23). "You will find him to be glittering with metaphors, rich in analogies, overflowing with illustrations, superabundant in reflections . . . Every minister ought to read Matthew Henry entirely and carefully through once at least" (Spurgeon, 3).

+Poole, Matthew. _A Commentary on the Holy Bible._ 3 vols. Reprint, Peabody, MA: Hendrickson, 1985.

> First published in 1686, this classic work is again out of print. For over 300 years, the set has been a mainstay of preachers in the English-speaking world. Poole died before completing his great work. From Isaiah 69 onward, his commentary was completed by others. "If I must have only one commentary, and have read Matthew Henry as I have, I do not know but what I should choose Poole. He is a very prudent and judicious commentator . . . not so pithy and witty by far as Matthew Henry, but he is perhaps more accurate, less a commentator, and more an expositor" (Spurgeon, 6). Reformed.

The Moody Bible Commentary. Edited by Michael Rydelnik and Michael Vanlaningham. Chicago: Moody, 2014.

> A one-volume work written by professors at the Moody Bible Institute. Dispensational.

!*_The New American Commentary._ Edited by E. Ray Clendenen, Nashville: B & H, 1991–2012.

> The commentaries in this series focus on two concerns. First, they allow the reader to understand the theological unity of each book and how they fit into Scripture as a whole. Second, they are non-technical in nature so that their message is accessible to a wider reading audience. This series is based on the _NIV_ and is written from a Baptist perspective. Authors are committed to a doctrine of inerrancy.

!*_The NIV Application Commentary._ Edited by Terry Muck. Grand Rapids: Zondervan, 1995–2014.

> Each commentary explores units of the text under three headings: original meaning, bridging contexts, and contemporary significance. This series has an impressive list of contributors and its volumes are particularly well-written for the most part. Although its commentaries are not geared toward the scholar, these volumes are not light-weight. Teachers and preachers would benefit from this series. "Clearly written, accessible to nonspecialists" (Evans, 56).

*_Story of God Bible Commentary._ Edited by Tremper Longman III and Scot McKnight. Grand Rapids: Zondervan, 2013-Present.

> The editors explain the intent of the series, "We want to explain each passage in light of the Bible's grand story." Each passage is examined from three angles: Listen to the Story, Explain the Story, and Live the Story. Thus, the big picture is never lost in the details of individual verses or passages. This series is far from complete, but the individual volumes that I have seen are promising. It's "story-centric" approach is accessible and easy-to-use making it extremely useful for laypeople and Bible study leaders.

!*Teach the Text*. Edited by Mark L. Strauss and John H. Walton. Grand Rapids: Baker, 2013–Present.

> This new set of commentaries on the entire Bible endeavors to bridge the gap between technical works and devotional ones. In each commentary, the discussion of each biblical text is limited to six pages and is divided into three main sections: Understanding the Text, Teaching the Text, and Illustrating the Text. There are four subsections under Understanding the Text: The Text in Context, Historical and Cultural Background, Interpretative Insights, and Theological Insights. As of this writing, twenty-one volumes are available out of twenty-two that were planned. However, according to the publisher, the series has been canceled. That is unfortunate because the volumes I have seen have been particularly well done.

Thru the Bible. J. Vernon McGee. 5 vols. Nashville: Thomas Nelson, 1981.

> This compilation of radio messages covers the entire Bible from Genesis to Revelation. McGee, 1904–1988, was a Presbyterian minister who was hugely popular among laypeople and very straightforward and homespun in his teaching style.

The Wycliffe Bible Commentary. Edited by Charles F. Pfeiffer and Everett F. Harrison. Chicago: Moody, 1990.

> This one-volume commentary at 1552 pages is an old standard that has served several generations of Christians well. It was written by forty-eight Bible scholars who used the KJV in most cases. The 1990 First Edition by Moody is essentially a reprint of the original 1962 edition. If you are going to be stranded on a desert island and you can only take one commentary along with your Bible, you cannot go wrong with this volume.

Zondervan NIV Bible Commentary. Edited by Kenneth L Barker and John R. Kohlenberger III. Grand Rapids: Zondervan, 1994.

> An abridgment of *The Expositor's Bible Commentary* in a two-volume set, this resource, based on the NIV, is an exceptional acquisition to any layperson's library. This is the best

two-volume commentary on the entire Bible, hands down. Winner of the ECPA's 1995 Gold Medallion Book Award in the Commentaries category.

OLD TESTAMENT

The Entire Old Testament

!*Apollos Old Testament Commentary.* Edited by David W. Baker and Gordon J. Wenham. Downers Grove: IVP Academic, 2002–Present.

> This exciting new commentary series is firmly rooted in the latest evangelical scholarship written by international scholars who are "exhibiting scholarly excellence along with practical insight for application." (Editor's Preface) Eleven volumes are currently available: Leviticus, Deuteronomy, Joshua, Ruth, 1 & 2 Samuel, 1 & 2 Kings, Ecclesiastes & the Song of Songs, Daniel, and Haggai, Zechariah. The aim of the editors is to keep "one foot firmly in the universe of the original text, and the other in that of the target audience, which consists of preachers, teachers, and students of the Bible." (Editors Preface) Each volume seeks to offer a detailed exegesis of the Hebrew text as well as the historical and theological meanings. The nine volumes completed thus far are very well written, which indicates great promise for the completion of this series.

!*New International Commentary on the Old Testament.* Edited by R. K. Harrison and R. L. Hubbard. Grand Rapids: Eerdmans, 1965–Present.

> This series is a scholarly effort written in the evangelical tradition, but accessible to general audiences. Its history has been one of fits and starts. It began with E. J. Young's three-volume Isaiah commentary under his editorship, but never really got off the ground. That commentary was later removed from the series. It took off again under the editorship of R. K. Harrison who, upon his death, was replaced by R. Hubbard. The list of contributors includes some of the foremost scholars in the

evangelical world. An extremely useful series that is consistently evangelical! Recommended for the motivated layperson.

Tyndale Old Testament Commentaries. Edited by D. J. Wiseman. Reprint, Downers Grove: IVP Academic, 2009–12.

The entries in this commentary series are authored by respected British, American, South African, and Australian evangelical scholars. They are fairly brief and written for the non-specialist. For the most part, they are very helpful and informative emphasizing exegesis while not getting bogged down in minutiae. These commentaries are now in the process of being updated with David Firth as the main editor and Tremper Longman III as consulting editor. They promise to maintain the high standards of the original series.

Zondervan Illustrated Bible Backgrounds Commentary: Old Testament. Edited by John H. Walton. Grand Rapids: Zondervan, 2009.

The aim of this series is to bring to life the cultural world of the Old Testament through informative entries and full-color photographs and graphics. The pages are high quality glossy and the format is extremely pleasing to the eye. This series is primarily for laypersons and other non-specialists. Winner of the ECPA's 2011 Christian Book Award in the Bible Reference & Study category.

The Pentateuch

*Wolf, Herbert. *An Introduction to the Old Testament: Pentateuch.* Chicago: Moody, 1991.

This commentary, written by an Old Testament professor at Wheaton College, is a handy easy-to-use handbook for understanding the Pentateuch. It is well suited for the undergraduate student, but could also be used as a seminary text along with supplementary material. The book lacks in-depth treatment of many of the current critical issues one would expect in an introductory work, but for its purpose, it succeeds well in providing a useful tool for beginning study.

Genesis

*Davis, John J. *Paradise to Prison: Studies in Genesis.* Grand Rapids: Baker, 1975.

> This helpful volume is not a commentary as such, but still is very helpful for students wanting a better understanding of Genesis. "This is an excellent, well-documented and readable survey on some of the key passages and problems in Genesis" (Rosscup, 43).

*Kidner, Derek. *Genesis: An Introduction and Commentary.* TOTC. Downers Grove: IVP, 1967.

> This book is a valuable, but concise, conservative treatment of the book. An excellent commentary for laypersons. "Kidner has packed in a lot of understanding of word meanings, movements of thought in different parts of Genesis customs, God's purposes, and relationship to other parts of Scripture" (Rosscup, 45).

*Walton, John H. *Genesis. Zondervan Illustrated Bible Backgrounds Commentary.* Edited by John H. Walton. Grand Rapids: Zondervan, 2013.

> This beautiful little commentary provides the reader with much help in understanding the cultural milieu of the book of Genesis by explaining ancient Near East customs and traditions and how they relate. The photographs and graphics are first rate! Do not confuse this volume with the author's controversial *The Lost World of Genesis One.*

*Wiersbe, Warren W. *Be Authentic: Exhibiting Real Faith in the Real World.* 2nd ed. Colorado Springs: David C. Cook, 2010.

> This is the author's treatment of Genesis 25–50 which is included in his six-volume compilation, *The Bible Exposition Commentary.*

*———. *Be Basic: Believing the Simple Truth of God's Word.* 2nd ed. Colorado Springs: David C. Cook, 2010.

> This is the author's treatment of Genesis 1–11 which is included in his six-volume compilation, *The Bible Exposition Commentary.*

Be Obedient: Learning the Secret of Living by Faith. 2nd ed. Colorado Springs: David C. Cook, 2010.

> This is the author's treatment of Genesis 12–25 which is included in his six-volume compilation, *The Bible Exposition Commentary.*

Special Subjects in Genesis 1–11

!*Brown, Walt. *In the Beginning: Compelling Evidence for Creation and the Flood.* Phoenix Center for Scientific Creation, 1980.

> A comprehensive reference book on the subject of origins. Accessible to the educated layperson. Most helpful and thought-provoking!

*Gish, Duane T. *Evolution: The Fossils Say NO!* 2nd ed. San Diego: Creation-Life Publishers, 1973.

> The author, who earned a Ph.D. in biochemistry from the University of CA Berkeley and was Associate Director of the Institute for Creation Research, argues in this volume that the fossil record does not support evolution as an explanation for human origins. Although this volume is now nearly fifty years old, it is easy-to-read and compelling.

Lammerts, Walter E., ed. *Special Studies in Special Creation*. Grand Rapids: Baker, 1971.

> The thirty-one articles in this volume were selected from the *Creation Research Society Quarterly* (Volumes I through V) published from 1964–68. Contributors include such well-known writers in the field as John C. Whitcomb, Jr., Henry M. Morris, Harold L. Armstrong, and Duane T. Gish. Quite dated! "A fascinating, scholarly volume which deals with the basic questions in the areas of special creation and presents arguments for its strong support" (Barber, 54).

*Lennox, John C. *Seven Days That Divide the World: The Beginning According to Genesis and Science*. Grand Rapids: Zondervan, 2011.

> This brief, extremely interesting, and easy-to-read book is by a Professor of Mathematics at the University of Oxford, who also wrote *God's Undertaker: Has Science Buried God?* Lennox attempts to define what the writer of Genesis meant in his account of the days of Genesis 1. Are they literal twenty-four hour periods or a series of indeterminate time periods? The author explores different views on the subject and concludes that the earth is 4.5 billion years old.

Morris, Henry M. *The Genesis Record: A Scientific and Devotional Commentary on the Book of Beginnings*. Grand Rapids: Baker, 1976.

> This volume covers the entire book of Genesis, but its real value is in its treatment of chapters 1–11. Keep in mind that both this book and *Scientific Creationism* are now over forty years old and not up on the latest scientific developments. "Valuable as corollary reading and of importance in any study of Genesis" (Barber).

———, ed. *Scientific Creationism*. San Diego: Creation-Life Publishers, 1974.

> This informative volume, prepared by the technical staff and consultants of the Institute for Creation Research, contains eight chapters that cover most of the discussion on the

subject from over fifty years ago. The chapters are: "Evolution or Creation?," " Chaos or Cosmos?," "Uphill or Downhill?," "Accident or Plan?," "Uniformitarianism or Catastrophism?," "Old or Young?," "Apes or Men?," and "Creation According to Scripture." "Well written and well researched" (Barber).

!*Walton, John H. *The Lost World of Adam and Eve*. Downers Grove: IVP, 2015.

This seminal work is an examination of Genesis 2–3 particularly in light of the ancient Near East context. The author attempts to allow for a faithful reading of the text of Scripture along with full engagement with scientific findings to advance the human origins debate. This book is the logical continuation of the author's groundbreaking *The Lost World of Genesis One*. Winner of *Christianity Today's* 2016 Book Award in the Biblical Studies category.

!* ———. *The Lost World of Genesis One: Ancient Cosmology and the Origins Debate*. Downers Grove: IVP Academic, 2009.

In this groundbreaking study, the author presents and defends eighteen propositions supporting a literary and theological understanding of Genesis 1. It is particularly helpful in that it emphasizes that ancient creation texts, including Genesis 1, are function oriented and that the Hebrew word for create concerns functions. Thus, he argues that days one to three in Genesis 1 establish functions and days four to six install functionaries. A seminal and mind-expanding work!

Young, Davis A. *Creation and the Flood: An Alternative to Flood Geology and Theistic Evolution*. Grand Rapids: Baker, 1977.

This book, by a professor of geology at the University of North Carolina at Wilmington, attempts to mediate between flood geologists and theistic evolutionists. He presents a mediating position that is both biblical and scientific.

Exodus

*Cole, R. Alan. *Exodus: An Introduction and Commentary.* TOTC. Downers Grove: IVP, 1973.

> This book is a good, albeit brief, treatment of the book from an evangelical perspective. This is one of the better offerings in the TOTC series.

*Davis, John J. *Moses and the Gods of Egypt.* Grand Rapids: Baker, 1971.

> This book, much like the author's Genesis volume, is not a commentary as such, but more a study guide. Its strength is in synthesizing exegetical observations from the text and making them accessible to the student and pastor. "A valuable and informative series of studies fully abreast of the more recent archaeological and historical information. Makes available to Bible students a vast amount of material not normally accessible" (Barber, 96). Updated in 1986.

!*Enns, Peter E. *Exodus. The NIV Application Commentary.* Edited by Terry Muck. Grand Rapids: Zondervan, 2000.

> An outstanding commentary that deals with the major themes of the book and their theological importance in a nontechnical, approachable way. Sometimes Enns can belabor the obvious, but there is much good to be said for this thoughtful study. "Incredibly insightful theological study" (Longman, 28).

+Meyer, F. B. *Devotional Commentary on Exodus.* London: Purnell, n.d.; Reprint, Grand Rapids: Kregel, 1978.

> As the title suggests, this is not an exegetical commentary and thus not of much help to the serious scholar or student. However, Meyer was a master preacher and his book is full of sermonic material and helpful applications. It is particularly good for the layperson. His devotional treatment will warm your heart.

*Pink, Arthur W. *Gleanings in Exodus*. Reprint, Chicago: Moody Press, 1981.

> Rich expositions written on a nontechnical level. Ideal for laypersons.

!*Stuart, Douglas K. *Exodus: An Exegetical and Theological Exposition of Holy Scripture*. NAC. Edited by E. Ray Clendenen. Nashville: Broadman, 2006

> An excellent contribution to the NAC series. Stuart is a highly respected Old Testament scholar who writes clearly and well and is a staunch evangelical.

Wiersbe, Warren W. *Be Delivered: Finding Freedom by Following God*. Revised, Colorado Springs: David C. Cook, 2010.

> This is the author's treatment of the book, which is included in his six-volume compilation, *The Bible Exposition Commentary*.

Ten Commandments

*Clowney, Edmund P. *How Jesus Transforms the Ten Commandments*. Edited by Rebecca Clowney Jones. Phillipsburg, NJ: Presbyterian & Reformed, 2007.

> This thoughtful volume was completed just prior to the author's death in 2005. This edition is annotated. Reformed.

*Davidman, Joy. *Smoke on the Mountain*. Philadelphia: Westminster, 1971.

> An engaging and readable study of the Ten Commandments by the wife of C. S. Lewis.

DeYoung, Kevin. *The Ten Commandments: What They Mean, Why They Matter, and Why We Should Obey Them*. Wheaton: Crossway, 2018.

> Highlights the timelessness and goodness of the Ten Commandments and how to understand, obey, and delight in them.

*Mohler, Jr., R. Albert. *Words From the Fire: Hearing the Voice of God in the 10 Commandments*. Chicago: Moody, 2009.

> A rich and penetrating exposition by the president and Joseph Emerson Professor of Christian Theology at The Southern Baptist Theological Seminary.

*Packer, J. I. *Keeping the Ten Commandments*. Wheaton: Crossway, 2008.

> Packer is certainly one of the most influential Christian thinkers of the past fifty years and any book that he has written is well worth reading. This book is a collection of brief, penetrating chapters that include discussion questions and ideas for further study at the end of each chapter. Any teacher teaching a series on the Ten Commandments ought to consult this volume. Reformed.

*Ryken, Philip Graham. *Written in Stone: The Ten Commandments and Today's Moral Crisis*. Phillipsburg, NJ: Presbyterian & Reformed, 2010.

> A collection of incisive sermons preached by the former pastor of Philadelphia's Tenth Presbyterian Church who is now president of Wheaton College. Highly recommended! Reformed.

+*Watson, Thomas. *The Ten Commandments*. Reprint, Edinburgh: Banner of Truth, 1965.

> This Puritan classic, first published in 1692 as part of *A Body of Practical Divinity*, is a warm and rich exposition of the Decalogue. When I preached a series on The Ten Commandments thirty-five years ago, I found Watson's writing to be a goldmine of practical application.

Leviticus

+*Bonar, Andrew. *A Commentary on Leviticus.* Reprint, Edinburgh: Banner of Truth, 1966.

> This book is a devotional commentary first published in 1846. This is arguably the best conservative older treatment of the book. It is a true classic in the field. "One of the great works on this portion of God's Word" (Barber, 97). "Very precious" (Spurgeon, 60). "A lovely devotional and theological exposition by one of the godliest ministers Scotland ever knew" (Evans, 89).

*Gane, Roy. *Leviticus, Numbers.* NIVAC. Grand Rapids: Zondervan, 2004.

> Extremely practical and helpful volume for wading through the maze of religious rituals particularly in Leviticus.

*Harrison, R. K. *Leviticus: An Introduction and Commentary.* TOTC. Downers Grove: IVP, 1980.

> This brief treatment is a very helpful generally conservative work by a noted OT scholar.

Wiersbe, Warren W. *Be Holy: Becoming "Set Apart" for God.* 2nd ed. Colorado Springs: David C. Cook, 2010.

> This is the author's treatment of the book, which is included in his six-volume compilation, *The Bible Exposition Commentary.*

Numbers

!*Cole, Dennis R. *Numbers: An Exegetical and Theological Exposition of Holy Scripture.* NAC. Nashville: Broadman, 2001.

> This excellent conservative commentary includes a substantial discussion of the book's literary structure. As its title indicates, it is also a very strong theological exposition of the book. Cole holds to essential Mosaic authorship of the book, but falters in

concluding that the large numbers in the census accounts are hyperbole. There is robust interaction with previous scholarship on the book.

*Gane, Roy. See section on Leviticus.

*Wenham, Gordon. *Numbers: An Introduction and Commentary.* TOTC. Downers Grove: IVP, 1981.

> As are all of the commentaries in the TOTC series, this volume is a brief treatment of the text, but is replete with helpful details and application. This is a very helpful volume for the pastor or teacher by a noted Old Testament scholar. "In short compass, you can't do any better" (Evans, 94).

Wiersbe, Warren W. *Be Counted: Living a Life That Counts for God.* 2nd ed. Colorado Springs: David C. Cook, 2010.

> This is the author's treatment of the book, which is included in his six-volume compilation, *The Bible Exposition Commentary.*

Deuteronomy

!*Block, Daniel I. *Deuteronomy.* NIVAC. Grand Rapids: Zondervan, 2012.

> At just over 800 pages, this commentary is a weighty volume both in length and in depth. True to the primary aim of the series, this volume endeavors to apply the text and to assist the reader in the process of moving from original meaning to contemporary significance. Block, a well-respected Old Testament scholar, accomplishes this admirably. The three headings under which each unit is examined are original meaning, bridging contexts, and contemporary significance. Anyone studying Deuteronomy would benefit much from reading this commentary, but preachers would especially find assistance. This is a worthwhile library acquisition for preachers and teachers. "Brilliant and stimulating work" (Evans, 97).

!*Merrill, Eugene H. *Deuteronomy.* NAC. Nashville: Broadman, 1994.

> A major commentary by a senior Old Testament scholar that really shines in exculpating the structure and unity of the book. As always, Merrill's writing is engaging and informative. The author, a longtime faculty member at Dallas Theological Seminary, is a staunch conservative and this volume reflects those evangelical values consistently. "This is a very good and full commentary" (Evans, 101).

*Wiersbe, Warren W. *Be Equipped: Acquiring the Tools for Spiritual Success.* Colorado Springs: David C. Cook, 2010.

> This is the author's treatment of the book, which is included in his six-volume compilation, *The Bible Exposition Commentary.*

*Woods, Edward J. *Deuteronomy.* TOTC. Downers Grove: IVP, 2011.

> This volume replaces the 1974 one by J. A. Thompson in the series. Woods holds to the conservative fifteenth century BC date for the composition of the book. A worthy replacement that is up-to-date on current scholarly issues.

The Historical Books

*Hamilton, Victor P. *Handbook on the Historical Books.* Grand Rapids: Baker, 2001.

> This volume is more of a survey of the Historical Books than an actual handbook. It abounds with charts and helpful discussions of problems, such as the offer of Jepthtah's daughter, along with helpful bibliographies after each section.

*Howard Jr., David M. *An Introduction to the Old Testament: Historical Books.* Chicago: Moody, 1993.

> This book is an excellent introduction to this section of the Old Testament by a noted scholar. Very helpful and concise!

Joshua

*Davis, John J. *Conquest and Crisis: Studies in Joshua, Judges and Ruth.* Grand Rapids: Baker, 1969.

> This study, like the author's similar works on Genesis and Exodus, is not a commentary as such, but rather an excellent treatment of the central themes of Joshua, Judges, and Ruth. The author, a noted Old Testament scholar and long-time professor at Grace Theological Seminary, grapples with the difficult problems in the books from a conservative perspective and valiantly defends the evangelical positions. Particularly good for lay readers.

!*Howard, David M. *Joshua: An Exegetical and Theological Exposition of Holy Scripture.* NAC. Nashville: Holman Reference, 1998.

> A thoroughly conservative treatment of the book by a noted OT scholar and Professor of OT at Bethel Seminary in St. Paul, MN. This volume is one of the strongest offerings in a weak field. The author is a previous president of the Evangelical Theological Society.

!*Hubbard, Robert L. *Joshua.* NIVAC. Grand Rapids: Zondervan, 2009.

> One of the better entry-level commentaries on this book. Good application, but challenging for the layman.

Pink, Arthur W. *Gleanings in Joshua.* Chicago: Moody, 1964.

> This book is a very rewarding devotional study, but like all of Pink's writings tends to overemphasize typology. Pink died before the completion of this book and most of the material in chapters 20–23 was written by James Gunn of Midland, Ontario. "Deeply devotional, manifests a comprehensive grasp of Scripture, contains clear outlines, and abounds in edifying material" (Barber, 99). This volume would be particularly useful for preachers and laypersons.

*Wiersbe, Warren W. *Be Strong: Putting God's Power to Work in Your Life.* Colorado Springs: David C. Cook, 2010.

>This is the author's treatment of the book, which is included in his six-volume compilation, *The Bible Exposition Commentary.*

Judges

*Cundall, Arthur E., and Leon Morris. *Judges and Ruth.* TOTC. Downers Grove: IVP, 1968.

>Cundall wrote the Judges portion and Morris the Ruth. The commentary by Morris is far superior to that by Cundall. Unfortunately, the two are bound together and cannot be purchased separately. For an excellent non-technical treatment of Judges, purchase Webb or Wood. "Judges follows many of the higher critical theories. The exposition, however, is clear and helpful" (Barber, 99).

*Davis, John J. See section on Joshua.

*Wiersbe, Warren W. *Be Available: Accepting the Challenge to Confront the Enemy.* Colorado Springs: David C. Cook, 2010.

>This is the author's treatment of the book, which is included in his six-volume compilation, *The Bible Exposition Commentary.*

*Wood, Leon. *Distressing Days of the Judges.* Grand Rapids: Zondervan, 1975.

>Written by a solid evangelical scholar, this study remains one of the best books available on Judges and Ruth. This treatment is a detailed exegetical study of the period from Othniel to Samuel and yet is easy to read and extremely helpful to scholar and layperson alike. "It is one of the most valuable books on the period of the judges and on character sketches of the main judges" (Rosscup, 82). Dispensational.

*Younger, K. Lawson. *Judges, Ruth*. NIVAC. Grand Rapids: Zondervan, 2002.

> An excellent commentary that is strong in explaining the text, but weaker in applying it to today's world.

Ruth

Atkinson, David. *The Wings of Refuge: The Message of Ruth*. BST. Downers Grove: IVP, 1983.

> This book is an excellent offering in the popular the Bible Speaks Today series. Atkinson ably sets forth the major themes of the book in an engaging and readable way. The author, chaplain of Corpus Christi College, Oxford, demonstrates an awareness of critical views, but there is little interaction with them. This is a book for the preacher or layperson, but the scholar will receive little help here in the exegesis of the text.

*Barber, Cyril J. *Ruth: An Expositional Commentary*. Chicago: Moody, 1983.

> As the title states, this study is an expositional rather than an exegetical commentary. The author includes an introduction which demonstrates an awareness of current scholarly research at the time of writing and which refutes liberal critical views. It also deals with such questions as date, authorship, and the book's place in the canon of the Old Testament. It is especially helpful for preachers and laypeople.

*Cundall, Arthur E., and Leon Morris. See section on Judges.

*Davis, John J. See section on Joshua.

*Wiersbe, Warren W. *Be Committed: Doing God's Will Whatever the Cost.* Colorado Springs: David C. Cook, 2010.

> This is the author's treatment of this book and *Esther*, which are included in his six-volume compilation, *The Bible Exposition Commentary*.

1 and 2 Samuel

*Arnold, Bill T. *1 & 2 Samuel.* NIVAC. Grand Rapids: Zondervan, 2003.

> Helpful commentary based on solid biblical interpretation.

*Baldwin, Joyce G. *1 and 2 Samuel.* TOTC. Downers Grove: IVP Academic, 1988.

> An excellent non-technical commentary for pastors and laypersons. Baldwin's work is always characterized by careful scholarship. "A concise, competent, clear evangelical work" (Rosscup, 86).

!*Bergen, Robert D. *1, 2 Samuel.* NAC. Nashville: B & H, 1996.

> This study is an important conservative work by a professor of Old Testament at Hannibal-LaGrange College in Hannibal, MO. This is one of the best and most complete commentaries available on these two books. "His excellent work reflects wide knowledge of biblical literature in the text and in footnotes" (Rosscup, 86). "Competent and readable . . . sensitive to historical, literary, and theological issues" (Longman, 52).

+*Blaikie, W. G. *The First Book of Samuel.* London: A. C. Armstrong and Son, 1887; Reprint, Minneapolis: Klock & Klock, 1978.

> This study is an exceptional exposition full of devotional insights and richness. It will warm the reader's heart. "One of the finest devotional commentaries ever produced" (Barber, 100).

+*Blaikie, W. G. *The Second Book of Samuel*. London: A. C. Armstrong and Son, 1893; Reprint, Minneapolis: Klock & Klock, 1978.

> See comments on the author's work of 1 Samuel. "A work that deserves a place in every Bible student's library. Perceptive and enlightening" (Barber, 101).

*Chisholm, Jr., Robert B. *1 & 2 Samuel*. TTCS. Grand Rapids: Baker, 2013.

> This interesting commentary, in the Teach the Text Commentary Series, is well-written, accessible, and non-technical. Chisholm, Professor of Old Testament and department chair at Dallas Theological Seminary, writes for pastors and well-informed laymen who do not have either the time or the expertise to wade through detailed, exegetical commentaries and want to grasp quickly the most important data on the text. Chisholm communicates that well. Particularly interesting and helpful are his insights in each section under "Teaching the Text." Many of his applications could be used as sermon outlines. His thoughts under "Illustrating the Text" are varied and imaginative such as his mention of writers including Bunyan, C. S. Lewis, and George MacDonald and film directors such as Speilberg and DeMille. A lot of thought went into the suggested applications in this volume.

*Davis, John J. *The Birth of a Kingdom: Studies in I–II Samuel and I Kings 1–11*. Grand Rapids: Baker, 1970.

> This fine survey treatment covers the period of Samuel and the united monarchy through I Kings 11. It is a very helpful volume, written by a professor of Old Testament at Grace Theological Seminary, and it possesses the virtues of being scholarly, conservative theologically, and well written. "Illuminates the historical record of the Books of Samuel and Kings, draws information from the comparative literature of the Ancient Near East on social and political conditions prevailing at the time, and highlights the Biblical text with material from archaeological investigations. A valuable book" (Barber, 100). Particularly valuable for a lay audience.

*Wiersbe, Warren W. *Be Successful: Attaining Wealth that Money Can't Buy.* Colorado Springs: David C. Cook, 2010.

> This is the author's treatment of the book, which is included in his six-volume compilation, *The Bible Exposition Commentary.*

1 and 2 Kings

*Davis, John J. See section on Samuel.

!*House, Paul. *1, 2 Kings.* NAC. Nashville: B & H, 1995.

> This book, by noted conservative Old Testament scholar and Beeson Divinity School professor, is an outstanding addition to the lauded NAC series. It is user friendly and scholarly, but not limited in usefulness to scholars. The author, a former president of the Evangelical Theological Society, is solid in his evangelical convictions and has produced one of the very best conservative treatments of these books. One often wishes that his exposition of the text were more detailed, but that is a minor quibble over such an excellent commentary. "The introduction to the commentary gives excellent and clear exposition of the issues surrounding the interpretation of the book" (Longman, 58). Reformed.

*Konkel, August H. *1 and 2 Kings.* NIVAC. Grand Rapids: Zondervan, 2006.

> A solid contribution in an excellent series.

*Whitcomb, John C. *Solomon to the Exile: Studies in Kings and Chronicles.* Grand Rapids: Baker, 1971.

> This study is an excellent, easy-to-read brief survey of Kings and Chronicles from a conservative perspective. The author was a noted Old Testament professor at Grace Theological Seminary for many years. This book is not a commentary as such, but follows a survey approach. It is especially useful for

undergraduate students and laypersons. It covers the period of history from 1 Kings 12 through 2 Kings.

*Wiersbe, Warren W. *Be Responsible: Being Good Stewards of God's Gifts.* Colorado Springs: David C. Cook, 2010.

This is the author's treatment of 1 Kings, which is included in his six-volume compilation, *The Bible Exposition Commentary.*

*———. *Be Distinct: Standing Firmly Against the World's Tides.* Colorado Springs: David C. Cook, 2010.

This is the author's treatment of 2 Kings and 2 Chronicles, which are included in his six-volume compilation, *The Bible Exposition Commentary.*

1 and 2 Chronicles

*Hill, Andrew E. *1 & 2 Chronicles.* NIVAC. Grand Rapids: Zondervan, 2003.

An excellent commentary that succeeds on many levels. It is a handful at about 700 pages.

*Selman, Martin J. *1 Chronicles.* TOTC. Downers Grove: IVP, 1994.

*———. *2 Chronicles.* TOTC. Downers Grove, IL: IVP, 1994.

At just under 600 pages, these two volumes are concise, evangelical, and readable. Although not a technical commentary, it is quite informative and aimed at pastors and informed laypersons. The extensive introduction is very helpful. Highly recommended!

*Thompson, J. A. *1, 2 Chronicles: An Exegetical and Theological Exposition of Holy Scripture.* NAC. Nashville: Holman Reference, 1994.

A serviceable conservative treatment aimed at pastors and students.

*Whitcomb, John C. See section on 1 and 2 Kings

*Wiersbe, Warren W. See sections on 1 and 2 Samuel, and 1 and 2 Kings.

Ezra

+*Adeney, Walter F. *Ezra and Nehemiah*. New York: Hodder & Stroughton, n.d.; Reprint, Minneapolis: Klock & Klock, 1980.

> This book by a noted British Congregationalist minister and Professor of New Testament Exegesis and Church History at London University in the late nineteenth and early twentieth centuries has been thankfully reprinted. The author allows the text to speak for itself in this able treatment. It is full of insight and golden nuggets. "A work which can be read with profit by both pastor and layperson" (Barber, 102).

!*Breneman, Mervin. *Ezra, Nehemiah, Esther: An Exegetical and Theological Exposition of Holy Scripture*. NAC. Nashville: Holman Reference, 1993

> A concise, conservative treatment of these three books. Well-written and engaging.

!*Fensham, F. Charles. *The Books of Ezra and Nehemiah*. NICOT. Grand Rapids: Eerdmans, 1982.

> This commentary is a fine evangelical treatment of these two books. The author's presentation of introductory matters is particularly helpful. For example, his discussion of the chronological sequence of Ezra and Nehemiah is conservative and traditional in its approach. He prefers the view that Ezra arrived in Jerusalem in 458 B.C. prior to Nehemiah's arrival in 445 B.C. This study is not as detailed as that of Williamson. "An evangelical effort knowledgeably rich in exegesis with a firm grasp of Hebrew, matters of introduction, and solid explanation of many of the verses. He shows a more meaningful grip on the relationship of the material in Ezra and Nehemiah than Williamson and is better overall." (Rosscup, 97–98)

*Kidner, Derek. *Ezra and Nehemiah: An Introduction and Commentary.* TOTC. Leicester: IVP, 1979.

> An exceptional brief treatment of these two books, Kidner is a master of simplifying complex material and making it understandable. Here he is concise, to-the-point and eminently readable as always. "Perhaps no one could write a short OT commentary as well as Kidner" (Evans, 141).

*Wiersbe, Warren W. *Be Heroic: Demonstrating Bravery By Your Walk.* 2nd ed. Colorado Springs: David C. Cook, 2010.

> This is the author's treatment of the book along with Haggai and Zechariah, which are included in his six-volume compilation, *The Bible Exposition Commentary.*

Nehemiah

+*Adeney, Walter F. See section on Ezra.

!*Breneman, Mervin. See section on Ezra.

*Campbell, Donald K. *Nehemiah: Man in Charge.* Wheaton, IL: Victor, 1979.

> The author, formerly academic dean and professor of Bible exposition at Dallas Theological Seminary, draws leadership lessons from Nehemiah. He answers questions such as—What kind of person does God pick for leadership? What are the prerequisites for successful leadership? What kind of prayers does God answer? How does God's leader respond to crisis? Nehemiah is often regarded as the epitome of the godly leader. This book demonstrates how God chooses and develops leaders for his work.

!*Fensham, F. Charles. See section on Ezra.

*Kidner, Derek. See section on Ezra.

*Swindoll, Charles R. *Hand Me Another Brick*. Nashville: Thomas Nelson, 1978.

> The author examines Nehemiah's experiences as a builder of the walls of Jerusalem and relates them, in his clear and engaging manner, to modern, everyday people. "Pastors, Bible teachers, and laypeople in general will find pointed principles to refresh their spiritual lives and direct them in service" (Rosscup, 100).

*Wiersbe, Warren W. *Be Determined: Standing Firm in the Face of Opposition*. 2nd ed. Colorado Springs: David C. Cook, 2010.

> This is the author's treatment of the book, which is included in his six-volume compilation, *The Bible Exposition Commentary*.

Esther

*Baldwin, Joyce G. *Esther: An Introduction and Commentary*. TOTC. Downers Grove: IVP, 1984.

> Baldwin, formerly dean of women at Trinity College, Bristol, has contributed several fine volumes in this series. This is a very fine commentary that is extremely helpful for scholar and student alike. However, that being said, she appears to doubt the historicity of some events in the book while holding to its having a "historical nucleus" (p. 24). "Baldwin combines a keen literary and theological sense with a firm and intelligent opinion concerning the book's historicity. The commentary is well written and based upon thorough research" (Longman, 66).

!*Breneman, Mervin. See section on Ezra.

!*Jobes, Karen. *Esther*. NIVAC. Grand Rapids: Zondervan, 1999.

> The author is a highly respected New Testament and LXX scholar and Bible translator whose works are of a uniformly excellent quality. Having done her dissertation at Westminster Theological Seminary on the LXX of Esther, she is right at

home here and has written a remarkable commentary. "Without a doubt this is the best commentary to buy on Esther" (Longman, 67).

*Stedman, Ray C. *The Queen and I: Studies in Esther.* Waco: Word, 1977.

> Many people who study the Bible find the book of Esther to be out of place in the canon of Scripture. For one thing, it has no mention of God anywhere in the book. There is no apparent mention of the Messiah. The author assists modern readers in making sense of this book by using Old Testament types and parables alongside New Testament truths to make it come alive with deep, spiritual meaning. Stedman sees the book as foreshadowing the Last Supper, the Crucifixion, and the coming of the Holy Spirit among other New Testament events.

*Wiersbe, Warren W. See section on Ruth.

The Poetical Books

The books of poetry of the Old Testament are Job, Psalms, Proverbs, Ecclesiastes, and Song of Songs. The wisdom books are considered a subgenre and include Job, Proverbs, and Ecclesiastes.

*Bullock, C. Hassell. *An Introduction to the Old Testament: Poetic Books.* Chicago: Moody, 1988.

> This helpful volume is an excellent introduction to the Poetical Books that is not too technical. Highly recommended!

Job

*Andersen, Francis I. *Job: An Introduction and Commentary.* TOTC. Downers Grove: IVP, 1976.

> This study is possibly the best conservative scholarly work available on Job. It is an exemplary and thorough work of scholarship that is presented in a concise and non-technical

manner. "An excellent treatment which maintains a high standard of evangelical scholarship" (Barber). "Andersen has provided one of the best modern and informed expositions of the text of Job" (Rosscup, 102).

!*Lawson, Steven J. *Job*. HOTC. Nashville: B & H, 2004.

"Job is one of those Old Testament books that is often passed over except for a few notable passages. It is long and sometimes difficult to understand particularly in Bible studies and Sunday School classes. Lawson's commentary is an excellent resource for individuals or for lesson preparation in a teaching setting. The format follows the standard one followed by most of the commentaries in the HOTC series, which is to cover one chapter in the book with verse-by-verse commentary. Each section begins with an introduction, which is a story or illustration which sets the focus for the rest of the lesson. Lawson then gives a conclusion along with a life application followed by a prayer. He also includes a section on deeper discoveries in which he goes into more detail concerning the translation of certain Hebrew words. All of this is followed by a teaching outline and questions for discussion. Whether studying individually or in a Bible study, this commentary is a sure guide laid out in an insightful and understandable format. It is a great resource for lay people and for those wanting to teach the book of job. His material is concise and clear for anyone to follow" (**Van Hook**).

*Walton, John H. *Job*. NIVAC. Grand Rapids: Zondervan, 2012.

This commentary takes on a different perspective on how to interpret Job and, in doing so, contributes fresh understanding to a most difficult book. Walton is a sure guide and an able interpreter. You can't go wrong with this book. "Stimulating" (Evans, 155).

*Wiersbe, Warren W. *Be Patient: Waiting on God in Difficult Times.* 2nd ed. Colorado Springs: David C. Cook, 2010.

This is the author's treatment of the book, which is included in his six-volume compilation, *The Bible Exposition Commentary.*

Psalms

+*Dickson, David. *A Commentary on the Psalms.* 2 vols. Glasgow, 1834; Reprint, Minneapolis: Klock & Klock, 1980.

A rich and warm exposition by a noted seventeenth century Scottish covenanter. This is the best Puritan commentary on the Psalms and a true classic. For those wise folks who love the Puritans, this is a must buy! Originally published in one volume in 1655 in London, this two-volume work is a reprint of the 1834 Glasgow edition. "Heavily laden with richness" (Rosscup, 109). "A rich volume dripping fatness. Invaluable to the preacher. Having read and re-read it, we can speak of its holy savour and suggestiveness. We commend it with much fervor" (Spurgeon, 84).

Kelso, Don. *The Psalms.* Delmar, NY: First Century Publishing, 2005.

Easy-to-read expositional devotional studies on each psalm that are brief with application at the end of each. This book was recommended to me by a layperson in my Sunday School class.

*Kidner, Derek. *Psalms: An Introduction and Commentary.* TOTC. 2 vols. Leicester: IVP, 1973.

As are all volumes in the generally helpful TOTC series, these two volumes are very brief but of uniform high quality. Kidner, a noted Old Testament scholar and warden of Tyndale House, Cambridge, has produced an excellent and helpful treatment of the English text, much like his commentary on Proverbs in the same series. "Highly recommended for its theological insight and practical bent. . . . The introductory material, particularly the discussion of the meaning of the difficult words in the psalm titles, is very helpful. This commentary is well worth the price" (Longman, 75). "He never fails me when I am looking for theological insights on the text" (Evans, 170).

*Scroggie, W. Graham. *The Psalms*. Old Tappan, NJ: Revell, 1965.

This helpful volume is a wonderful collection of brief studies on each of the 150 psalms written with the general reader in mind. This volume is highly recommended for the layperson. "This is an excellent *synthesis* on each of the 150 psalms, with homiletical outlines, choice quotes and concise glimpses of the thought" (Rosscup, 113).

+*Spurgeon, C. H. *The Treasury of David*. Reprint, Peabody, MA: Hendrickson, 1988.

This classic set seems never to go out of print. Spurgeon was a giant of the pulpit in nineteenth century London and is still read and often quoted today. He read widely, particularly the Puritans, and his preaching and writings show the rich results. He can still be read with profit and enrichment today. When you read Spurgeon, you are feeding your soul. "Richly rewarding, deeply devotional and pleasingly relevant" (Barber, 106).

*Wiersbe, Warren W. *Be Worshipful: Glorifying God for Who He Is*. 2nd ed. Colorado Springs: David C. Cook, 2010.

This is the author's treatment of Psalms 1–89, which is included in his six-volume compilation, *The Bible Exposition Commentary*.

*———. *Be Exultant: Praising God for His Mighty Works*. 2nd ed. Colorado Springs: David C. Cook, 2010.

This is the author's treatment of Psalms 90–150, which is included in his six-volume compilation, *The Bible Exposition Commentary*.

Proverbs

*Alden, Robert L. *Proverbs: A Commentary on an Ancient Book of Timeless Advice.* Grand Rapids: Baker, 1983.

> This study is a brief treatment of the book in which the author comments on each verse in capsule form. This book is very illuminating to the beginning student or layperson. "Helpful for its practical suggestions" (Evans, 176).

!*Garrett, Duane A. *Proverbs, Ecclesiastes, Song of Songs.* NAC. Nashville: Broadman, 1993.

> A very helpful, conservative treatment of these three books. Of particular value to pastors and Bible study leaders.

*Kidner, Derek. *The Proverbs: An Introduction and Commentary.* TOTC. Downers Grove: IVP, 1964.

> This study is a useful, albeit brief work, that focuses on key themes in Proverbs. The textual treatment is brief, but the author does compare it with apocryphal wisdom books and parallels in ancient Near Eastern literature. "He often helps on proverbs that seem to clash, and has insights on how to view the ones that generalize and do not work in some cases" (Rosscup, 117).

!*Longman, Tremper III. *Proverbs.* Baker Commentary on the Old Testament Wisdom and Psalms. Grand Rapids: Baker Academic, 2007.

> An exceptional commentary exceeded only by Waltke's massive work. It is exceedingly helpful for both the scholar and the student. The book also contains a very helpful appendix containing twenty-eight brief essays on topics ranging from Anger to Women/Wife. Every Bible study teacher who teaches on the Proverbs should consult this commentary.

!*Waltke, Bruce K. *The Book of Proverbs.* NICOT. 2 vols. Grand Rapids: Eerdmans, 2004.

> This is "hands down" the very best commentary, new or old, on the Proverbs. Waltke, a highly respected Old Testament scholar, who has taught at Dallas Theological Seminary and Reformed Theological Seminary, has produced a massive work of scholarship that is mid-level and very helpful to scholar, pastor, and motivated layperson. It is simply magisterial and without peer. Highly recommended!

*Wiersbe, Warren W. *Be Skillful: God's Guidebook to Wise Living.* 2nd ed. Colorado Springs: David C. Cook, 2010.

> This is the author's treatment of the book, which is included in his six-volume compilation, *The Bible Exposition Commentary.*

Ecclesiastes

DeHaan, Richard W., and Herbert Vander Lugt. *The Art of Staying Off Dead-End Streets.* Wheaton: Victor, 1974.

> This book is not a commentary, but rather a compilation of reflections on Ecclesiastes. The stated purpose of the authors was to "present a work designed for the general Christian public." De Haan was for many years the voice of the Radio Bible Class which in 1994 became known as RBC Ministries and in 2015 as Our Daily Bread Ministries.

Eaton, Michael A. *Ecclesiastes: An Introduction and Commentary.* TOTC. Downers Grove: IVP, 1983.

> Not the strongest volume in the TOTC series, but still worth having. "Many good insights into the text" (Longman, 83).

!*Fredericks, Daniel C., and Daniel J. Estes. *Ecclesiastes & The Song of Songs*. AOTC. Downers Grove: IVP, 2010.

> An excellent mid-level commentary that vies with Longman for supremacy on the book of Ecclesiastes. Fredericks wrote on Ecclesiastes and Estes on Song of Songs. Both are extremely well-done and worth obtaining. About Estes' contribution, "This is a wise, mature work and a dependable tool for pastors and teachers" (Evans, 187).

!*Garrett, Duane A. See section on Proverbs.

!*Longman, Tremper III. *The Book of Ecclesiastes*. NICOT. Grand Rapids: Eerdmans, 1998.

> Although the author does not hold to Solomonic authorship, this is still, along with Fredericks, one of the two best mid-level commentaries on the book. Longman is a careful scholar who has given great thought to the weighty issues raised in this book and deserves to be heard. "Excellent in moving from the original significance of the text to Christian reflection and contemporary application" (Bauer, 162).

*Provan, Iain. *Ecclesiastes, Song of Songs*. NIVAC. Grand Rapids: Zondervan, 2001.

> He explains the latter book as a drama with three main characters. Provocative!

+*Wardlaw, Ralph. *Exposition of Ecclesiastes*. Philadelphia: Rentoul, 1868; Reprint, Minneapolis: Klock & Klock, 1982.

> A rare and hard-to-obtain classic. Wardlaw (1779–1853) was one of Scotland's most distinguished theologians who also pastored a church in Glasgow. He was a master expository preacher and this book contains messages delivered to his congregation between 1810–11. "Is always good" (Spurgeon, 110). "Well worth reading" (Barber).

*Wiersbe, Warren W. *Be Satisfied: Looking for the Answer to the Meaning of Life*. 2nd ed. Colorado Springs: David C. Cook, 2010.

> This is the author's treatment of the book, which is included in his six-volume compilation, *The Bible Exposition Commentary*.

Song of Songs

*Carr, G. Lloyd. *The Song of Solomon: An Introduction and Commentary*. TOTC. Downers Grove: IVP, 1984.

> This commentary is one of the better offerings in the TOTC series. Carr takes a literal approach to interpreting the book. The author, a professor at Gordon College in Boston, is solidly evangelical and careful in his scholarly approach. "This is a good popular exposition of the Song. Much scholarly research stands behind it" (Longman, 88).

!*Fredericks, Daniel C., and Daniel J. Esters. See section on Ecclesiastes.

!*Garrett, Duane A. See section of Proverbs.

Glickman, S. Craig. *A Song for Lovers*. Downers Grove: IVP, 1976.

> This book was an outgrowth of Glickman's 1974 Th.M. thesis at Dallas Theological Seminary titled "The Unity of the Song of Solomon." This is a generally helpful volume that takes a consistently literal interpretation of the book and applies it to love and marriage today.

!*Longman, Tremper III. *Song of Songs*. NICOT. Grand Rapids: Eerdmans, 1998.

> This book and that of Estes are the two best mid-level commentaries on the Song. He sees the book as best understood as an anthology of twenty-three love poems.

*Provan, Iain. See section on Ecclesiastes.

The Prophets

*Bullock, C. Hassell. *An Introduction to the Old Testament: Prophetic Books*. Revised edition. Chicago: Moody, 2007.

> First published in 1986, this book remains an excellent introductory guide to the prophetic books. The 2007 revision was basically cosmetic. Bullock's treatment is not detailed enough to delve into all of the complex scholarly issues in any depth, but he does provide a useful overview of the major issues. His approach to the text is chronological, not canonical, as he moves from the Neo-Assyrian Period to the Neo-Babylonian Period and finally to the Persian Period. Highly recommended for the undergraduate level or for the layperson!

*Wood, Leon J. *The Prophets of Israel*. Grand Rapids: Baker, 1979.

> The author, a noted professor of Old Testament at Grand Rapids Baptist Seminary until 1976, has provided an excellent introduction to the study of the prophets of Israel. He pays particular attention to the continuity between both writing and non-writing prophets. According to the book's dust jacket, "A continuity exists between Israel's earlier non-writing prophets and its later prophets. Both must be studied to acquire a thorough understanding of Israelite prophecy." "A careful and reverent treatment of the place, importance, and teaching of the OT prophets. Should be in every preacher's library" (Barber). Premillennial.

Isaiah

*Motyer, J. Alec. *Isaiah: An Introduction and Commentary*. TOTC. Reprint, Downers Grove: IVP, 2009.

> This volume, first published in 1994, is an excellent, non-technical treatment of Isaiah, which will be of inestimable value to pastors, students, and laypersons. Do not confuse this book with the author's 1993 stand-alone work on the same subject. Both are excellent.

!*Oswalt, John N. *The Book of Isaiah, Chapters 1–39*. NICOT. Grand Rapids: Eerdmans, 1986.

!*———. *The Book of Isaiah, Chapters 40–66*. NICOT. Grand Rapids: Eerdmans, 1998.

> The best mid-level evangelical commentary by far. Not for the faint of heart. For those wanting less of a challenge, purchase the author's NIVAC volume on Isaiah (see below). Amillennial. "Dependably conservative approach" (Evans, 197)).

*———. *Isaiah*. NIVAC. Grand Rapids: Zondervan, 2003.

> This volume is a more accessible and less technical treatment than his massive two volume NICOT commentary. This book is outstanding and will be of great value to pastors, students, and laypersons. Highly recommended!

*Webb, Barry G. *The Message of Isaiah*. BST. Downers Grove: IVP, 1997.

> A fine commentary that I highly recommend. "Exactly the kind of approach that makes the OT come alive" (Evans, 198).

*Wiersbe, Warren W. *Be Comforted: Feeling Secure in the Arms of God*. 2nd ed. Colorado Springs: David C. Cook, 2010.

> This is the author's treatment of the book, which is included in his six-volume compilation, *The Bible Exposition Commentary*. Dispensational.

Jeremiah

Harrison, R. K. *Jeremiah and Lamentations*. TOTC. Downers Grove: IVP, 1973.

> At one time revered for its solid scholarship and conservative point of view, it is now dated and of limited value. Superseded by Lalleman's volume in the series.

*Lalleman, Hetty. *Jeremiah and Lamentations.* TOTC. Downers Grove: IVP, 2013.

>This volume is a replacement for Harrison's 1973 commentary. Lalleman, tutor in Old Testament studies at Spurgeon's College in London, wrote her Ph.D. thesis titled *Jeremiah in Prophetic Tradition.* Her treatment of the text is exceptional.

!*Thompson, J. A. *The Book of Jeremiah.* NICOT. Grand Rapids: Eerdmans, 1980.

>An evangelical standard for forty years, this is still perhaps the best mid-level conservative commentary for the motivated layperson. "Well worth getting" (Longman, 104).

*Wiersbe, Warren W. *Be Decisive: Taking a Stand for the Truth.* 2nd ed. Colorado Springs: David C. Cook, 2010.

>This is the author's treatment of the book, which is included in his six-volume compilation, *The Bible Exposition Commentary.*

Lamentations

Harrison, R. K. See section on Jeremiah.

*Lalleman, Hetty. See section on Jeremiah.

*Wright, Christopher J. H. *The Message of Lamentations.* BST. Downers Grove: IVP Academic, 2015.

>A brief, but eminently useful, exposition of particular value for pastors.

Ezekiel

*Duguid, Iain M. *Ezekiel.* NIVAC. Grand Rapids: Zondervan, 1999.

>A solid non-technical treatment particularly useful for pastors.

!+*Fairbairn, Patrick. *An Exposition of Ezekiel*. Edinburgh: T. & T. Clark, 1851; Reprint, Minneapolis: Klock & Klock, 1979.

> This classic commentary is a breath of fresh air to the reader. It is a bedrock conservative treatment of the English text with extensive references to the Hebrew. It is accessible to general readers and helpful to pastors and scholars. Amillennial.

Feinberg, Charles Lee. *The Prophecy of Ezekiel: The Glory of the Lord*. Chicago: Moody, 1969.

> This study is a helpful treatment for pastors, students, and laypersons based upon the English text. The material in this commentary first appeared in serial form in the missionary magazine *The Chosen People*. "The best work on the subject" (Barber, 112)! Premillennial. Dispensational.

*Taylor, John B. *Ezekiel: An Introduction and Commentary*. TOTC. Downers Grove: IVP, 1969.

> This handy little volume in keeping with the series goals is particularly helpful for the pastor and beginning student. "Quite readable; I read it all the way through" (Evans, 222). Anglican.

*Wiersbe, Warren W. *Be Reverent: Bowing Before Our Awesome God*. 2nd ed. Colorado Springs: David C. Cook, 2010.

> This is the author's treatment of the book, which is included in his six-volume compilation, *The Bible Exposition Commentary*.

*Wright, Christopher J. H. Wright. *The Message of Ezekiel: A New Heart and a New Spirit*. BST. Downers Grove: IVP Academic, 2001.

> An excellent non-technical exposition that is particularly valuable for pastors and laypersons.

Daniel

*Baldwin, Joyce G. *Daniel: An Introduction and Commentary.* TOTC. Downers Grove: IVP, 1978.

> As are all of the books in this series, this is a fairly brief, but capable, verse-by-verse treatment of the text. The Introduction is substantial, over sixty pages and particularly well done. There is much interaction with liberal viewpoints throughout the book. "This commentary contains a wealth of information and careful exegetical insight. Baldwin is a balanced and sane exegete, which is important to note in a commentary on a book that attracts some wild ideas. Baldwin is solidly conservative but not rigid" (Longman, 111).

*Longman III, Tremper. *Daniel.* NIVAC. Grand Rapids: Zondervan, 1999.

> An excellent treatment by a seasoned Old Testament scholar who taught at Westminster Theological Seminary and Westmont College. The best way to summarize the theme is to let the author do it himself. "The theme of the whole book is that in spite of present difficult circumstances, God is in control and will defeat the forces of evil and oppression" (Longman, 113). "A great expositional and theological help" (Evans, 224).

*———. *How to Read Daniel.* Downers Grove: IVP Academic, 2020.

> A reliable guide to an often-baffling book of the Bible by one of the foremost evangelical Old Testament scholars of this generation. According to the author, "it was written for pastors and lay people." This is the sixth volume in the author's How to Read series. Other fine books in this series are on Genesis, Exodus, Job, Proverbs, and Psalms.

Walvoord, John F. *Daniel: The Key to Prophetic Revelation.* Chicago: Moody, 1971.

> This commentary by the late president of Dallas Theological Seminary remains one of the finest works available from a

dispensational premillennial perspective. Dispensationalism has been in a state of evolution in recent decades and this volume does not reflect those discussions. "Strongly dispensational and more oriented toward dogmatics than OT interpretation" (Evans, 229). "Emphasizes the genuineness of the prophet and his writings, and provides a clear interpretation of the book. Thorough, well outlined, and well documented" (Barber, 113). Premillennial. Dispensational.

*Wiersbe, Warren W. *Be Resolute: Determining to Go God's Direction.* 2nd ed. Colorado Springs: David C. Cook, 2010.

This is the author's treatment of the book, which is included in his six-volume compilation, *The Bible Exposition Commentary.* Premillennial. Dispensational.

*Wood, Leon. *A Commentary on Daniel.* Grand Rapids: Zondervan, 1973.

This study is a fine verse-by-verse commentary by a noted professor of Old Testament at Grand Rapids Baptist Bible Seminary. Can be used by the more advanced student and pastor as well as by the layperson. "A fascinating and enlightening commentary which expounds the historical setting of the book, unfolds its prophetic message, and provides readers with a fresh, accurate translation of the text" (Barber, 113). Premillennial. Dispensational.

Minor Prophets

The pickings are indeed slim when it comes to non-technical commentaries on the Minor Prophets. You can't go wrong with Craigie's two-volumes for a more scholarly approach. For a more popular approach, Wiersbe would be my first choice.

*Craigie, Peter C. *Twelve Prophets.* The Daily Study Bible Series. 2 vols. Louisville: Westminster John Knox, 1984–85.

In the spirit of William Barclay's New Testament series, Craigie, a noted Old Testament scholar, carries on the tradition with an eminently readable commentary that ably bridges the gap between serious Bible study and devotional use. The author covers all twelve minor prophets in just under 500 pages so the reader is not encumbered with scholarly details. Ideal for a lay audience.

*Feinberg, Charles L. *The Minor Prophets*. Chicago: Moody, 1976.

This compilation by a former professor of Old Testament at Dallas Theological Seminary and Talbot Seminary, was originally published in five volumes from 1948 to 1952. It is rather dated now and not up to date on current research trends, but is still valuable for giving an overview of each book. "These studies are valuable for their historical and cultural contribution" (Barber). Premillennial. Dispensational.

*Hailey, Homer. *A Commentary on the Minor Prophets*. Grand Rapids: Baker, 1972.

This very accessible study is ideal for pastors and laypersons. Amillennial.

*Laetsch, Theo. *The Minor Prophets*. St. Louis: Concordia, 1956.

An excellent commentary that has stood the test of time. "Valuable devotional studies with . . . helpful exposition" (Barber, 114). Amillennial. Lutheran.

*Tatford, Frederick Albert. *The Minor Prophets*. 2 vols. Reprint, Minneapolis: Klock & Klock, 1982.

An excellent entry-level study of the twelve prophets.

Hosea

!*Dearman, J. Andrew. *The Book of Hosea.* NICOT. Grand Rapids: Eerdmans, 2010.

> This excellent commentary is perhaps the best mid-level treatment of this book available. It is particularly well done. "Hosea is a complex book, but Dearman is up to the task" (Longman, 115).

!*Garrett, Duane A. *Hosea, Joel.* NAC. Nashville: Holman Reference, 1997.

> A stellar nontechnical treatment of these two books. Garrett is an engaging and careful writer. Excellent for Bible teachers and serious-minded laypersons.

*Hubbard, David Allan. *Hosea.* TOTC. Downers Grove: IVP Academic, 2009.

> A well-researched and well-written commentary that is surprisingly scholarly for the series. "Sound scholarship and extensive research" (Longman, 116).

+*Morgan, G. Campbell. *Hosea: The Heart and Holiness of God.* Westwood, NJ: Fleming H. Revell, 1934; Reprint, Grand Rapids: Baker, 1974.

> A collection of brilliant sermons by a true master of the pulpit. Morgan was the pastor of Westminster Chapel in London prior to D. Martyn Lloyd-Jones. Even today nearly a century after he preached, Morgan's sermons are models of the art of exposition. Pastors will love this volume. Laypersons will be greatly blessed, too.

*Smith, Gary V. *Hosea, Amos, Micah.* NIVAC. Grand Rapids: Zondervan, 2001.

> An outstanding treatment of these three books that will be especially appreciated by pastors. Although this is not a technical commentary, Smith does not skimp on the exegesis. Anyone teaching through these books will want to purchase this work.

*Wiersbe, Warren W. *Be Amazed: Restoring an Attitude of Wonder and Worship.* 2nd ed. Colorado Springs: David C. Cook, 2010.

> This is the author's treatment of the book along with Joel, Nahum, Habakkuk, and Malachi, which are included in his six-volume compilation, *The Bible Exposition Commentary.* Premillennial. Dispensational.

Joel

*Baker, David W. *Joel, Obadiah, Malachi.* NIVAC. Grand Rapids: Zondervan, 2006.

> A very solid and satisfying exposition and application of these three brief books that will particularly benefit Bible study teachers.

!*Garrett, Duane A. See section on Hosea.

*Hubbard, David A. *Joel and Amos: An Introduction and Commentary.* TOTC. Downers Grove: IVP, 1989.

> An excellent non-technical treatment of these two books. Particularly useful for pastors and laypersons.

*Motyer, J. A. *The Day of the Lion: The Message of Amos.* BST. Downers Grove: IVP, 1974.

> This study is a well-written and helpful commentary, written on a popular level but with a substantial research base. Motyer is a top Old Testament scholar. "A helpful examination of the Book of Amos which relates the message of this OT prophet to the needs of the present day" (Barber). "Succeeds in making the message articulate, often bringing out stimulating and refreshing lessons and applying them to people today" (Rosscup, 176).

*Wiersbe, Warren W. See section on Hosea.

Amos

*Hubbard, David A. See section on Joel.

*Smith, Gary V. See section on Hosea.

*Wiersbe, Warren W. *Be Concerned: Making a Difference in Your Lifetime.* 2nd ed. Colorado Springs: David C. Cook, 2010.

> This is the author's treatment of the book along with Obadiah, Micah, and Zephaniah, which are included in his six-volume compilation, *The Bible Exposition Commentary.*

Obadiah

*Alexander, T. Desmond, David W. Baker, and Bruce Waltke. *Jonah, Obadiah, and Micah.* TOTC. Downers Grove: IVP, 1988.

> Baker, a top-notch Old Testament scholar and professor at Ashland Theological Seminary, wrote the Obadiah portion of this commentary, Alexander the Jonah section, and Waltke on Micah. At just over 200 pages, this little volume seems to cover all of the bases. The Bible teacher not delving into technical areas of the text will find this book to be a tremendous help and a trustworthy guide.

*Baker, David W. See section on Joel.

*Gaebelein, Frank E. *Four Minor Prophets: Obadiah, Jonah, Habakkuk, and Haggai.* Chicago: Moody Press, 1970.

> This little book is a devotional commentary of particular value for laymen. The author attempts to distill the message of the prophets Obadiah, Jonah, Habakkuk, and Haggai for today's world.

Jonah

*Alexander, T. Desmond, David W. Baker, and Bruce Waltke. See section on Obadiah.

*Bruckner, James K. *Jonah, Nahum, Habakkuk, Zephaniah.* NIVAC. Grand Rapids: Zondervan, 2004.

> An excellent non-technical treatment of these four short books. Bible teachers will particularly love this volume.

+*Fairbairn, Patrick. *Jonah: His Life, Character, and Mission.* Reprint, Grand Rapids: Baker, 1980.

> First published in 1849, this book has rightly achieved classic status. It is not a technical commentary on the Hebrew text, but is rich in insight and application. "Regarded as one of the ablest expository treatments available" (Barber, 116). "This work is well done, and is by far the ablest English treatise on this prophet" (Spurgeon, 136).

Gaebelein, Frank E. See section on Obadiah.

+*Martin, Hugh. *The Prophet Jonah: His Character and Mission to Nineveh.* Reprint, London: Banner of Truth, 1958.

> This edition is a reprint of the 1877 edition. A warm, devotional exposition. Spurgeon perhaps engaged in hyperbole in his comments particularly in light of his endorsement of Fairbairn. "A first-class exposition of Jonah! No one who has it will need any other" (Spurgeon, 137).

Micah

*Alexander, T. Desmond, David W. Baker, and Bruce Waltke. See section on Obadiah.

*Smith, Gary V. See section on Hosea.

Nahum

*Baker, David W. *Nahum, Habakkuk, Zephaniah*. TOTC. Downers Grove: IVP Academic, 2009.

> One of the new second-generation commentaries in this series, this very brief treatment (120 pages) of these three prophetic books is well written and enlightening. It is unfortunate that the constraints of the series did not allow for more elucidation. This commentary is most helpful for laypersons and pastors with little Bible training. "An engaging writing style and an emphasis on theology and historical background" (Longman, 133). Wesleyan.

*Bruckner, James K. See section on Jonah.

*Wiersbe, Warren W. See section on Hosea.

Habakkuk

*Baker, David W. See section on Nahum.

*Bruckner, James K. See section on Jonah.

Gaebelein, Frank E. See section on Obadiah.

Henderson, E. Harold. *The Triumph of Trust*. Little Rock, AK: Baptist Publishing House, 1980.

> This book is a slim volume for general readers that deals primarily with the three questions posed and answered by the prophet Habakkuk. It concludes with a chapter titled, "The Continuing Significance of Habakkuk." The outlines would make this work especially valuable for Bible teachers.

*Wiersbe, Warren W. See section on Hosea.

Zephaniah

*Baker, David W. See section on Nahum.

*Bruckner, James K. See section on Jonah.

Haggai

*Baldwin, Joyce G. *Haggai, Zechariah, Malachi*. TOTC. Downers Grove: IVP, 1972.

> As are all of the books in this series, this study is a fairly brief, but capable, verse-by-verse treatment of the text by a frequent contributor, Joyce G. Baldwin of Trinity College, Bristol. "A very insightful, conservative commentary" (Longman, 140).

!*Boda, Mark J. *Haggai, Zechariah*. NIVAC. Grand Rapids: Zondervan, 2004.

> This volume is one of the more substantial volumes in the series. Although it is excellent on application, it deals with some of the more technical issues as well as theological ones. "Both exegetically and theologically, this work is deeply satisfying" (Evans, 262).

Gaebelein, Frank E. See section on Obadiah.

!*Petterson, Anthony R. *Haggai, Zechariah, & Malachi*. AOTC. Downers Grove: IVP Academic, 2015.

> This brief commentary attempts to treat three prophetic books in just over 400 pages of text. Less than a hundred pages each are devoted to Haggai and Malachi, with Zechariah getting the longest treatment at just over 200 pages. Thus, this volume is not exhaustive by any means and some things get short shrift. The project is simply too ambitious considering the page restraints. Having said that, Petterson is an evangelical who takes the authority of the text seriously. He holds to one author of Zechariah, for example. This is a well-written and

interesting commentary primarily aimed at the non-specialist or pastor. Motivated laypersons will find it useful.

*Wiersbe, Warren W. See section on Ezra.

Zechariah

*Baldwin, Joyce G. See section on Haggai.

!*Boda, Mark J. See section on Haggai.

+*Moore, Thomas V. *A Commentary on Zechariah.* New York: Robert Carter, 1856; Reprint, Edinburgh: Banner of Truth, 1958.

This study is a Reformed devotional commentary by a nineteenth century U.S. Presbyterian. It is not a technical commentary, but rather an exposition whose stated purpose in the Publishers Foreword "combines such scholarship and devotion in a form which the ordinary believer is well able to follow" (p. 5). "A capital book. Most useful to ministers" (Spurgeon, 139). Amillennial.

!*Petterson, Anthony R. See section on Haggai.

*Wiersbe, Warren W. See section on Ezra.

Malachi

*Baker, David W. See section on Joel

*Baldwin, Joyce G. See section on Haggai.

!*Petterson, Anthony R. See section on Haggai.

*Wiersbe, Warren W. See section on Hosea.

NEW TESTAMENT

The Entire New Testament

Daily Study Bible. William Barclay. 17 vols. Reprint, Louisville: Westminster John Knox, 1979.

> This hugely popular set of commentaries was originally published by Saint Andrew Press, the Church of Scotland's publishing house. Barclay, Professor of Divinity and Biblical Criticism at the University of Glasgow in the middle of the twentieth century, intended to make the best of biblical scholarship available to the average reader. The result was a tremendously popular set of commentaries known for the author's turn of phrase and homiletical insight. His questionable interpretations of the Gospels are quite obviously influenced by critical scholarship and negate the value of this set. However, if it can be obtained second-hand at a reasonable price, this set is worth obtaining if one can sift the wheat from the chaff. Featured in Petersen and Petersen's *100 Christian Books That Changed the Century.*

*Jewish New Testament Commentary. David H. Stern. Messianic Jewish Publishers, 1989.

> "After accepting Yeshua as Messiah in 1972, Stern became a theologian devoted to helping Christians understand the Jewish roots of their faith. This is a companion to his Complete Jewish Bible translation. It is a uniquely relevant guide to the New Testament from a Jewish perspective. Stern adroitly explains texts in light of various theological issues, ancient cultural practices, and Old Testament references. A must-read for friends of Jewish people, and for those who seek to better understand Jesus the Jew. Stern also authored Messianic Jewish Manifesto which outlines the destiny, history, theology and program of today's Messianic Jewish movement, and Restoring the Jewishness of the Gospel: A Message for Christians. Education/background: Ph.D. from Princeton, professor at UCLA, Master of Divinity at Fuller and taught their first course in 'Judaism and Christianity,' graduate work at American Jewish

University. Stern was an officer of the Messianic Jewish Alliance of America, and remains active in the Messianic Jewish community in Israel where he now resides" (**Juster**).

The MacArthur New Testament Commentary. John MacArthur. 34 vols. Chicago: Moody, 2015.

John MacArthur is a master communicator and his teaching and illustrations are always practical and down-to-earth. Dispensational.

New Testament Commentary. William Hendriksen and Simon Kistemaker. 15 vols. Grand Rapids: Baker.

This hugely popular series was begun by William Hendriksen who produced eleven volumes prior to his death: Matthew, Mark, Luke, John, Romans, Galatians, Ephesians, Philippians, Colossians-Philemon, I–II Thessalonians, and I–II Timothy–Titus. Upon his death, Simon Kistemaker agreed to complete the series, which is now complete. The series is evangelical and often of great help to students and preachers. The volumes across the board are bedrock conservative, extremely practical, and of great value to preachers and laypersons. Reformed. Amillennial.

!*Pillar New Testament Commentary.* Edited by D. A. Carson. Grand Rapids: Eerdmans.

The series editor is D. A. Carson, a first-rate, solidly evangelical scholar. This is a top-notch midlevel series that is not too technical for the motivated layperson. It is similar in style and scope to the NICNT series. Although not yet completed, it promises to stand alongside the NICNT as the standard for conservatives. "Strongly evangelical, well-grounded in scholarship, insightful, and warmly recommended" (Evans, 60).

Tyndale New Testament Commentaries. Edited by Eckhard Schnabel. Downers Grove: IVP.

> This series covers the New Testament in twenty volumes and was begun in the late 1950s. The volumes were revised once; the process was completed in 2004. Now it is undergoing another revision. The series is evangelical, trustworthy, and its authors steer away from technical issues. For a layperson who is teaching Bible studies, this set would be my first choice.

Zondervan Illustrated Bible Backgrounds Commentary: New Testament. Edited by Clinton E. Arnold. 4 vols. Grand Rapids: Zondervan, 2002.

> Winner of the ECPA's 2003 Gold Medallion Book Award in the Reference Works/Commentaries category.

The Gospels

!*Blomberg, Craig L. *Jesus and the Gospels: An Introduction and Survey.* 2nd ed. Nashville: B & H Academic, 2009.

> This is an excellent and comprehensive study that leaves few stones unturned. I used this book as a textbook this year for a master's level class on the Gospels and found it to be the best resource available. I read it through cover to cover (all 482 pages) along with my students and was thoroughly impressed. May be a challenge for some, but very worthwhile. Winner of the ECPA's 1998 Gold Medallion Award in the Theology/Doctrine category. "I have not found a better accessible evangelical-content survey" (Evans, 273).

Hiebert, D. Edmond. *The Gospels and Acts. An Introduction to the New Testament.* Chicago: Moody, 1975.

> This introduction is a helpful guide to the study of the Gospels and the Book of Acts. Published in 1975, it is now a bit dated and should be supplemented with more current works. But still very helpful particularly for undergraduate students and lay Bible teachers.

*Scroggie, Graham. *A Guide to the Gospels.* Old Tappan, NJ: Revell, n.d.

> This book is an exceptional treatment of the Gospels. It is thorough and extremely helpful. Even after more than half a century of age, it is still worth consulting. Highly recommended! "Worth an entire shelf of books on the same subject" (Barber, 139).

Matthew

!*Blomberg, Craig. *Matthew.* NAC. Nashville: B & H, 1992.

> An extremely helpful work by a noted New Testament scholar. A wonderful resource for Bible teachers! Blomberg is an incredibly prolific writer and extremely solid. "A work containing great insight" (Evans, 280).

!*France, Richard T. *The Gospel of Matthew.* NICNT. Grand Rapids: Eerdmans, 2007.

> Perhaps the best mid-level commentary for the serious lay student. "A careful, judicious commentary" (Bauer, 304). Do not confuse with the author's TNTC volume which is more of an introductory work.

*———. *Matthew: An Introduction and Commentary.* TNTC. Downers Grove: IVP Academic, 2008.

> At less than half the length of Wilkins' book, this is my choice for an entry-level commentary for this gospel. Do not confuse with the author's NICNT volume, which is much more detailed and technical.

!*Morris, Leon. *The Gospel According to Matthew.* PNTC. Grand Rapids: Eerdmans, 1992.

> A very helpful work for the serious lay student. "Solid, basic, and dependable" (Evans, 285).

*Wiersbe, Warren W. *Be Loyal: Following the King of Kings*. Colorado Springs: David C. Cook, 2008.

> This is the author's treatment of the book, which is included in his six-volume compilation, *The Bible Exposition Commentary*.

*Wilkins, Michael J. *Matthew*. NIVAC. Grand Rapids: Zondervan, 2004.

> An extremely helpful and practical volume. At over 1,000 pages, it is quite detailed.

The Sermon on the Mount

*Lloyd-Jones, D. Martyn. *Studies in the Sermon on the Mount*. 2 vols. Grand Rapids: Eerdmans, 1959–60.

> These two volumes contain an exceptional compilation of sermons preached at Westminster Chapel in London on successive Sunday mornings. The form of the messages in the book is just as they were preached. They were not edited for a reading audience, but dictated as is. This is expository preaching at its very best. My heart was warmed and my mind challenged as I worked through both volumes a few years ago. Just wonderful!!! "This is one of the finest expositions of the sermon by an evangelical preacher of the modern era, a deeply perceptive man relevant to his age and a man of scholarly awareness. He is stimulating, practical, often wise in his interpretations of problem verses. It is well worth the money" (Rosscup, 215). "A lengthy, reverent, penetrating exposition, which deserves a place on every pastor's shelf" (Evans, 288)!

*McKnight, Scot. *Sermon on the Mount*. SGBC. Grand Rapids: Zondervan, 2013.

> This study is a scholarly treatment of the Sermon on the Mount that is also eminently readable. In the SGBC series, each passage of Scripture is examined from three angles: Listen to the Story, Explain the Story, and Live the Story. It is in the third section of each chapter that McKnight really shines. The

author examines the text and seeks to apply it to today's world, how the text might be lived out in the contemporary life of the Church. McKnight is especially helpful in his discussion on the divorce question that is both scholarly in its examination of the many different views while, at the same time, pastoral in its application. The bibliographic notations are found in the footnotes which can be annoying if one is looking for a separate bibliography.

*Palmer, Earl F. *The Enormous Exception: Meeting Christ in the Sermon on the Mount.* Waco: Word, 1986.

A tremendously practical and insightful compilation of fifteen studies by a leading Presbyterian preacher.

*Stott, John R. W. *The Message of the Sermon on the Mount (Matthew 5–7).* BST. Downers Grove: IVP, 1978.

This book is an outstanding exposition of the Sermon on the Mount by one of the leading evangelical writers of the twentieth century. Any book written by Stott is well worth obtaining. This book suffers from the lack of an index and bibliography.

Mark

Cole, Alan. *The Gospel According to St. Mark.* TNTC. Grand Rapids: Eerdmans, 1961.

Though now rather dated, this volume is still fairly serviceable for pastors and laypersons. "A provocative, evangelical study" (Barber, 144).

!*Edwards, James R. *The Gospel According to Mark.* PNTC. Grand Rapids: Eerdmans, 2009.

An excellent mid-level commentary for the serious layperson. Gets the nod over Lane if for no other reason than it is more current. One can't go wrong with either.

*Garland, David E. *Mark*. NIVAC. Grand Rapids: Zondervan, 1996.

> An excellent and helpful offering in a very practical series. For an introductory work, I would chose this or Schnabel over Cole.

*Hiebert, David Edmond. *Mark: A Portrait of the Servant*. Chicago: Moody, 1974.

> A conservative commentary that focuses thematically on Christ as the servant. A popular treatment that is quite dated, but is still tremendously helpful to the preacher. "A reverent and insightful treatment which deserves the attention of the Bible teacher and expository preacher" (Barber).

!*Lane, William L. *The Gospel According to Mark*. NICNT. Grand Rapids: Eerdmans, 1974.

> An older work that along with Edwards is one of the two best mid-level commentaries for the serious lay reader. Of course, the Edwards book is much more up-to-date.

*Schnabel, Eckhard J. *Mark: An Introduction and Commentary*. TNTC. Downers Grove: IVP Academic, 2017.

> This volume replaces Cole in the TNTC series and should be used instead for the introductory student.

*Wiersbe, Warren W. *Be Diligent: Serving Others as You Walk with the Master Servant*. 2nd ed. Colorado Springs: David C. Cook, 2010.

> This is the author's treatment of the book, which is included in his six-volume compilation, *The Bible Exposition Commentary*.

Luke

*Bock, Darrell. * *Luke*. NIVAC. Edited by Terry Muck. Grand Rapids: Zondervan, 1996.

> A most practical and accessible work which distills the essence of the author's BECNT work and makes it more accessible for the layperson. "None can match his thoroughness" (Evans, 298).

!*Edwards, James R. *The Gospel According to Luke*. PNTC. Grand Rapids: Eerdmans, 2015.

> Along with Green, this commentary is perhaps the best mid-level evangelical work for the layperson seeking to do serious Bible study on Luke. One cannot go wrong with either one. "Thorough, lucid, and reliable" (Evans, 298).

Erdman, Charles R. *The Gospel of Luke*. Philadelphia: Westminster, 1956.

> This brief study is helpful to the layperson. "A devotional and practical exposition of the theme of Luke's Gospel. Excellent as a study guide" (Barber, 147). Reformed.

!*Green, Joel B. *The Gospel of Luke*. NICNT. Grand Rapids: Eerdmans, 1997.

> This is the replacement volume in the fine NICNT series for the Geldenhuys book, which came out in 1951. I still recommend Geldenhuys; he is a bit more conservative than Green. In any event, this commentary is a fine piece of work for the serious student.

*Hendriksen, William. *Exposition of the Gospel of Luke*. NTC. Grand Rapids: Baker, 1978.

> At 1,082 pages of text, this commentary is a handful for the average layperson and not for the faint in heart. It is well-written and would be helpful to anyone studying this gospel.

+*Kelly, William. *An Exposition of the Gospel of Luke*. London: Pickering and Inglis, n.d. Reprint, Minneapolis: Klock & Klock, 1981.

> This commentary is a devotional classic. It is nontechnical, easy to read, and characterized by evangelical warmth. "A clear readable exposition. . . . Readers will find themselves blessed and enriched" (Barber). "Useful" (Carson, 62).

+*Morgan, G. Campbell. *The Gospel According to Luke*. Old Tappan, NJ: Fleming H. Revell, 1931.

> This volume is one of Morgan's stronger offerings. A masterful exposition by the predecessor of Lloyd-Jones at Westminster Chapel in London. "A carefully reasoned exposition which adheres quite closely to Luke's argument and provides an example of expository preaching at its best" (Barber, 147). Premillennial.

*Morris, Leon. *The Gospel According to St. Luke*. TNTC. Grand Rapids: Eerdmans, 1974.

> This volume is an excellent commentary that is surprisingly detailed in light of the limitations of the series. Morris is a careful and lucid New Testament scholar and always worth reading. Very helpful volume for the layperson. "A clear, forthright presentation of the facts surrounding the authorship and date of this Gospel . . . A handy and helpful volume" (Barber). "Good value, one of the better volumes in the series . . . he skates over some difficult questions and skirts some contemporary issues" (Carson, 61).

*Wiersbe, Warren W. *Be Compassionate: Let the World Know That Jesus Cares*. 2nd ed. Colorado Springs: David C. Cook, 2010.

> This is the author's treatment of Luke 1–13, which is included in his six-volume compilation, *The Bible Exposition Commentary*.

———. *Be Courageous: Take Heart from Christ's Example.* 2nd ed. Colorado Springs: David C. Cook, 2010.

> This is the author's treatment of Luke 14–24, which is included in his six-volume compilation, *The Bible Exposition Commentary*.

John

*Bruce, F. F. *The Gospel of John.* Grand Rapids: Eerdmans, 1983.

> F. F. Bruce was perhaps the evangelical world's leading New Testament scholar of the twentieth century. Any book by him is well worth obtaining. This commentary is no exception. It is very readable and not overly technical. "Probably the best of the 'popular' commentaries" (Carson, 71). "Overall, it is a very fine commentary by one of the leading evangelicals of recent decades" (Rosscup, 232).

*Burge, Gary M. *John.* NIVAC. Grand Rapids: Zondervan, 2000.

> A capable and practical treatment based upon solid scholarship that is highly recommended for pastors and laypersons. "Bold, thought-provoking application" (Evans, 304).

!*Carson, D. A. *The Gospel According to John.* PNTC. Grand Rapids: Eerdmans, 1991.

> Although almost thirty years old, this remains one of the very best mid-level commentaries on this gospel from an evangelical perspective. The author staunchly defends apostolic authorship.

Erdman, Charles R. *The Gospel of John.* Philadelphia, PA: Westminster, 1944.

> This study is a devotional treatment based upon the ASV primarily for the non-specialist. Ideal for laypersons.

!*Morris, Leon. *The Gospel According to John*. NICNT. Grand Rapids: Eerdmans, 1971.

> This study is an outstanding commentary in the usually reliable NICNT series. Morris was one of the most respected New Testament scholars of the twentieth century and principal of Ridley College, Melbourne. It has been replaced by Ramsey Michaels in the series. I hesitate to recommend Michael's commentary for a lay audience because of its roughly 1,100 pages of intricate detail. For pastors, seminary students, and scholars? Absolutely! But for the serious-minded layperson, Morris will suffice nicely. "One of the major conservative commentaries on John" (Carson, 66).

*Palmer, Earl F. *The Intimate Gospel: Studies in John*. Waco: Word, 1978.

> This delightful study is not a verse-by-verse commentary, but rather is comprised of forty-two brief sequential chapters of expositions on this gospel. This book by a prominent Presbyterian pastor and master preacher is highly recommended. I just love this book!

*Wiersbe, Warren W. *Be Alive: Get to Know the Living Savior*. 2nd ed. Colorado Springs: David C. Cook, 2009.

> This is the author's treatment of John 1–12, which is included in his six-volume compilation, *The Bible Exposition Commentary*.

*———. *Be Transformed: Christ's Triumph Means Your Transformation*. 2nd ed. Colorado Springs: David C. Cook, 2009.

> This is the author's treatment of John 13–21, which is included in his six-volume compilation, *The Bible Exposition Commentary*.

Acts of the Apostles

!*Bruce, F. F. *Commentary on the Book of Acts*. NICNT. Grand Rapids: Eerdmans, 1952.

> Although this commentary came out the same year that I was born, it has aged better than I have. A jewel of a commentary that has been revered by pastors and students who wanted a general work that was not too technical. Bruce revised and enlarged this work prior to his passing in 1990.

*Erdman, Charles R. *The Acts: An Exposition*. Philadelphia: Westminster, 1919.

> This commentary is a brief, but helpful, exposition of the text based on the ASV. It is geared toward the non-specialist. Perfect for a lay audience. "A devotional and practical commentary of great help to preachers" (Barber, 152).

*Fernando, Ajith. *Acts*. NIVAC. Grand Rapids: Zondervan, 1998.

> A capable and practical exposition by the National Director of Youth for Christ in Sri Lanka. A layperson would not go wrong with this commentary. It has everything that one could want in an introductory work. "Very good indeed" (Carson, 78). "A very well-done exposition" (Evans, 319).

*Harrison, Everett F. *Acts: The Expanding Church*. Chicago: Moody, 1975.

> This commentary is a readable treatment of the English text geared to the pastor, layperson, or student. It is weak on its approach to problem passages. This is a really good introductory study for a layperson who wants to see the big picture. "A well-organized and non-technical commentary by a fine evangelical scholar . . . The commentary reads easily and comes directly to the point" (Rosscup, 243).

*Kistemaker, Simon J. *Acts*. NTC. Grand Rapids: Baker, 1991.

> At over 1,000 pages, this volume is a handful, but is most helpful and should be consulted if you are teaching a class on the

Acts of the Apostles. Winner of the ECPA's 1992 Gold Medallion Book Award for Commentaries. Reformed.

*Marshall, I. Howard. *The Acts of the Apostles.* TNTC. Tasker. Grand Rapids: Eerdmans, 1980.

> This volume replaces the 1959 offering by E. M. Blaiklock. It is an excellent treatment of the text and much more detailed than one might expect in the TNTC series, which has a deserved reputation for brevity. Published in 1980, it should be supplemented with more recent works. "Very useful" (Carson, 77). "This, with Bruce's NIC work, is one of the finer, more often helpful evangelical commentaries on Acts in recent times" (Rosscup, 246).

+*Morgan, G. Campbell. *The Acts of the Apostles.* Old Tappan, NJ: Revell, 1924.

> This study is a fine exposition of the English text by the "prince of expositors." It is not a verse- by-verse commentary. It is almost a century old and not much help on critical matters, but its application of the text is second to none. "By many regarded as being *the* most important single expository work for the pastor" (Barber, 153). "One of Morgan's better commentaries and one which the student can profitably consult" (Rosscup, 246).

!*Peterson, David G. *The Acts of the Apostles.* PNTC. Grand Rapids: Eerdmans, 2009.

> This helpful commentary is perhaps the best mid-level commentary available. It is more up-to-date than Bruce. Highly recommended!

!*Pohill, John B. *Acts.* NAC. Nashville: Holman Reference, 1992.

> A solid, but brief, commentary that will particularly benefit a lay audience by a professor of New Testament at the Southern Baptist Theological Seminary in Louisville, KY. A brief, popular and genuinely helpful exposition. Ideal for home Bible

classes and Bible study groups. Premillennial. Dispensational. "Well worth buying" (Evans, 323).

*Wiersbe, Warren W. *Be Dynamic: Experience the Power of God's People*. 2nd ed. Colorado Springs: David C. Cook, 2009.

This is the author's treatment of Acts 1–12, which is included in his six-volume compilation, *The Bible Exposition Commentary*.

*———. *Be Daring: Put Your Faith Where the Action Is*. 2nd ed. Colorado Springs: David C. Cook, 2009.

This is the author's treatment of Acts 13–28, which is included in his six-volume compilation, *The Bible Exposition Commentary*.

Pauline Epistles

+*Bruce, F. F. *Paul: Apostle of the Heart Set Free*. Grand Rapids: Eerdmans, 1977.

A recognized modern classic, this volume explores the life of the Apostle Paul and the main themes of his letters.

*———. *The Pauline Circle*. Grand Rapids: Eerdmans, 1985.

This slim volume (100 pages) examines the closest friends and associates of the Apostle Paul. Included are Ananias, Barnabas, Silas, Timothy, Luke, Priscilla and Aquila, Apollos, Titus, Onesimus, and Mark.

Hiebert, D. Edmond. *An Introduction to the Pauline Epistles*. Chicago: Moody, 1954.

This book is a rather dated introductory guide to the Pauline Epistles. It is intended for college students approaching this body of literature for the first time. Not a bad choice for the layperson. "Among the best introductory studies available. Thoroughly conservative" (Barber, 157).

!*Longenecker, Bruce W., and Todd D. Still. *Thinking Through Paul: A Survey of His Life, Letters, and Theology.* Grand Rapids: Zondervan, 2014.

> This well-written volume is an engaging survey of Paul's life, letters, and theology. It is intended to serve as a textbook for university and seminary students. It is very "user friendly" as the beginning of each chapter includes a chapter overview as well as a section titled "Key Verses." At the end of each chapter, there is a helpful listing of key people, places, and terms, questions for review and discussion, and contemporary theological reflection questions to enhance further thinking. Finally, there is a helpful bibliography concluding each chapter divided into two sections: "Commentaries" and "Special Studies." Some of their conclusions may be questionable to evangelicals.

+*Ramsay, W. M. *The Cities of St. Paul: Their Influence on His Life and Thought.* New York: Armstrong, 1908; Reprint, Minneapolis: James Family, n.d.

> This out of print classic examines the life and culture of five cities from the life of the Apostle Paul—Tarsus, Psidian, Iconium, Derbe, and Lystra—and seeks to determine how their culture and social milieu influenced his thought and writings. Ramsay was the greatest Pauline expert of his day and deserves to be read today over a century later. A true classic!

+*———. *St. Paul the Traveler and the Roman Citizen.* London: Hodder and Stoughton, 1897; Reprint, Grand Rapids: Baker, 1962.

> Also out of print, this classic examines the cities that the Apostle Paul visited in the Acts of the Apostles.

!*Schreiner, Thomas R. *Paul, Apostle of God's Glory in Christ.* Downers Grove: IVP Academic, 2001.

> An accessible guide to Pauline theology. Reformed. "Well worth buying as an introductory study" (Evans, 326).

*Stalker, James. *The Life of St. Paul*. Westwood, NJ: Revell, 1950.

> A popular biography of the Apostle Paul that is particularly suited for laypersons.

*Ware James P. *Paul's Theology in Context: Creation, Incarnation, Covenant, and Kingdom*. Grand Rapids: Eerdmans, 2019.

> Intended for a general audience, this book provides an informative and satisfying introduction to Paul's theology that is perfect for the motivated layperson. Well-written and engaging!

Romans

There is an embarrassment of riches available for those who would endeavor to study the Epistle to the Romans. From technical works (see the author's 2017 *The Pastor's Library*) to devotional commentaries, there is something for everyone.

*Barnhouse, Donald Grey. *Expositions of Bible Doctrines Taking the Epistle to the Romans as the Point of Departure*. 4 vols. Grand Rapids: Eerdmans, 1952–63.

> This set, by the late editor of *Eternity Magazine* and pastor of 10th Presbyterian Church in Philadelphia, is a masterful examination of Bible doctrines using the epistle to the Romans as a point of departure. It is not a commentary, but will reward careful reading. Masterful! "Very rich. His many striking illustrations help make the series especially valuable to the pastor as well as the teacher" (Rosscup, 248). "An exposition of Bible doctrine which is very full, well-illustrated and appropriately applied" (Barber, 162).

*Boice, James Montgomery. *Romans: An Expositional Commentary*. 4 vols. Grand Rapids: Baker, 1991–95.

> "Well-known Reformed theologian, author, Bible teacher, speaker and co-founder of the Alliance of Confessing Evangelicals.

Boice served as Senior Pastor of Tenth Street Presbyterian Church in Philadelphia from 1968 until his death in 2000. This four-volume set is based on Boice's 239 sermons preached as his church over a five-year period of time. The 2000+ pages of this set might seem intimidating, but Boice's expertise on expository teaching balanced with contemporary insight makes the commentary clear, concise, and understandable to laypersons and biblical scholars alike. This verse-by-verse commentary, written by an outstanding Reformed theologian, is an invaluable resource for any serious student of Paul's majestic letter to the Romans" **(VanHook)**.

*Bruce, F. F. *The Epistle to the Romans*. TNTC. Grand Rapids: Eerdmans, 1963.

This brief study is now dated and uneven in spots mostly due to the limitations of the TNTC series. It was revised in 1986 prior to the author's death, but the revision was not as extensive as warranted. However, any book by Bruce is certainly worth acquiring. "Draws upon a wide knowledge of literature, frequently cites theological writers, and provides an understandable, and, in many ways, significant exposition of this epistle. Occasionally the comments are too brief to be of help to the pastor and at other times exceptionally full" (Barber, 162).

!*Kruse, Colin. *Paul's Letter to the Romans*. PNTC. Grand Rapids: Eerdmans, 2012.

This volume vies with Moo for pride of place for the best mid-level commentary. A fine and helpful study. With either Kruse or Moo, one cannot go wrong.

!*Moo, Douglas. *The Epistle to the Romans*. NICNT. Grand Rapids: Eerdmans, 1996.

Perhaps the best mid-level commentary available to the serious lay scholar. The author teaches New Testament at Wheaton College and is widely respected. Highly recommended!

*———. *Romans*. NIVAC. Grand Rapids: Zondervan, 2000.

> This volume distills the essence of his NICNT commentary and makes it accessible for general audiences. "Great for pastors" (Evans, 342).

!*Murray, John. *The Epistle to the Romans*. NICNT. Grand Rapids: Eerdmans, 1959–65.

> This magnificent commentary by the late professor at Westminster Theological Seminary is a fine treatment of the book particularly in the areas of exegesis and theology. For decades it has been one of the standard conservative works on this epistle. It has been replaced in the NICNT series by Moo, but hardly eclipsed. Though this work is now dated, it remains one of the outstanding mid-level commentaries available. "Murray deals with problem verses with careful scholarship and good insight, leaving few stones unturned. It is one of the most helpful works on the epistle for the teacher ... who is serious about his Bible study" (Rosscup, 257). "A superb theological commentary which shows good exegetical judgment" (Evans, 342). Reformed. Postmillennial.

*Sproul, R. C. *The Gospel of God: Romans*. Focus on the Bible Commentary. Rev. ed. Ross-Shire, Scotland: Christian Focus, 2011.

> "The late R. C. Sproul was found of Ligonier Ministries and the first president of Reformed Bible College. His books, the Renewing Your Mind daily radio Bible broadcast, and the popular Ligonier Conferences made Sproul one of the most well-known and respected Reformed theologians in the world. Needless to say, his commentary on Romans reflects his Reformed perspective of Scripture. There are numerous commentaries on the Book of Romans, many in multiple sets, so this 316-page book seems small in comparison. But Sproul has a way of getting to the heart of Scripture in a way that is informative, detailed, and concise, but at the same time easy to understand. His unique gift of making biblical truth clear and insightful is a hallmark of his teaching and ministry. The commentary begins with an outline and summary of the book

and moves from there to a verse-by-verse exposition of the book. Chapter summaries, comments, and illustrations help in understanding the context and relevance of each passage. After each chapter, Sproul includes questions not only about the scriptural content, but also personal application. The questions can be used for individual reflection as well as for the basis for group discussion. The *Gospel of God* is an easy to understand, clearly-presented commentary on Romans from a Reformed Theology viewpoint" (**VanHook**).

Stifler, James M. *The Epistle to the Romans*. Chicago: Moody, 1960.

This brief commentary, by the late longtime professor of Greek at Crozier Theological Seminary, is geared to the lay reader and is useful to the preacher or Bible teacher. "Traces the argument of the epistle very well so that the reader receives help in a nutshell form in thinking his way through Paul's profound reasoning" (Rosscup, 258). Premillennial. Dispensational.

*Thomas, W. H. Griffith. *St. Paul's Epistle to the Romans: A Devotional Commentary*. Grand Rapids: Eerdmans, 1946.

As the title indicates, this study is a devotional commentary useful mainly to the non-specialist and layperson. Griffith was very helpful to me as a baby Christian. "Excellent outlines and illustrations" (Barber, 164).

*Wiersbe, Warren W. *Be Right: How to Be Right with God, Yourself, and Others*. 2nd ed. Colorado Springs: David C. Cook, 2008.

This is the author's treatment of the book, which is included in his six-volume compilation, *The Bible Exposition Commentary*.

1 Corinthians

*Blomberg, Craig L. *1 Corinthians*. NIVAC. Grand Rapids: Zondervan, 1995.

> A capable and eminently practical work that is of great value to pastors. Blomberg is one of the evangelical luminaries writing today and this volume is not to be missed! "A thoughtful, suggestive work" (Evans, 345).

!*Ciampa, Roy E., and Brian S. Rosner. *The First Letter to the Corinthians*. PNTC. Grand Rapids: Eerdmans, 2010.

> This fine commentary is massive at 867 pages of text and would serve as an excellent mid-level choice for the serious student. However, Fee is my first choice here. Very helpful in the introduction is a lengthy section on how to interpret the epistle. "Very full, but on occasion not easy to follow and not very plausible" (Carson, 93).

!*Fee, Gordon D. *The First Epistle to the Corinthians*. NICNT. Grand Rapids: Eerdmans, 1987.

> This is an exceptional commentary and my first choice for a mid-level commentary on this epistle. The author's denominational affiliation is Assemblies of God, so the reader may disagree with his positions on some issues. For example, Fee views 14:34–35 as a textual gloss essentially dismissing those arguments against a more limited role for women in the church. "This is the all-around best evangelical commentary on the epistle" (Rosscup, 262). "Fee's commentary is lucid, informed, sensible, and written with great verve. Occasionally the passion that marks this commentary is grating, especially when Fee is passionate about a position with which one disagrees" (Carson, 93)!

*Kistemaker, Simon. *Exposition of the First Epistle to the Corinthians.* NTC. Grand Rapids: Baker, 1993.

> A fine mid-level commentary that is solid theologically. Winner of the ECPA's 1994 Gold Medallion Book Award in the Commentaries category. Reformed.

+*Morgan, G. Campbell. *The Corinthian Letters of Paul.* Old Tappan, NJ: Revell, 1956.

> G. Campbell Morgan, who lived from 1863–1945, was highly regarded as a preacher and was rightly known as the "prince of expositors" throughout the English-speaking world. Although this book is not an exegetical commentary, any book by Morgan is well worth reading. Of particular value to preachers, but will be treasured by laypersons. "A renowned pulpiteer addresses himself to the problems which plague the church. His statements are timely and show a mastery of the subject matter" (Barber, 166).

*Prior, David. *The Message of 1 Corinthians: Life in the Local Church.* BST. Downers Grove: IVP, 1985.

> This middle level popular treatment is by a practitioner who has pastored churches in South Africa and Oxford, England. It is not a verse-by-verse treatment, but rather paragraph-by-paragraph. It is well-written and eminently practical. "Many will appreciate his insightful strokes that are relevant today on areas such as divorce, remarriage, and tongues" (Rosscup, 265).

*Redpath, Alan. *The Royal Route to Heaven: Studies in First Corinthians.* Old Tappan, NJ: Revell, 1960.

> This book is not a commentary, but rather a compilation of sermons delivered from the pulpit at the Moody Memorial Church in Chicago. These sermons are warm, devotional, and pastoral expositions that would benefit any Bible teacher who plans to teach from this epistle. "They rebuke shallowness and ineffectiveness in the church, expose the tragedy of living in sinfulness and worldliness, and vigorously apply the message

of this epistle to the lives of believers today" (Barber, 166). "Remarkably practical" (Carson, 96).

*Wiersbe, Warren W. *Be Wise: Discern the Difference Between Man's Knowledge and God's Wisdom.* 2nd ed. Colorado Springs: David C. Cook, 2010.

This is the author's treatment of the book, which is included in his six-volume compilation, *The Bible Exposition Commentary.*

2 Corinthians

!*Garland, David E. *2 Corinthians.* NAC. Nashville: Holman Reference, 1999.

An exceptional non-technical work by a Baylor University New Testament scholar. Can be used with profit by motivated laypersons. "Deserves serious consideration as a priority purchase for evangelical pastors" (Evans, 351).

*Hafemann, Scott J. *2 Corinthians,* NIVAC. Grand Rapids: Zondervan, 2000.

One of the best in the series, this volume is of immense value to Bible teachers. "A superior entry" (Carson, 99).

!*Hughes, Philip Edgcumbe. *Paul's Second Epistle to the Corinthians.* NICNT. Grand Rapids: Eerdmans, 1962.

At forty years of age, this is still a solid mid-level guide for the serious student. "Dependable, and especially valued for its theological insights" (Evans, 354).

*Kruse, Colin G. *2 Corinthians.* TNTC. 2nd ed. Downers Grove: IVP Academic, 2015.

Originally published in 1987, this work capably replaces the quite serviceable 1963 volume by Tasker in the series. Probably the best entry level commentary for the layperson.

!*Seifrid, Mark A. *The Second Letter to the Corinthians.* PNTC. Grand Rapids: Eerdmans, 2014.

> A fine offering that vies with Barnett and Garland as the best mid-level commentary on this epistle. Actually, one cannot go wrong with any of the three. They are all very good. Seifrid approaches this epistle as a unified letter, rather than, as many modern liberal scholars argue, a composite of fragments and excerpts. The author has produced a well-written and exegetically sound commentary that is theologically rich.

*Wiersbe, Warren W. *Be Encouraged: God Can Turn Your Trials into Triumphs.* 2nd ed. Colorado Springs: David C. Cook, 2010.

> This is the author's treatment of the book, which is included in his six-volume compilation, *The Bible Exposition Commentary.*

Galatians

+*Brown, John. *An Exposition of the Epistle of Paul to the Galatians.* Edinburgh: Oliphant, 1853; Reprint, Minneapolis: James Family, 1979.

> Again, out of print, this is a very rare classic indeed and would be found treasure if discovered second-hand. The author was a noted Presbyterian pastor and seminary professor in Scotland. His expositions are comprehensive, warmly devotional, and first rate. "Brown is a modern Puritan. All his expositions are of the utmost value" (Spurgeon, 175).

*Cole, Alan. *The Epistle of Paul to the Galatians: An Introduction and Commentary.* TNTC. Grand Rapids: Eerdmans, 1965.

> This helpful little commentary was revised in 1989. It offers help with the Greek text, but is not technical and is aimed at the general reader. Not one of the better volumes in the series, but serviceable. Particularly helpful for a lay audience. "It is a good evangelical commentary, well-informed, solid, clear with good help at times on problem verses" (Rosscup, 274). "Readable, informative, and suggestive" (Barber, 167).

!*DeSilva, David A. *The Letter to the Galatians*. NICNT. Grand Rapids: Eerdmans, 2018.

> This is the third Galatians volume in the NICNT series and the best by far. My first choice for a mid-level commentary for the serious lay student.

!*Fung, Ronald Y. K. *The Epistle to the Galatians*. NICNT. Grand Rapids: Eerdmans, 1988.

> This is the second Galatians volume in the NICNT series and a third with DeSilva came out in 2018. This volume is a real improvement over the 1953 Ridderbos contribution. Fung is solidly evangelical. A good, but not great, mid-level commentary. My recommendation is George over Fung and DeSilva over both.

!*George, Timothy. *Galatians*. NAC. Nashville: Holman Reference, 1994.

> This well-done study, by the founding dean of Beeson Divinity School, is rich theologically and will benefit laypersons. Until DeSilva's volume, probably the best mid-level commentary for the serious lay student available. "There is much to appreciate about this theologically astute, traditionally-styled commentary" (Evans, 360).

*Gromacki, Robert G. *Stand Fast in Liberty: An Exposition of Galatians*. Grand Rapids: Baker, 1979.

> This little guide is a popular commentary for the non-specialist by a professor of Greek and New Testament at Cedarville College (now Cedarville University). It is practical and competent and ideal for Bible study groups. The Questions for Discussion at the end of each chapter are especially thought provoking.

*Hendriksen, William. *Exposition of Galatians*. NTC. Grand Rapids: Baker, 1968.

> With good reason, Hendriksen has earned a wide following among pastors. His commentaries are practical and devotional in spirit. "Warmhearted" (Carson, 105). Reformed.

*Keller, Timothy. *Galatians for You: For Reading, for Feeding, for Leading*. God's Word for You. Surrey: The Good Book Company, 2013.

> A satisfying beginner's introduction to the epistle by a noted Presbyterian pastor.

*McKnight, Scot. *Galatians*. NIVAC. Grand Rapids: Zondervan, 1995.

> A lucid and accessible treatment that abounds in practical insights. An excellent entry level volume for the layperson.

Tenney, Merrill C. *Galatians: The Charter of Christian Liberty*. Revised and enlarged edition. Grand Rapids: Eerdmans, 1957.

> This interesting little volume is a brief treatment of the book using different methods of Bible study. This is definitely for the beginning student, but can be helpful to the pastor in approaching the book. It gives little exegetical assistance. "Designed to help students of the Word grapple with the text firsthand. Approaches the epistle from synthetic, critical, biographical, and devotional points of view. Excellent" (Barber, 168)!

*Wiersbe, Warren W. *Be Free: Exchange Legalism for True Spirituality*. 2nd ed. Colorado Springs: David C. Cook, 2009.

> This is the author's treatment of the book, which is included in his six-volume compilation, *The Bible Exposition Commentary*.

Ephesians

+*Calvin, John. *Sermons on the Epistle to the Ephesians.* Translated by Arthur Golding in 1577; Revised translation, 1973. Reprint, Edinburgh: Banner of Truth, 1973.

> This gem is a true classic of the Christian faith. First published in 1562, this collection of sermons by the eminent Swiss reformer, is a gold mine of teaching material that serves as a model for conveying Christian doctrine. These forty-eight sermons were preached at Geneva on consecutive Sundays in 1558–59 when Calvin was forty-nine years of age. "The sermons are priceless" (Spurgeon, 177).

*Kent, Homer. *Ephesians: The Glory of the Church.* Chicago: Moody, 1971.

> Like all of the author's works, this book is a concise and lucid treatment of the main themes of the book with an emphasis on the practical. At 127 pages this book is not as detailed or as helpful as his commentary on The Pastoral Epistles. This book is mainly for the beginning student and non-specialist. Ideal for laypersons.

+*Moule, H. C. G. *Grace and Godliness: Studies in the Epistle to the Ephesians.* London: Seeley and Co. Limited, 1895. Reprint, Minneapolis: Klock & Klock, 1983.

> This brief devotional gem was published together in one volume along with Pattison's *Exposition of Ephesians: Lessons in Grace and Godliness* by Klock & Klock. It is now regrettably out of print. This volume came about in 1894 when ministers gathered at Cambridge for the "Long Vacation" and requested Professor Moule, at that time principal of Ridley Hall, to provide them with a series of Bible readings. These studies are the result of that request.

!*O'Brien, Peter T. *The Letter to the Ephesians*. PNTC. Grand Rapids: Eerdmans, 1999.

> A detailed commentary at close to 500 pages of text, this is my choice for a mid-level commentary for the serious student.

*Snodgrass, Klyne. *Ephesians*. NIVAC. Edited by Terry Muck. Grand Rapids: Zondervan, 1996.

> One of the better volumes in the series, this is an eminently practical guide to the epistle that laypersons will greatly appreciate. Please note that Snodgrass has a weak view of election.

*Stott, John *God's New Society: The Message of Ephesians*. BST. Downers Grove: IVP, 1980.

> Exceptional introductory study for laypersons. My first choice for beginning study. One can never go wrong with Stott.

*Wiersbe, Warren W. *Be Rich: Gaining the Things That Money Can't Buy*. 2nd ed. Colorado Springs: David C. Cook, 2009.

> This is the author's treatment of the book, which is included in his six-volume compilation, *The Bible Exposition Commentary*.

Philippians

*Boice, James Montgomery. *Philippians: An Expositional Commentary*. Grand Rapids: Zondervan, 1971.

> Boice was the pastor for many years of 10th Presbyterian Church in Philadelphia and successor to Donald Gray Barnhouse. This work is similar to most of the late author's other works on books of the Bible in that it is a series of expositions on the text. It is particularly well suited to laypersons and beginning students. He is extremely practical and does not get bogged down in technical details. Preachers and teachers will find Boice to be quite suggestive. "A lucid and very readable simple exposition that is helpful and competent on many of

the issues . . . The exposition is practical and sermonic, with sometimes good background and comparison with relevant passages from other Scripture. He illustrates heavily from literature, history, and contemporary life" (Rosscup, 285).

*Bruce, F. F. *Philippians*. NIBC. Peabody: Hendrickson, 1989.

This commentary, based on the NIV by the esteemed New Testament scholar and professor at the University of Manchester, is concise, very accessible to the non-specialist, and well worth acquiring. The serious student will want to supplement it with more detailed works such as that of Fee. A good introduction for laypersons by perhaps the top evangelical New Testament scholar of the twentieth century.

*Cohick, Lynn H. *Philippians*. SGBC. Grand Rapids: Zondervan, 2013.

Although the series' intentions are laudable and this volume does a good job of highlighting the Bible's grand story in Philippians, it is not strong on the details. For example, the introduction at twenty-one pages is much too brief and it lacks a bibliography.

!*Fee, Gordon D. *Paul's Letter to the Philippians*. NICNT. Grand Rapids: Eerdmans, 1995.

An outstanding commentary by one of the top New Testament scholars of the past generation. Fee has written what is arguably the best mid-level work on this epistle. It is beautifully written and accessible. This is my top choice for the serious lay student.

Getz, Gene A. *A Profile of Christian Maturity: A Study of Philippians*. Grand Rapids: Zondervan, 1976.

This little book is not a verse-by-verse commentary, but rather a series of studies "With 20th Century Lessons for Your Church." Each chapter begins with "Something to Think About" and ends with "A Personal Life Response." Very practical for laypersons and pastors.

+*Johnstone, Robert. *Lectures on the Epistle to the Philippians.* Edinburgh: T. & T. Clark, 1875. Reprint, Minneapolis: Klock & Klock, 1977.

> This delightful book is a collection of thirty lectures on the epistle that were delivered from the pulpit in successive Sunday services. Johnstone, late professor of New Testament Literature and Exegesis, United Presbyterian College, Edinburgh, shares the insights he learned as a student of the law and a New Testament scholar in these brilliant expositions. I read this book during my devotions while a student in seminary over forty years ago and was enthralled and greatly blessed. I felt as if I were in the presence of pulpit royalty. It is true that preachers do not preach this way in the twenty-first century, but perhaps the Church would be less superficial if they did. "A thorough, practical, and homiletical exposition, which warns against the fallacies of churchianity, strongly defends the preexistence of Christ, and remains one of the leading expository works on the subject" (Barber, 170). "A noble volume. A real boon to the man who purchases it" (Spurgeon, 180). Reformed.

*Martin, Ralph P. *The Epistle of Paul to the Philippians.* TNTC. Grand Rapids: Eerdmans, 1959.

> This volume is not to be confused with the author's Philippians volume in the New Century Bible series published in 1976. Also, avoid the author's 1987 revision of this work which is questionable in some of its views and certainly not in line with evangelical theology. However, this book is a fine introduction to the book for laity.

!*Melick, Richard R. Philippians, Colossians, Philemon. NAC. Nashville: Holman Reference, 1991.

> A helpful volume particularly for pastors and serious lay students by a professor of New Testament at Golden Gate Theological Seminary in Mill Valley, CA. "Workmanlike but not outstanding" (Carson, 115). Baptist.

*Moule, H. C. G. *Studies in Philippians.* Cambridge: University Press, 1893. Reprint, Grand Rapids: Kregel Publications, 1977.

> This brief treatment was originally published in 1893 in the series, Cambridge Bible for Schools and Colleges. Although now quite dated on technical matters, it is still worth obtaining for its devotional emphasis. "A beautifully written, deeply devotional treatment which expounds the affectionate character of this epistle and relates its message to the lives of believers" (Barber, 171). "Warm devotional tone that bathes his exegesis" (Carson, 117).

*Robertson, A. T. *Paul's Joy in Christ: Studies in Philippians.* Old Tappan: Revell, 1917. Reprint, Grand Rapids: Baker, 1979.

> This little volume, by perhaps the foremost Greek grammarian the U.S. has ever produced, is a sheer delight to read. It is not a detailed commentary, but rather a series of expositions on the text. It is not technical and is easily accessible to the beginning student or layperson. "He is rich in word studies and in the explanation of the text" (Rosscup, 291).

*Thielman, Frank. *Philippians.* NIVAC. Grand Rapids: Zondervan, 1995.

> An exceptional commentary suitable for laypersons. I used this book last year when I taught an adult Sunday School class on Philippians and I found it exceedingly user-friendly and practical. I recommend this volume without hesitation for the introductory lay student.

*Wiersbe, Warren W. *Be Joyful: Even When Things Go Wrong, You Can Have Joy.* 2nd ed. Colorado Springs: David C. Cook, 2008.

> This is the author's treatment of the book, which is included in his six-volume compilation, *The Bible Exposition Commentary.*

Colossians

*Garland, David E. *Colossians, Philemon*. NIVAC. Grand Rapids: Zondervan, 1998.

> This volume is the rare practical commentary that has substantial interaction with scholarly writings. It is quite helpful for laypersons.

*Harrison, Everett F. *Colossians: Christ All-Sufficient*. Chicago: Moody, 1971.

> This book is an extremely brief treatment by a former professor of New Testament at Dallas Theological Seminary and Fuller Theological Seminary. It is well written, but its brevity makes it of interest only to the beginning students and other non-specialists. "Good things frequently come in small packages. This is one of them" (Barber, 172).

*Lucas, R. C. *The Message of Colossians and Philemon*. BST. Downers Grove: IVP Academic, 1984.

> A popular treatment of these epistles that will particularly help Bible study teachers.

!*Melick, Richard R. See section on Philippians.

!*Moo, Douglas J. *The Letters to the Colossians and to Philemon*. PNTC. Grand Rapids: Eerdmans, 2008.

> This commentary is a mid-level work by a front-rank evangelical scholar and is my top choice for serious lay students. Highly recommended!

*Moule, H. C. G. *Studies in Colossians & Philemon*. Cambridge: The University Press, 1893. Reprint, Grand Rapids: Kregel, 1977.

> This volume is a devotional commentary on these epistles first published in 1877 by the noted Cambridge professor of the late eighteenth/early twentieth century. It is for general audiences and should be supplemented with more substantial

works. "Moule was known for his saintliness and evangelical fervor. These studies bear testimony to his ability as an expositor. They deal adequately with the text and deftly apply the message of these epistles" (Barber, 172).

*Wiersbe, Warren W. *Be Complete: Become the Whole Person God Intends You to Be*. 2nd ed. Colorado Springs: David C. Cook, 2008.

This is the author's treatment of the book, which is included in his six-volume compilation, *The Bible Exposition Commentary*.

*Wright, N. T. *Colossians and Philemon*. TNTC. Downers Grove: IVP Academic, 1986.

An exceptional brief treatment by the controversial and prolific New Testament scholar who was formerly the Bishop of Durham in the Church of England. This commentary retires Carson's 1960 work in the series.

1 and 2 Thessalonians

*Beale, G. K. *1-2 Thessalonians*. IVPNTC. Downers Grove: IVP, 2003.

This non-technical commentary provides a good mix of exegesis, theology, Old Testament background, and application of the text to the modern reader. As usual, Beale's work is meticulous and well worth reading. "Very well done" (Evans, 381). Reformed. Amillennial.

!*Fee, Gordon D. *The First and Second Letters to the Thessalonians*. NICNT. Grand Rapids: Eerdmans, 2009.

Perhaps the strongest mid-level commentary for the serious lay Bible student. Fee is always a disciplined scholar who focuses on the text and doesn't go off on tangents. My first choice with Green a close second.

!*Green, Gene. *The Letters to the Thessalonians.* PNTC. Grand Rapids: Eerdmans, 2002.

> A fine mid-level work for the serious lay student. "Well-done, thoroughly evangelical" (Evans, 380).

*Hiebert, D. Edmond. *The Thessalonian Epistles: A Call to Readiness.* Chicago: Moody, 1971.

> This commentary by the late professor of Greek and New Testament at the Mennonite Brethren Biblical Seminary in Fresno, CA is user-friendly, warm, and quite readable. Now somewhat dated, it sets forth the pretribulational, premillennial viewpoints in an exemplary fashion. "An outstanding exposition based upon unusually comprehensive and complete exegesis. A leader among commentaries for accuracy and reliability" (Barber, 173). "Many features make this volume valuable: background information, extensive bibliography up to its day, numerous footnotes, and a rich use of the original Greek" (Rosscup, 296). Premillennial.

*Holmes, Michael W. *1 and 2 Thessalonians.* NIVAC. Grand Rapids: Zondervan, 1998.

> A practical commentary that is exceedingly helpful for laypersons. I highly recommend it! "Judicious in its pastoral application" (Carson, 125).

*Martin, D. Michael. *1, 2 Thessalonians.* NAC. Nashville: Holman Reference, 1995.

> A workmanlike study by a professor at Golden Gate Baptist Seminary. Helpful for pastors. Premillennial. Posttribulational. Baptist.

!*Morris, Leon. *The First and Second Epistles to the Thessalonians.* NICNT. Grand Rapids: Eerdmans, 1959.

> A perfectly fine mid-level commentary that was replaced in the NICNT by Fee's volume. Fee and Green are superior now

mainly because this is over a half century old, but I have always been partial to Morris' work. Still recommended!

*———. *1 and 2 Thessalonians*. TNTC. Downers Grove: IVP, 1957.

> This commentary is a less technical distillation of the ideas in the author's NICNT volume (see above). It was revised in 1984. It is still perfectly fine for introductory students and laypersons.

*Stott, John. *The Gospel and End of Time: The Message of 1 & 2 Thessalonians*. BST. Downers Grove: IVP, 1991.

> This commentary is excellent for laypersons or for study groups. Includes a study guide both for individuals and groups. Stott, who died in 2011, served as an Anglican rector at All Souls Church in London for a quarter century and was the epitome of the pastor-scholar. His writings were hugely influential and I highly recommend that you acquaint yourself with him.

*Wiersbe, Warren W. *Be Ready: Living in Light of Christ's Return*. 2nd ed. Colorado Springs: David C. Cook, 2010.

> This is the author's treatment of these books, which is included in his six-volume compilation, *The Bible Exposition Commentary*.

The Pastoral Epistles

The books, 1 and 2 Timothy and Titus, are usually designated by the special term The Pastoral Epistles.

Getz, Gene A. *A Profile for a Christian Life Style: A Study of Titus with 20th-Century Lessons for Your Church*. Grand Rapids: Zondervan, 1978.

> This little book is an interesting compilation of expositions on this epistle with helpful sermonic outlines at the beginning of

each chapter and pointed questions at the end to aid in review and internalization of the material. This is a general treatment for the non-specialist.

*Guthrie, Donald. *The Pastoral Epistles: An Introduction and Commentary.* TNTC. Grand Rapids: Eerdmans, 1957.

This commentary is a good basic treatment of the text for the non-specialist by the former Tutor in New Testament Language and Literature at London Bible College. It is brief, but very helpful on introductory matters particularly with summaries of conflicting interpretations.

*Hughes, R. Kent, and Chapell, Bryan. *1 & 2 Timothy and Titus: To Guard the Deposit. Preaching the Word.* Wheaton: Crossway, 2000.

Hughes wrote the 1 and 2 Timothy sections and Chapell wrote the Titus potion. Both are noted masters of the homiletical craft and offer much here of value for pastors, teachers, and students. Illustrations abound.

*Kent Jr., Homer A. *The Pastoral Epistles.* Chicago: Moody, 1958.

This is an outstanding commentary for the non-specialist. Very helpful especially in comparing different views. I used it extensively many years ago and found it to be quite useful for preaching. "A work of quality and reliability. Admirably bridges the gap between a laborious, technical treatment and a superficial, popular one" (Barber, 175).

*Liefeld, Walter L. *1 and 2 Timothy, Titus.* NIVAC. Grand Rapids: Zondervan, 1999.

A most helpful introductory work for laypersons and Bible teachers. Has good application. "Very fine work" (Evans, 390).

Moule, H. C. G. *Studies in II Timothy.* London: Religious Tract Society, n.d.; Reprint, Grand Rapids: Kregel, 1977.

This little book is a brief devotional study for the non-specialist. The author, who lived from 1841–1920, served as Principal of Ridley Hall, Cambridge, for nineteen years and was a popular speaker at Keswick Conventions and church conferences. He was well-known for his piety and practical application.

*Stott, John R. W. *Guard the Gospel: The Message of 2 Timothy.* BST. Downers Grove: IVP, 1973.

This little commentary is a brief, but rich, exposition that will be particularly helpful for teachers. Anything written by Stott is worth purchasing and consulting regularly. "Will be treasured by preachers" (Carson, 132). "Deserves to be read by all who are interested in living dynamically for Christ in this present era" (Barber). "Stott has quite good insight into the meaning of verse, and has a rare ability to state truth succinctly" (Rosscup, 304).

*———. *Guard the Truth: The Message of 1 Timothy and Titus.* BST. Downers Grove: IVP, 1996.

See above description.

+*Taylor, Thomas. *Exposition of Titus.* Cambridge, 1619. Reprint, Minneapolis: Klock & Klock, 1980.

This commentary is a classic exposition by a Puritan writer. First published in 1619, it is rich, thorough, and warm. "This commentary will well repay the reader" (Spurgeon, 185).

!*Towner, Philip H. *The Letters to Timothy and Titus.* NICNT. Grand Rapids: Eerdmans, 2006.

This is a massive mid-level commentary at just over 800 pages. This is my first choice for the serious layperson wanting to delve into these epistles.

*Wiersbe, Warren W. *Be Faithful: It's Always Too Soon to Quit.* 2nd ed. Colorado Springs: David C. Cook, 2009.

This is the author's treatment of the Pastoral Epistles and Philemon, which is included in his six-volume compilation, *The Bible Exposition Commentary.*

Woychuk, N. A. *An Exposition of Second Timothy: Inspirational and Practical.* Old Tappan: Revell, 1973.

> This brief commentary, by the founder of Bible Memory Association, is for the non-specialist. "An original and creative exposition which abounds in illustrative material" (Barber).

Philemon

*Garland, David E. See section on Colossians.

*Lucas, R. C. See section on Colossians.

!*McKnight, Scot. *The Letter to Philemon.* NICNT. Grand Rapids: Eerdmans, 2017.

> I am glad the editors at Eerdmans saw fit to give Philemon its own stand-alone commentary. So often, it is simply appended to Colossians. McKnight is the perfect person to tackle this short book. For the serious lay student, this is hands down the best mid-level commentary on this book. By the way, for the layperson wanting to study a book of the Bible seriously and not wanting to commit to a lengthy tome such as Romans, this would be an easy one to attempt for a first try. Philemon itself is one short chapter and this volume is just over 100 pages. Highly recommended!

!*Melick, Richard R. See section on Philippians.

!*Moo, Douglas J. See section on Colossians.

Moule, H. C. G. See section on Colossians.

*Wiersbe, Warren W. See section on The Pastoral Epistles.

*Wright, N. T. See section on Colossians.

General Epistles

The term General Epistles refers to the epistles James, 1 and 2 Peter, 1, 2, and 3 John, and Jude. They have also been referred to as the Catholic Epistles or Universal Epistles. These terms indicate that these letters were addressed to the general church and not to specific congregations, such as with Paul's epistles.

*Hiebert, D. Edmond. *An Introduction to the Non-Pauline Epistle.* Chicago: Moody, 1962.

> This helpful book is a well done, but dated, introduction to the general epistles. Hebrews is not included. Each section deals with such introductory matters as canonicity and authorship. There is an outline for each book and a brief bibliography, which sorely needs updating. Good for the general reader, but should be supplemented with a more recent volume such as Jobes' new work. "Lucid, accurate, and reliable" (Barber).

!*Jobes, Karen H. *Letters to the Church: A Survey of Hebrews and the General Epistles.* Grand Rapids: Zondervan Academic, 2011.

> The standard evangelical treatment of these books since its publication. Jobes' work is always top-notch!

Hebrews

+*Brown, John. *Hebrews.* Reprint, Edinburgh: Banner of Truth, 1961.

> First published in 1862, this commentary was treasured by Spurgeon for its thorough exposition, boldness, and evangelical warmth. Like Spurgeon, Brown was something of a nineteenth century Puritan. "Spiritually edifying" (Evans, 396). Reformed.

!*Bruce, F. F. *The Epistle to the Hebrews*. NICNT. Grand Rapids: Eerdmans, 1964.

> F. F. Bruce was the Rylands Professor of Biblical Criticism and Exegesis at the University of Manchester, England, and editor of the *Evangelical Quarterly*. He was the author of dozens of books and one of the evangelical world's shining scholarly lights of the twentieth century. Upon its publication in 1964, this commentary assumed pride of place as the finest evangelical commentary on this epistle. Prior to his death in 1990, Bruce revised this work, but the differences are marginal at best. My judgment is that this still remains one of the very finest expositions of this epistle. Retired in the series by Cockerill in 2012, but never eclipsed. For the motivated layperson, this volume by Bruce will suffice nicely, but so will Cockerill and O'Brien.

!*Cockerill, Gareth Lee. *The Epistle to the Hebrews*. NICNT. Grand Rapids: Eerdmans, 2012.

> A worthy successor to Bruce's 1964 commentary is this fine volume by the research professor of New Testament and biblical theology at Wesley Biblical Seminary. Since I am Reformed, I found myself disagreeing with many of Cockerill's positions particularly in chapter 6. In fact, because of his Arminian positions, I would choose O'Brien, or even Bruce, as my first choice for a mid-level work. However, there is much to like in this stimulating and fresh treatment. "His treatment of the use of the Old Testament in Hebrews is frequently disappointing" (Carson, 134). Wesleyan.

English, E. Schuyler. *Studies in the Epistle to the Hebrews*. Neptune, NJ: Loizeaux Brothers, 1955.

> This commentary is a popular treatment of the epistle for the non-specialist. "A capable exposition of the theme of this epistle" (Barber, 176).

!*Guthrie, George H. *Hebrews*. NIVAC. Grand Rapids: Zondervan, 1998.

> This volume is one of the strongest in the series and is great help to both pastors looking for homiletical assistance and students seeking exegetical insight. It will also be of assistance to the motivated layperson wanting to dig a bit deeper into the text. A real treat!

*———. *Hebrews*. TNTC. Downers Grove: IVP Academic, 2009.

> A fine replacement to the Hewitt volume in this series. This is my first choice for an introductory work for the layperson.

Hewitt, Thomas. *The Epistle to the Hebrews: An Introduction and Commentary*. TNTC. Grand Rapids: Eerdmans, 1960.

> This volume was one of the weakest offerings in the TNTC series. The author sees Silas as the likely author and takes a bizarre position on the warning passages. Replaced in the series by Guthrie. Use him instead. Reformed.

*Kent, Jr., Homer A. *The Epistle to the Hebrews*. Grand Rapids: Baker, 1972.

> This volume is an excellent commentary for the non-specialist by the former Dean and Professor of NT and Greek at Grace Theological Seminary. It is well organized, like all of Kent's works, quite readable, and is easily accessible to the layperson. "A helpful evangelical commentary, especially from the standpoint of clarity on the Greek where this is crucial to the interpretation, without being technical" (Rosscup, 310). "A work which the pastor or seminary student will welcome. Adequately explains the theme of the epistle, builds exposition upon a very capable exegesis of the text, and ably elucidates the theological facets of the epistle" (Barber, 177).

!*O'Brien, Peter T. *The Letter to the Hebrews.* PNTC. Grand Rapids: Eerdmans, 2010.

> This volume has surpassed Bruce's work as the best mid-level work on this epistle for the serious lay student. Highly recommended! Reformed.

*Thomas, W. H. Griffith. *Hebrews: A Devotional Commentary.* Grand Rapids: Eerdmans, 1961.

> A collection of forty-one devotional messages on the epistle first delivered at Wycliffe Hall, Oxford, 1905–10, and then at the Moody Bible Institute in 1911. It focuses on the main themes of the epistle and the necessity and conditions of spiritual progress. This was the first commentary that I ever read along with the epistle when I began studying the Bible decades ago. I still have my highlighted copy. I never realized that Bible study could be so much fun.

*Wiersbe, Warren W. *Be Confident: Live by Faith, Not by Sight.* 2nd ed. Colorado Springs: David C. Cook, 2009.

> This is the author's treatment of the book, which is included in his six-volume compilation, *The Bible Exposition Commentary.*

James

*Adamson, James B. *The Epistle of James.* NICNT. Grand Rapids: Eerdmans, 1976.

> A fine commentary that has been replaced in the NICNT series by McKnight. Still a very good choice for the motivated layperson and very helpful. McKnight and Moo are better choices though.

*Hiebert, D. Edmond. *The Epistle of James: Tests of a Living Faith*. Chicago: Moody, 1979.

> This volume is a helpful treatment of the English text by a professor of New Testament at Mennonite Brethren Biblical Seminary in Fresno, CA. An excellent choice for the layperson. "A lucid evangelical work that looks at every verse, discussing exegetical matters, views, supports, and the relevance to a practical spiritual life" (Rosscup, 315). "The product of mature scholarship" (Barber).

!*McKnight, Scot. *The Letter of James*. NICNT. Grand Rapids: Eerdmans, 2011.

> Replaces Adamson's 1976 volume. This would be an excellent choice for a mid-level commentary for the serious student, but, in my judgment, Moo is better. "This work is admirably researched, written with verve and clarity" (Carson, 140).

*Moo, Douglas J. *James*. TNTC. Second edition. Downers Grove: IVP, 2015.

> The first edition, which was published in 1986, was a fine offering ably superseding the brief volume by Tasker (1957). Whether first or second edition, this would be an excellent commentary for the introductory student. Moo is a careful writer and top-drawer New Testament scholar who always exercises good judgment and sound exegesis. Suffice it to say that any work by Moo is uniformly excellent in its quality and worth acquiring. Do not confuse this book with the author's 2000 PNTC volume. This is my choice for the top entry-level introduction for the layperson.

!*————. *The Letter of James*. PNTC. Grand Rapids: Eerdmans, 2000.

> This fine volume, not to be confused with the author's 2015 TNTC commentary, is an excellent contribution to the series. Moo, the Kenneth T. Wessner Professor of New Testament at Wheaton Graduate School, is one of the top evangelical New Testament scholars writing today. He concludes that James,

the Lord's brother, was the author and is sound on his other judgments. This is my pick for the best mid-level commentary for the serious lay student. "A lovely blend of good judgment, good writing, good theology, and sometimes good application" (Carson, 140).

*Motyer, J. A. *The Tests of Faith*. London: IVP, 1970.

This book is a very brief but helpful volume that deals primarily with the themes running through this epistle. This was one of the first books I read as a baby Christian. Excellent for laypersons. Very well done. Anglican.

Nystrom, David P. *James*. NIVAC. Grand Rapids: Zondervan, 1997.

Not one of the stronger volumes in the series. The homiletical applications are fine, but the exegesis is weak. Though they are dated, Motyer and Hiebert would be more helpful.

+*Stier, Rudolf. *Commentary on James*. Edinburgh: T. & T. Clark, 1864. Reprint, Lynchburg: James Family, n.d.

This volume is not a commentary, but rather a series of thirty-two sermons on the book. Though first published over 150 years ago, these discourses are still useful and challenging and the book should be obtained if available. "No one can be expected to receive all that Stier has to say, but he must be dull indeed who cannot learn much from him. Read with care he is a great instructor" (Spurgeon, 149).

Tasker, R. V. G. *The General Epistle of James: An Introduction and Commentary*. TNTC. Grand Rapids: Eerdmans, 1956.

This slim volume is a well written, albeit brief, exposition of the book for the non-specialist. Moo's updated volume in the same series supersedes this commentary. "Introductory data is carefully outlined, and the verse-by-verse exposition is practical and helpful" (Barber, 179).

*Wiersbe, Warren W. *Be Mature: Growing Up in Christ*. 2nd ed. Colorado Springs: David C. Cook, 2008.

> This is the author's treatment of the book, which is included in his six-volume compilation, *The Bible Exposition Commentary*.

1 Peter

+*Brown, John. *Expository Discourses on 1 Peter*. 2 vols. Reprint, Edinburgh: Banner of Truth, 1975.

> First published in three volumes in 1848, this is a collection of warmly devotional discourses on 1 Peter from a Reformed perspective by the well-known John Brown of Haddington. They are almost 200 years old, but still worth reading for the good they can provide one's soul. "Dr. Brown produced what is substantially a commentary, and one of the best. It affords us a grammatical interpretation, together with an exposition, at once exegetical, doctrinal, and practical. It is a standard work, and the indices increase its value" (Spurgeon, 192). "Rich and suggestive theologically" (Evans, 410). Reformed.

*Clowney, Edmund. *The Message of 1 Peter*. BST. Downers Grove: IVP Academic, 1989.

> An excellent entry-level commentary for the layperson. Clowney was the president of Westminster Theological Seminary in Philadelphia. This is my first choice for the layperson edging out Grudem. "A favorite of mine . . . This work is interesting from start to finish; you can read it straight through" (Evans, 408–9). Reformed.

!*Davids, Peter H. *The First Epistle of Peter*. NICNT. Grand Rapids: Eerdmans, 1990.

> This is probably the best evangelical treatment that is accessible to the layperson. "This is an ideal commentary: careful exegesis, superb theological reflection, thorough yet pithy" (Evans, 409).

*Grudem, Wayne. *1 Peter*. TNTC. Downers Grove: IVP Academic, 1988.

> A fine commentary that replaced Stibbs in the TNTC series. Perfect for pastors and motivated laypersons. Reformed.

*Hiebert, D. Edmond. *First Peter: An Expositional Commentary*. Chicago: Moody, 1984.

> This book is a helpful treatment of the English text that would particularly benefit the layperson or pastor without seminary training. It is well-written and very readable. "Gentle, cautious, and pious (in the best sense), but essentially a distillation of older work" (Carson, 147).

*Kistemaker, Simon J. *Exposition of the Epistles of Peter and the Epistle of Jude*. NTC. Grand Rapids: Baker Academic, 2011.

> A dependable and workmanlike commentary by a bedrock conservative who accepts the authenticity of both Petrine epistles. Very helpful. Straddles the line between introductory and mid-level. Reformed.

!*Schreiner, Thomas. *1, 2 Peter, Jude*. NAC. Nashville: Holman Reference, 2003.

> An outstanding work that for some reason is not even listed by Bauer as either recommended or significant, this commentary was written by one of the evangelical world's top New Testament scholars and it rightly towers over most of the other mid-level offerings. The writings of Schreiner have greatly impressed me over the years and this volume is no exception. It is well-written and eminently practical, a top choice for motivated laypersons. "This is one of most impressive volumes in the series, nicely displaying Schreiner's combination of exegesis and theological reflection coached in admirable clarity" (Carson, 145). Baptist.

*Wiersbe, Warren W. *Be Hopeful: How to Make the Best of Times Out of Your Worst of Times*. 2nd ed. Colorado Springs: David C. Cook, 2009.

> This is the author's treatment of the book, which is included in his six-volume compilation, *The Bible Exposition Commentary*.

2 Peter

The epistles of 2 Peter and Jude are often grouped together because they share a direct literary relationship. However, it is difficult to determine who borrowed from whom. Suffice to say that commentaries on 2 Peter often include Jude.

!*Davids, Peter H. *The Letters of 2 Peter and Jude*. PNTC. Grand Rapids: Eerdmans, 2006.

> This is a top-notch commentary on these two epistles by a noted scholar who specializes in the General Epistles. This is my top choice for a mid-level commentary for the serious lay student with Schreiner a close second.

*Kistemaker, Simon J. See section on 1 Peter.

+*Lloyd-Jones, D. M. *Expository Sermons on 2 Peter*. Edinburgh: Banner of Truth, 1983.

> These twenty-five sermons, by the matchless English preacher, D. M. Lloyd-Jones, were preached on consecutive Sunday mornings at Westminster Chapel in London during 1946–47 and were first compiled in The Westminster Record from 1948–50. It is my opinion that anything published by Lloyd-Jones is worth acquiring. His insights are penetrating and he pulls no punches in his preaching. "One is soon aware that Lloyd-Jones has much insight, explaining the essentials of the text adeptly and developing how these have vital force for living in this world. This book is a primer for expositors and refreshing for Christians in general" (Rosscup, 327).

*Moo, Douglas J. *2 Peter, Jude.* NIVAC. Grand Rapids: Zondervan, 1996.

> This exceptional work builds upon a solid exegetical base and is tremendously helpful for pastors and informed laypersons. An excellent choice for an introductory work.

!*Schreiner, Thomas. See section on 1 Peter.

*Wiersbe, Warren W. *Be Alert: Beware of the Religious Imposters.* 2nd ed. Colorado Springs: David C. Cook, 2010.

> This is the author's treatment of the book along with 2 and 3 John and Jude, which is included in his six-volume compilation, *The Bible Exposition Commentary.*

1, 2, 3 John

!Akin, Daniel L. *1, 2, 3 John.* NAC. Nashville: Holman Reference, 2001.

> A workmanlike commentary that is of particular value to pastors. The author is the president of Southeastern Baptist Theological Seminary. Baptist.

*Boice, James Montgomery. *The Epistles of John.* Grand Rapids: Zondervan, 1979.

> This well-written and informative volume is a popular compilation of expositions of the text by a noted Presbyterian pastor. This commentary is very helpful for the pastor or general reader. Reformed.

*Burge, Gary. *Letters of John.* NIVAC. Grand Rapids: Zondervan, 1996.

> This commentary is a particularly strong addition to the series. I used it along with Stott and Campbell when I taught my adult Sunday School class on the Johannine Epistles and found all three to be excellent and quite helpful. Highly recommended! Good particularly in the area of application. A very good choice for the entry-level beginning student.

*Campbell, Constantine R. *1, 2, & 3 John*. SGBC. Grand Rapids: Zondervan, 2017.

> This volume is a very fine contribution to the SGBC series by a professor of New Testament at Trinity Evangelical School of Divinity in Deerfield, IL. Extremely easy-to-use and helpful. I have been using it along with Stott and Burge in preparing for my adult Sunday School class and highly recommend it. Excellent discussions on propitiation versus expiation (1 John 2:2) and the extent of the atonement.

!*Kruse, Colin G. *The Letters of John*. PNTC. Grand Rapids: Eerdmans, 2000.

> This is one of the very finest commentaries published over the past two decades and is geared at the student (and pastor) with limited Greek skills. Kruse argues for apostolic authorship of all three epistles. Throughout the commentary, there are useful discussions on topics of interest and the meaning of different terms such as "fellowship," "propitiation," and "antichrist." These helpful discussions enhance the value of this volume. Along with Marshall, a fine first choice for a mid-level commentary. With either or both, one could hardly go wrong.

!*Marshall, I. Howard. *The Epistles of John*. NICNT. Grand Rapids: Eerdmans, 1978.

> This commentary is a very fine treatment of these epistles by the late senior lecturer in New Testament exegesis at the University of Aberdeen, Scotland, and one of the foremost New Testament scholars of the past generation. Marshall's approach is scholarly, but also accessible to the motivated non-specialist. An excellent effort! A good first choice for the serious layperson. "Keen ability to follow the thought of a book and articulate it with clarity" (Rosscup, 331). "The book is simply written and ably brings together a good deal of previous scholarship without getting bogged down in minutiae. . . . A very good commentary" (Carson, 153). Arminian.

*Stott, John R. W. *The Epistles of John.* TNTC. Grand Rapids: Eerdmans, 1964.

> This volume, which was revised in 1988, is one of the finest offerings in the TNTC series. Stott, an Anglican and until his death in 2011 one of the elder statesmen of the evangelical world, has written an outstanding commentary that, in spite of its age, has continued to hold its own alongside other more recent works. Any book written by Stott is worth obtaining. Age has not tarnished its luster. This is a nontechnical work that can be used by both pastors and laypersons. A cannot think of a better introductory-level work for these epistles. "A beautiful blending of Bible teaching and practical theology" (Barber, 182). "One of the most useful conservative commentaries on these epistles" (Carson, 154).

*Wiersbe, Warren W. *Be Real: Turning from Hypocrisy to Truth.* 2nd ed. Colorado Springs: David C. Cook, 2009.

> This is the author's treatment of the first epistle, which is included in his six-volume compilation, *The Bible Exposition Commentary.*

*———. For 2 and 3 John, see 2 Peter.

Jude

!*Davids, Peter H. See section on 2 Peter.

*Kistemaker, Simon J. See section on 1 Peter.

*MacArthur, John, Jr. *Beware the Pretenders: Who are the Spiritual Masqueraders Jude Warns Against?* Wheaton: Victor, 1980.

> This helpful little book (ninety-six pages) attempts to answer three questions: (1) What is apostasy? (2) Who are the apostates? (3) What will happen to them? Perfect for a lay audience.

+*Manton, Thomas. *An Exposition on the Epistle of Jude.* London, 1658; Reprint, Minneapolis: Klock & Klock, 1978.

> This massive volume is a monumental treatment of the text by a noted Puritan writer. Manton was one of the most prolific writers of his day and his writing style was characterized by clarity and simplicity (if one could describe any Puritan writing by those words). A masterpiece! "Manton's work is most commendable" (Spurgeon, 197). "Manton has an ease and clarity of style which immediately alerts the reader to the fact that he so thought through the issues as to be able to make even the most complex thoughts clear and understandable" (Barber). If you like Manton's work and want to dig even deeper into the Puritans, see William Jenkyn, *An Exposition upon the Epistle of Jude.* Revised by James Sherman. London: James Nisbet, 1653; Reprint, Minneapolis: James & Klock, 1976. I believe it can be found online for free.

*Moo, Douglas J. See section on 2 Peter.

!*Schreiner, Thomas. See section on 1 Peter.

*Wiersbe, Warren W. See section on 2 Peter.

Revelation

I am hesitant to recommend commentaries on Revelation for the simple reason that there are so many different positions on the interpretation of the book as well as its eschatology. Perhaps that is why John Calvin was reluctant to write a commentary on the book even though he wrote on just about every other book of the Bible. I am certainly no expert on Revelation. My understanding of the book is pretty simplistic, but I think fairly accurate: Jesus wins! For an excellent brief discussion of some of the approaches to this book, see John Evans' *A Guide to Biblical Commentaries and Reference Works,* pages 426–27. For what it is worth, my humble evaluations are as follows.

Cohen, Gary G. *Understanding Revelation: An Investigation of the Key Interpretational and Chronological Questions Which Surround the Book of Revelation.* Chicago: Moody, 1968.

> This book, by the former president of Graham Bible College in Bristol, TN, is not a commentary, but rather an attempt to provide a chronological framework for understanding the book of Revelation. It outlines six basic approaches (critical, allegorical, preterit, historical, topical, and futuristic) and then attempts to wrestle with the chronological problems in chapters 2–3, 4–5, 6–19, and 20–22. "A definitive work which develops a chronological framework for the interpretation of John's Apocalypse" (Barber). Premillennial.

!*Keener, Craig S. *Revelation.* NIVAC. Grand Rapids: Zondervan, 1999.

> At 576 pages, this commentary is longer than some exegetical commentaries. Of course, Keener is well-known for producing prodigious works. This book is no exception. Although this is an "application" commentary, there is ample scholarly interaction with other works and Keener treats fairly the different views of interpretation. The author told me that he was looking to convey "the book's principles and how we can apply them (not an idealist approach, but still looking for principles that are applicable)." I hesitate to give this commentary an ! because it quite helpful for the beginning student though challenging. Carson feels that this volume is uncharacteristically weak on exegesis and theological reflection (157). Motivated laypersons will find much to like here. Premillennial. Posttribulational.

*Kistemaker, Simon J. *Revelation.* NTC. Grand Rapids: Baker, 2001.

> An excellent beginning to mid-level commentary that completes the project he inherited from William Hendriksen. In my judgment, it is a major upgrade over Hendriksen's *More Than Conquerors* (which I declined to list in this book). Reformed. Amillennial.

!*Mounce, Robert. *The Book of Revelation*. NICNT. Grand Rapids: Eerdmans, 1977.

> This volume is an especially well-done commentary by the former president of Whitworth College in Spokane, WA. Its prose is easily accessible to both student and layperson. This book is still the best mid-level, nontechnical commentary available. "A learned and well-written work that not only explains the text satisfactorily in most instances but also introduces the student to the best of the secondary literature" (Carson, 157). Premillennial.

Newell, William R. *The Book of The Revelation*. Chicago: Moody, 1935.

> This commentary, based on the English text by an American Bible teacher and evangelist who worked closely with Dwight L. Moody, is aimed primarily at laypersons and beginning Bible students. "A careful unfolding of the theme and purpose of the Revelation" (Barber, 184). Premillennial. Dispensational.

!Patterson, Paige. *Revelation*. NAC. Nashville: Holman Reference, 2012.

> Patterson is the former president of the Southwestern Baptist Theological Seminary and a towering figure in Southern Baptist circles. This commentary presents a more progressive dispensational stance towards the interpretation of the prophecy rather than the more militant approach of Walvoord. If you lean toward the dispensational position, this is a pretty fair treatment of that school of thought. Premillennial. Dispensational.

Phillips, John. *Exploring Revelation*. Chicago: Moody, 1974.

> This commentary, like Newell's book, is aimed primarily at laypersons and beginning Bible students. It is not detailed and is rather superficial in approach. "Here is a light dispensational work, often alliterative, picturesque, with frequent illustrations (some quite good), but scant in supporting interpretation. Often Phillips shows no real attempt to grapple with meaning... The work as a whole offers minimal light to help

any but elemental readers grasp some points" (Rosscup, 347). Premillennial. Dispensational.

!+*Ramsay, William. *The Letters to the Seven Churches of Asia.* New York: Armstrong, 1904; Reprint, Minneapolis: James Family, 1978.

Although dated, this book remains an outstanding treatment on the historical background of the seven churches in chapters 2–3. The scholarly discussions have been updated in recent years, but this still remains a true classic. "A brilliant study of the historical and archaeological material relating to these churches" (Barber, 185). Preterist.

!Smith, J. B. *A Revelation of Jesus Christ: A Commentary on the Book of Revelation.* Scottdale, PA: Herald, 1961.

This commentary, by a former professor of New Testament at Hesston College in Hesston, KS, was completed by J. Otis Yoder after the death of Smith in 1951. It is based on the Greek text and is considered in dispensationalist circles to be one of the better older commentaries on Revelation. "Based on careful exegesis and providing rich source material. Well-substantiated conclusions" (Barber, 184). Premillennial. Dispensational.

*Stott, John R. W. *What Christ Thinks of the Church: Insights from Revelation 2–3.* Grand Rapids: Eerdmans, 1958.

The contents of this slender volume began in embryo form as a series of sermons at All Souls Church in London during the Lenten season 1957. Stott's applications are needed today. It is the writer's experience that anything published by Stott is well worth reading and should be purchased if available. "Characteristic of the writer's penetrating insight and usual brilliant exposition, these messages on Revelation 2 and 3 set forth the ideal qualities of the church" (Barber, 185).

Walvoord, John F. *The Revelation of Jesus Christ*. Chicago: Moody Press, 1966.

> This commentary, based upon the English text, by the former president of Dallas Theological Seminary is considered a classic by many in dispensational circles. One weakness of the book is that little exegetical support is offered to buttress the positions advanced. This was one of the first books that I purchased while a seminary student, but I cannot now recommend it as a faithful guide to interpreting the prophecy. It takes a rather militant approach. "This book is a lucid exposition of the Revelation which combines textual exposition with theological orientation" (Rosscup, 349). "Illustrates what old-style dispensationalists do with the book" (Evans, 437). Premillennial. Dispensational.

*Wiersbe, Warren W. *Be Victorious: In Christ You Are an Overcomer*. 2nd ed. Colorado Springs: David C. Cook, 2008.

> This is the author's treatment of the book, which is included in his six-volume compilation, *The Bible Exposition Commentary*.

4

Devotional Literature

BIBLE CHARACTERS

The apostle Paul, in writing to the Corinthians, speaks of the desert wanderings of the Israelites and states, "Now these things occurred as examples" (1 Cor 10:6). The characters of Scripture serve as examples for believers, both positive and negative. That is one reason that Christians ought to familiarize themselves with Bible characters so that they can emulate the godly characteristics and avoid the not-so-godly ones. We can learn a lot about godly living by acquainting ourselves with the lives of those who inhabit the pages of the Bible. We learn to avoid the spiritual traps into which men such as David fell and we also learn to imitate their positive qualities.

+*Blaikie, W. Garden. *David, King of Israel.* London: James Nisbet & Co., 1861; Reprint, Minneapolis: Klock & Klock, 1981.

> A classic exposition of the life of David. Blaikie was a nineteenth century Scottish professor and pastor who wrote several Christian classics. His writing is always a blessing.

+*———. *Heroes of Israel*. London: Thomas Nelson and Sons, 1894; Reprint, Minneapolis: Klock & Klock, 1981.

> A classic exposition of the lives of Abraham, Isaac, Jacob, Joseph, and Moses. Out of print for decades, this wonderful book should be purchased if found. A treasure!

*Boice, James Montgomery. *Ordinary Men Called By God*. Wheaton: Victor, 1982.

> An enriching study of the lives of Abraham, Moses, and David by the late pastor of Tenth Presbyterian Church in Philadelphia. Boice had a marvelous way of making Bible truths live and this volume is no exception. A masterful Bible teacher!

+*Edersheim, Alfred. *Practical Truths from Elisha*. London: Religious Tract Society, 1882; Reprint, Grand Rapids: Kregel, 1982.

> A wonderful exposition of the life of the great prophet by a great biblical scholar who was a Jewish Christ-follower. Originally published as *Elisha, the Prophet*.

Getz, Gene A. *Joseph: From Prison to Palace*. Ventura, CA: Regal, 1983.

> A popular exposition of the life of Joseph by the former director of the Center for Church Renewal in Dallas, senior pastor of Fellowship Bible Church-North, and professor at Dallas Theological Seminary.

———. *When the Pressure's On: Take a Lesson from Elijah*. Ventura, CA: Regal, 1984.

> This satisfying study of the life of Elijah offers many practical applications.

Gill, David W. *Peter the Rock: Extraordinary Insights from an Ordinary Man*. Downers Grove: IVP, 1986.

> Gill, who was the dean and associate professor of Christian ethics at New College, Berkeley, draws lessons in evangelism,

discipleship, conversion, apologetics, and the meaning of the church from the life of Peter.

+*Hamilton, James. *Moses, the Man of God*. London: James Nisbet & Co., 1874; Reprint, Minneapolis: Klock & Klock, 1984.

Another jewel from the pen of a Scottish minister, this book was revered by no less than Charles Spurgeon. "Beautiful as a poem, like everything which fell from Dr. Hamilton's pen. It would be impossible to study it without profit" (Spurgeon, 56). A masterpiece!

+*Kirk, Thomas. *The Life of Joseph*. Edinburgh: Andrew Elliot, 1900; Reprint, Minneapolis: Klock & Klock, 1985.

Few studies of the life of Joseph compare with this one. Exceptional! "Stimulating, as are all of Kirk's writings" (Barber, 89).

*Lockyer, Herbert. *All the Men of the Bible*. Grand Rapids: Zondervan, 1958.

*———. *All the Women of the Bible*. Grand Rapids: Zondervan, 1967.

Two helpful resources that list every man and woman whose name occurs in the Bible and where they are found. The men's book in itself contains more than 3000 characters. Indispensable for Bible and Sunday School teachers.

*MacArthur, John. *Twelve Extraordinary Women: How God Shaped Women of the Bible and What He Wants to Do with You*. Nashville: Thomas Nelson, 2005.

"This book was published three years after respected pastor and author John MacArthur's best-selling book, *Twelve Ordinary Men*, a comprehensive study of Jesus' disciples. Here MacArthur presents an in-depth look at both well-known as well as lesser-known women in the Bible. Women examined are Eve, Sarah, Rahab, Ruth, Hannah, Mary, Anna, the Samaritan Woman, Mary and Martha, Mary Magdalene, and Lydia. The chapters include the historical and cultural background of the life and times of each of the women. Understanding the struggles and pressures each woman experienced gives the reader added insight and appreciation of their incredible challenges and remarkable victories. The lessons learned are the same as today: redemption through faith, trust, and commitment to God. Study questions at the end of the book help the reader to ponder the life lessons in each of the chapters. While obviously an excellent Bible study guide for individual or group study, men too, would do well to learn about the lives of the women who played such an important role in biblical history" **(VanHook).**

*———. *Twelve Ordinary Men.* Nashville: Nelson, 2002.

"John MacArthur, the well-known author, pastor of Grace Community Church in Sun Valley, CA, chancellor emeritus of the Master's College and Seminary, and teacher on the syndicated radio program, "Grace to You," has written a most useful book that provides an in-depth look into the personalities, backgrounds, strengths, and weaknesses of each of the disciples that Jesus chose, not only as his companions during his earthly ministry, but also as his apostles, who would turn the world upside down with the gospel message. Each disciple is highlighted with most of the emphasis on Jesus' inner circle of Peter, Andrew, James, and John. Some of the material is somewhat speculative because there is not much biblical information on a few of the disciples, but MacArthur's clear and insightful writing is both interesting and thought-provoking as he describes the ordinary men who were chosen to live extraordinary lives. He challenges the reader to consider how everyday people can be used in remarkable ways to serve the Lord and to spread the message of the gospel in today's world. There is also an accompanying study guide, which is an excellent resource for group study and discussion" **(VanHook).**

+*MacDuff, John Ross. *Elijah, the Prophet of Fire*. London: James Nisbet & Co., 1861; Reprint, Minneapolis: Klock & Klock, 1982.

> A masterful recreation of the life and times of the great prophet with graphic portrayals of him, as well as of Ahab and Jezebel, by one of the greatest Scottish preachers of the nineteenth century. A delightful classic that should not be missed! "The reading of this book is a moving experience. The writer's power of description can hardly be equaled. Dramatic and dynamic" (Barber, 87). Available in a 2013 paperback edition from Bottom of the Hill Publishing that is 160 pages. Since the Klock & Klock edition is 351 pages, it is likely that this new edition is an abridgement. Personally, I would avoid any condensed versions.

+*Meyer, F. B. *New Testament Men of Faith*. Reprint, Westchester, IL: Good News Publishers, 1979.

+*———. *Old Testament Men of Faith*. Reprint, Westchester, IL: Good News Publishers, 1979.

> Exceptional character studies by a British preacher who is considered by Warren Wiersbe as one of the "giants" of the faith. Meyer's devotional studies will always warm your heart.

*Owen, J. Glyn. *From Simon to Peter*. Welwyn, Herts, England: Evangelical Press, 1985.

> Originally presented in sermon form, these studies brilliantly trace the progression of a Galilean fisherman with cowardly inclinations to a courageous preacher who became one of the leaders of the apostolic church. Owen followed the great D. Martyn Lloyd-Jones as pastor of Westminster Chapel in London.

*Pink, Arthur W. *Elijah*. Carlisle, PA: Banner of Truth, 1963.

> This rewarding study, first published posthumously in 1956, is the British revised edition. "An in-depth study. Revealing and challenging" (Barber, 88).

———. *Gleanings from Elisha: His Life & Miracles.* Reprint, Chicago: Moody, 1972.

> Pink was an early twentieth century English preacher who served congregations in both the U.S. and England and served as a Bible teacher and evangelist in Australia. He was a prolific author and his writings have blessed untold multitudes of both preachers and laypersons including the late great British preacher D. Martyn Lloyd-Jones. This book is one of seven in the Gleanings series and is a rich and rewarding study.

*———. *The Life of David.* Reprint, Grand Rapids: Baker, 1981.

> Originally published in two volumes, this classic is apparently out of print in paper form. It may be found used through online sources such as AbeBooks.com. It is also available in Kindle. "A masterful exposition" (Barber, 87).

Redpath, Alan. *The Making of a Man of God.* Grand Rapids: Revell, 1962.

> This study of the life of David is comprised of sermons preached from the pulpit of the Moody Memorial Church in Chicago. As always, Redpath is practical and engaging.

*Swindoll, Charles R. *Hand Me Another Brick.* Nashville: Thomas Nelson, 1978.

> Originally presented as sermons in the First Evangelical Free Church in Fullerton, CA, this excellent series of leadership case studies uses Nehemiah to teach how an effective leader leads.

+*Whyte, Alexander. *Bible Characters.* Edinburgh: Oliphant, Anderson, and Ferrier, 1898–1902; Reprint, Grand Rapids: Zondervan, 1967.

> A massive collection of brilliant character studies by one of the greatest Scottish preachers of all time. Originally published in six volumes over a period of five years, this classic deserves to be read and re-read. It will warm your heart. Warren Wiersbe in his *Walking with the Giants* speaks most highly of this book.

CHRISTIAN BIOGRAPHY AND MEMOIR

The genre of biography is a very early form of literature in the church. Accounts of the early martyrs of the church were common reading material and served to both instruct and inspire believers. Phillips Brooks, that great nineteenth century preacher who is probably best known for his wonderful hymn "O Little Town of Bethlehem," in 1886 addressed the students of Phillips Exeter Academy in New Hampshire. In his lecture, he said, "The object of reading biography, it cannot be said too earnestly or too often said, is not imitation, but inspiration." That said, it is important that we read Christian biography and memoir for the lessons that we can learn about the Christian life and the inspiration that they provide.

This section was an afterthought to this book, which, once started, took on a life of its own. As the list of titles grew, I had to decide which titles to include and which to reject. Apologies to those who feel that I did not include a worthy title. The fault is all my own.

!+*Augustine, Aurelius. *Confessions.* Translated by Henry Chadwick. Oxford: Oxford University Press, 2009.

> Written in Latin between AD 397 and 400, this autobiographical spiritual classic consists of thirteen books which outline St. Augustine's spiritual pilgrimage from childhood, through his profligate youth, to his conversion. It is widely regarded as the first Western autobiography written. Hugely influential!

*Bacon, Ernest W. *John Bunyan: Pilgrim and Dreamer.* Grand Rapids: Baker, 1983.

> Bunyan would be a towering figure among the Puritans if the only thing he ever did was write *The Pilgrim's Progress.* Of course, he did so much more. Among his classics are *Grace Abounding to the Chief of Sinners* and *The Holy War.* For a tinker who spent twelve years in prison for his faith, Bunyan was a hugely influential figure who is still revered today.

+*Bainton, Roland H. *Here I Stand: A Life of Martin Luther.* New York: Abingdon-Cokesbury, 1950.

> An honest and very readable portrayal of Martin Luther, warts and all. Sets the standard for all future religious biography. Featured in Petersen and Petersen's *100 Christian Books That Changed the Century.* "A brilliant treatment of the life of the great Reformer. Authoritative and well written" (Barber, 353).

Butler, Alban. *Lives of the Saints.* Reprint, Charlotte: Tan Books, 1995.

> "This eighteenth century Roman Catholic author has written what is usually regarded as the definitive reference book on Catholic saints. However, the stories in the book can be a blessing to both Catholics and Protestants, It is a good reference book to the lives of hundreds of great Christians through the ages" (**Fleming**).

*Colson, Charles. *Born Again.* Old Tappan, NJ: Chosen Books, 1976.

> This book, by the former "hatchet man" for Richard Nixon before the Watergate scandal, became one of the biggest news stories of the twentieth century that chronicled his subsequent conversion and personal transformation. The phrase "born again" became part of the common parlance of that age and Colson's book was no small part of that. Featured in Petersen and Petersen's *100 Christian Books That Changed the Century.*

+*Dalimore, Arnold A. *George Whitefield.* 2 vols. Westchester, IL: Cornerstone Books, 1970.

> Whitefield was the towering figure of English-speaking Christianity during the nineteenth century and a profound influence on C. H. Spurgeon. He was widely considered to be the greatest English-speaking preacher of the century, at least until Spurgeon came onto the scene. In terms of Christian influence, according to the author, "Whitefield was the foremost figure and Wesley the secondary one." This is THE definitive biography of the architect of the Great Awakening and a modern classic.

*Eareckson, Joni, and Joe Musser. *Joni*. 1976.

> The story about how a young woman overcame a tragic diving accident that left her a quadriplegic. She was plagued by thoughts of anger, depression, suicide, and religious doubts. Through her faith in Jesus Christ, she learned not only to overcome her negative thoughts, she also learned to paint with a brush between her teeth and was able to sell her artwork. She also learned how to write using voice recognition software and has published dozens of books, recorded several albums of her singing, and is an advocate for people with disabilities. She starred in a 1979 movie about her life. This is one of the best books that deal with the problem of adversity and pain. Featured in Petersen and Petersen's *100 Books That Changed the Christian Century*.

!+*Edwards, Jonathan. *The Life of David Brainerd*. The Works of Jonathan Edwards Series, Volume 7. Edited by Norman Pettit. New Haven, CT: Yale University Press, 1984.

> Published in 1749, this book became a spiritual classic almost immediately upon publication. I had almost left it out of this book when I read John Piper's assessment of Brainerd's life and this book as having changed the world. Brainerd had a very brief and obscure missionary career of five years (1743–1747) to the Indians of New England. He was prone to depression and would certainly not been considered a success by any stretch of the imagination in the eyes of the secular world. Yet, his life and ministry inspired the modern Protestant missionary movement more than anyone for twenty centuries since the Apostle Paul. He died at age twenty-nine in Edwards' house.

*Graham, Billy. *Just As I Am: The Autobiography of Billy Graham*. Grand Rapids: Zondervan, 1997.

> The compelling and disarmingly honest portrayal of the Southern Baptist preacher who became one of the most influential religious figures of the twentieth century and the spiritual adviser to presidents from Harry S. Truman to Barack Obama. I read it a few years ago and was captivated and enthralled.

This book was *Christianity Today's* 1998 Book of the Year as well as the ECPA's Gold Medallion Book Award winner for Biography/Autobiography. Not to be missed!

*Graham, Franklin. *Rebel With a Cause*. Nashville: Thomas Nelson, 1995.

PKs (preacher's kids) are notorious for being rebellious. The son of Billy Graham writes about the challenges he faced growing up as the son of the most famous preacher in the world as well as his work with Samaritan's Purse. Winner of the ECPA's 1996 Gold Medallion Award for Biography/Autobiography.

Harmon, Rebecca Lamar. *Susanna: Mother of the Wesleys*. Nashville: Abingdon, 1968.

Susanna Wesley was a remarkable woman. In addition to giving birth to nineteen children, ten of whom survived childhood, she raised two of the most influential men of her time, John and Charles Wesley. She has been widely regarded as the Mother of Methodism because of the stellar spiritual example she gave her children. "A candid evaluation of the powerful influence Susanna Wesley exerted on her family" (Barber, 359).

*Hillenbrand, Laura. *Unbroken: A World War II Story of Survival, Resilience, and Redemption*. New York: Random House, 2010.

The incredible story of Louis Zamperini, an Olympic distance runner who represented the U.S. in the 1936 Berlin Olympics running in the 5,000 meter event. During a World War II search and rescue mission, he survived a plane crash, drifting at sea for forty-seven days, and internment at a Japanese prison camp where he was tortured. After the war, he attended a Billy Graham evangelistic crusade and surrendered his life to Christ, after which he became an evangelist. He later visited Japan and expressed forgiveness to many of the guards from his POW days including a visit to Sugamo prison where many war criminals were imprisoned. An inspiring tale that was made into a major motion picture by the Coen brothers, this book enthralled me and intrigued me. I highly recommend it as well as the movie!

*Jacobs, Alan. *The Narnian: The Life and Imagination of C. S. Lewis.* San Francisco: HarperSanFrancisco, 2005.

> This book is not a biography in the usual sense of the word according to the author. He omits many details that most biographers might include to focus on a chronicle of Lewis' mind and imagination. How was it that an Oxford don and scholar of medieval literature could not only write a classic work of children's literature, but also become one of the foremost Christian apologists of his time? If you can read just one Lewis biography, this is the one. A delight to read! Winner of *Christianity Today's* 2006 Book Award for History/Biography.

*Marshall, Catherine. *A Man Called Peter.* New York: McGraw, 1951.

> The biography of the fiery Presbyterian pastor of the historic New York Avenue Presbyterian Church in Washington, DC and United States Senate chaplain, this book was the basis of a 20th Century-Fox movie in 1955. Written by his wife, Catherine, after his fatal heart attack in 1948, this heartwarming book has been an inspiration to millions and is not to be missed. Featured in Petersen and Petersen's *100 Christian Books That Changed the Century.*

*Marshall, Michael. *The Restless Heart: The Life and Influence of St. Augustine.* Grand Rapids: Eerdmans, 1987.

> A handsome and engaging volume that is beautifully illustrated. Augustine was the most influential figure of the Church fathers after the Apostolic Period and this is a most accessible introduction to his life and work. For the truly ambitious, try Augustine's famous *Confessions.*

*McGrath, Alister. *C. S. Lewis—A Life: Eccentric Genius, Reluctant Prophet.* Carol Stream, IL: Tyndale House, 2013.

> Winner of the ECPA's 2014 Christian Book Award for Nonfiction. The author is a highly respected British theologian.

+*Newton, John. *Out of the Depths*. Reprint, New Canaan, CT: Keats Publishing, 1981.

> Originally written in the form of letters to the Rev. T. Haweis, D.D., this classic autobiography was first published in 1764. Newton was a slave trader who converted to Christianity and became a noted minister. He is best known today as the author of the beloved hymn *Amazing Grace*. His life story can be summed up in his immortal words, "I once was lost but now am found, Was blind but now I see."

*Pollock, John. *Moody*. Reprint, Chicago: Moody, 1983.

> Originally published as *Moody without Sankey* by Hodder & Stoughton in 1966, this popular biography tells the story of how a former shoe salesman became the greatest evangelist of the nineteenth century. Although Moody was not seminary trained, he was used mightily of God and was the Billy Graham of his time. The author is the leading evangelical biographer of the second half of the twentieth century.

*———. *Wilberforce*. Belleville, MI: Lion Publishing, 1977.

> An exceptional treatment of the life of a remarkable man. Wilberforce is chiefly remembered as the driving force behind the abolition of the slave trade in the British Empire. The author has chronicled the lives of many of the heavyweights of the Christian world including Billy Graham, D. L. Moody, George Whitefield, and Hudson Taylor.

*Roe, Earl O., ed. *Dream Big: The Henrietta Mears Story*. Ventura, CA: Regal Books, 1990.

> "Every Christian library should include Henrietta Mears' Bible handbook, *What the Bible is All About*. Almost as extraordinary as her Bible handbook is the story of her own life. While Mears' accomplishments are legendary: founder of the National Sunday School Association, Director of Education at First Presbyterian Church in Hollywood, CA for over three decades, and founder of Gospel Light Publications, her

biography is even more remarkable. Born in 1890 at a time when the role of women in society, let alone the church, was very limited, Mears was blessed with a rich family heritage of godly men and women. Her maternal grandfather, a Baptist pastor, and her mother, a Baptist laywoman and notable Bible teacher, were significant influences in her life. At seven years old, Mears became a Christian and set her heart and mind on serving the Lord. Already struggling with debilitating nearsightedness, she suffered a severe eye injury at the age of sixteen. But her courage, sense of humor, love for people and passion for the Lord never wavered in the face of difficulty. Her sister, Margaret, dedicated her life to be her sister's companion so that Henrietta could accomplish all that God called her to do. In addition to a fascinating life story, the book is a study on the techniques and strategies she developed which produced remarkable successes in teaching the life-changing message of God's love to those of all ages. Her influence on others, especially teens and young adults, resulted in hundreds of men and women dedicating their lives to full-time Christian service, including Billy Graham, Bill Bright, and Richard Halverson. Mears' life demonstrates the amazing accomplishments that can be achieved through one woman totally committed to serving the Lord. Portions of this book were previously published under the title, *Henrietta Mears and How She Did It!* by Ethel May Baldwin and David B. Benson" (**VanHook**).

*Schaeffer, Edith. *The Tapestry: The Life and Times of Francis and Edith Schaeffer.* Waco: Word, 1981.

This is the remarkable story of Francis and Edith Schaeffer, the founders of the international Christian community known as *L'Abri* (The Shelter) in Switzerland. Thousands of questioning men and women from many cultures traveled there and were assured that there is a God in heaven and that he is both personal and knowable. Francis Schaeffer was one of the towering evangelical figures of the twentieth century and an able apologist for the Christian faith. Two of his books, *How Should We Then Live?* and *Whatever Became of the Human Race?*, became

*Selderhuis, Herman. *Martin Luther: A Spiritual Biography*. Wheaton, IL: Crossway, 2017.

> An engaging study of the spiritual and intellectual complexity of a most intriguing figure in church history. Stands alongside Roland Bainton's classic 1950 work, *Here I Stand*. Winner of *Christianity Today's* 2018 Book Award in the History/Biography category.

*Shepard, Valerie. *Devotedly: The Personal Letter and Love Story of Jim and Elisabeth Elliot*. Nashville: B & H Books, 2019.

> The daughter of Jim and Elisabeth Eliot was only ten months old when her father was killed in January 1956. More than sixty years after her father's untimely death, the author unseals and publishes letters and personal journals that reveal the two hearts becoming one of these beloved missionaries. Winner of the ECPA's 2020 Christian Book Award for Biography & Memoir.

*Solganick, Harvey E. *Lessons from C. S. Lewis: Becoming an Evangelical Apologetic Disciple for Christ*. Bloomington, IN: Archway, 2018.

> An important study that takes a bit of a different slant to Lewis in that Solganick focuses on him from an evangelical perspective regarding his stand on the philosophical and ethical issues that concern evangelical Christians today. A good companion piece to the Jacobs book for Lewis fans.

+*Solzhenitsyn, Aleksandr. *The Gulag Archipelago*. New York: Harper & Row, 1973.

> "A massive multi-volume work which sold over thirty million copies in thirty-five languages. Divided into seven parts, it recounts the slave labor systems in Soviet Russia over four decades from the perspective of those who experienced it firsthand. Each part deals with a particular component of the

Gulag system. For example, Part I ('The Prison Industry') covers the arrest, trial, and sentencing of people who did nothing wrong but whose punishment (often after confession obtained by torture) was 'expedient' for the Communist party, if only to instill fear in others. Part II covers the transportation network and transit prisons, moving millions to permanent camps where they were starved and worked to death. Solzhenitsyn himself was a prisoner for eight years, and his great contribution was to see it all and describe it powerfully in human terms—the desperate hopes of families, the cynical abuse by prison guards, the cunning but mostly futile survival strategies of the prisoners—and refuse to dismiss it as 'Stalinism.' He saw, rather, as he later expressly claimed, that 'Men have forgotten God; that's why all this has happened.' From a Christian perspective, arguably the twentieth century's most important book about human evil" (**Brafford**). Aleksandr Solzhenitsyn was awarded the 1970 Nobel Prize in Literature.

*Stanley, Charles. *Courageous Faith: My Story from a Life of Obedience.* Brentwood, TN: Howard Books, 2017.

The author, pastor of First Baptist Church of Atlanta, GA since 1971 and a popular television preacher, provides an intimate look at the challenges and joys of his many years of ministry. Winner of ECPA's 2017 Christian Book Award for Biography & Memoir.

*Ten Boom, Corrie. *The Hiding Place.* Reprint, Lincoln, VA: Chosen Books, 2006.

This is the story of how, after the Germans invaded the Netherlands in 1940, the Christian ten Boom family welcomed and hid Jewish neighbors during the German occupation. Corrie and her Sister Bessie opened their home not only to Jewish refugees, but also to Gentiles who were part of the resistance movement. Corrie and other members of her family were arrested by the Nazis for their efforts. The book was made into a major motion picture in 1975 and received a Golden Globe nomination. Featured in Petersen and Petersen's *100 Christian*

Books That Changed the Century. Originally published in 1971. One of the very best modern Christian memoirs.

*Vanauken, Sheldon. *A Severe Mercy*. Reprint, San Francisco: HarperOne, 2009.

"This profound and moving book tells the story of Sheldon Vanauken, his friendship with C. S. Lewis, his marriage, and his struggle for faith after his wife's untimely death. A beautiful look at what happens when faith and suffering meet" **(Fleming)**.

*Wacker, Grant. *One Soul at a Time: The Story of Billy Graham*. Grand Rapids: Eerdmans, 2019.

There have been many accounts of the life of this prominent evangelist. This is one of the best. Winner of *Christianity Today's* 2020 Award of Merit in the History/Biography category.

*Wigger, John. *PTL: The Rise and Fall of Jim and Tammy Faye Bakker's Evangelical Empire*. New York: Oxford University Press, 2017.

During the 1980s, PTL and Jim and Tammy Faye Bakker were the poster children for the prosperity gospel and the conspicuous consumption they practiced. This is a balanced account of their rise and fall that portrays them as basically sincere, but who somehow got derailed and finally toppled. Winner of *Christianity Today's* 2018 Award of Merit in the History/Biography category.

*Wilkerson, David. *The Cross and the Switchblade*. Reprint, Grand Rapids: Chosen, 2018.

"This book tells the inspiring story of David Wilkerson, a Pentecostal preacher who went to the ghettoes of New York to work with street gangs. The center of the book is the conversion of Nicky Cruz, a young Hispanic tough who went on to become a preacher and evangelist. It is a classic story, though a little dated. Nevertheless, this true story has never lost its ability to inspire" **(Fleming)**.

*Winner, Lauren F. *Still: Notes on a Mid-Faith Crisis.* New York: HarperOne, 2012.

> A spiritual memoir that elegantly and profoundly reflects the author's spiritual pilgrimage through the loss of her mother and a failed marriage. Winner of *Christianity Today's* 2013 Book Award in the Spirituality category.

*Zaleski, Philip, and Carol Zaleski. *The Fellowship: The Literary Lives of the Inklings: J. R. R. Tolkien, C. S. Lewis, Owen Barfield, Charles Williams.* Reprint, New York: Farrar, Straus, and Giroux, 2016.

> The Inklings were a group of Oxford intellectuals who met frequently during the 1930s and 40s to discuss literature, in particular their own works in progress. They praised the value of narrative in fiction and engaged in the writing of fantasy. C. S. Lewis was arguably the best-known of the group with Tolkien a close second. Lewis was probably the most influential Christian writer of the twentieth century and Christianity's most prolific apologist. He wrote children's fantasy such as *The Chronicles of Narnia* as well as technical literary criticism. In addition to *Narnia,* his best-known works are *The Screwtape Letters* and *Mere Christianity.* Tolkien, of course, is best-known for his works of fantasy, *The Hobbit, The Lord of the Rings,* and *The Silmarillion.* Two of the lesser-known members of this informal group were Owen Barfield and Charles Williams. Others who were more-or-less regular members were J. A. W. Bennett, Lord David Cecil, Nevill Coghill, Hugo Dyson, Adam Fox, J. H. Grant III, Roger Lancelyn Green, Robert Havard, Camille Smith (cousin of C. S. Lewis), Warren Lewis (Lewis' elder brother), and Christopher Tolkien (Tolkien's son). Dorothy Sayers, though not officially a member of the group, was certainly linked to them in thought and spirit. This account of four of the more influential members of the group is by a husband and wife who have both taught at Smith College in Massachusetts. She is a professor of World Religions there.

CHRISTIAN CONDUCT

*Issler, Klaus. *Living into the Life of Jesus.* Downers Grove: IVP, 2012.

> This book is much more than just one more "how to" guide to the Christian life. There are many such books that teach how to model Christian behavior. Issler, professor of Christian Education and Theology at Talbot School of Theology, Biola University, sounds a clarion call to believers that the core problem in their Christian profession and walk is the huge gap between "willing" and "doing" and that the main issue is not so much behavior as it is the transformation of the heart. Issler, in an engaging and entertaining manner, offers sound biblical strategies to help bridge that gap. This is a must read for anyone who wants to form Christian character. I suggest that you read it twice: The first time to allow the concepts to digest and marinate in the mind and heart, as well as for conviction. I confess that I was terribly convicted at times. The second reading should be for implementation. Highly recommended!

+*Kempis, Thomas á. *On the Imitation of Christ.* Reprint, London: Chapman and Hall, 1878.

> This venerated book is, next to the Bible, perhaps the most widely read devotional work and is regarded as a true classic. Composed in Latin in the fifteenth century (ca. 1418–1427), it is a handbook for spiritual life. It is comprised of four books, which provide detailed spiritual instructions: Admonitions Useful for a Spiritual Life, Admonitions Concerning Inward Things, Of Internal Consolation, and Concerning the Communion. This book arose from the *Devotio Moderna* movement of which Kempis was a member. The book's emphasis is on the interior life and withdrawal from the world. It is widely available in inexpensive paperback from numerous publishers. It should not be missed!

+*Miller, Keith. *The Taste of New Wine.* Waco: Word, 1965.

> A seminal work that upon its publication challenged the status quo in the church and called upon believers to live their

lives according to their profession of faith in Christ. Miller, using the wine metaphor, saw the church as manufacturing, bottling, and marketing wine, but not many were actually tasting it. He saw the Christian life as a relationship with Jesus Christ rather than a religion and his book rocked the church of that time. Featured in Petersen and Petersen's *100 Christian Books That Changed the Century.* "A vigorous call for personal renewal among laymen in the church" (Barber, 241).

Sweeting, George. *You Can Climb Higher: The Christian's Pursuit of Excellence.* Nashville: Thomas Nelson, 1985.

The author, former president of the Moody Bible Institute and editor-in-chief of *Moody Monthly*, believes that it is incumbent on each believer to pursue excellence in the Christian life. Drawing from his many years as a pastor as well as his time in college administration, Sweeting develops nine marks of Christian excellence: faith, character, action, single-mindedness, love, suffering, prayer, wisdom, and staying power. He then applies these truths to the life of D. L. Moody and other nineteenth and twentieth century heroes of excellence. Very readable and inspiring.

*Swindoll, Charles R. *Living Above the Level of Mediocrity.* Waco: Word, 1987.

Popular preacher, Swindoll, sounds a clarion call for believers to overcome the tendency we have to stagnate and to be selfish, which leads to mediocrity. The author calls for Christians to soar like eagles in our spiritual lives rather than settle for mediocrity. Swindoll writes compellingly and passionately for the common man.

CHRISTIAN FICTION

I debated for some time whether to include this section or not. However, the reality is that many people read fiction and there are many Christians who read both secular fiction and Christian fiction. To cater to those who do read fiction with a Christian thread running through it, hopefully these selections will be suggestive as to what good Christian fiction is.

One problem that we face is that good Christian fiction is hard to define much less quantify. What makes a work of fiction a Christian work? Is it a work of fiction by a Christian author or is it a work with a Christian or spiritual theme? These are difficult questions to answer. Sometimes the faith of an author is not obvious and sometimes the spiritual theme is not easy to discover. Fantasy has been a favorite medium for some Christian writers such as the works of Lewis, Tolkien, and L'Engle would suggest. Tolkien said that myth and fantasy (fairy-story) reflect and contain elements of moral and religious truth and that creativity is part of our endowment as the image of God.

I am especially indebted to the monthly magazine *Christianity Today*, which since 1992 has been publishing their annual Book Awards. I have designated those winners. Their Book Award is the top award with the Award of Merit being given to the runner-up. If you are looking for good Christian fiction, you can't go wrong reading any of their winners. I also mentioned the annual Christian Book Awards given by the ECPA (Evangelical Christian Publishers Association). I researched their awards going back thirty years.

I am also indebted to my good friend, Bill Fleming, a retired Presbyterian pastor and former department head at my college/seminary for his invaluable suggestions and annotations. He is much better-read than I am and his reading taste more sophisticated. This section would be the poorer were it not for his contributions. His insights into the value of Christian fiction are invaluable. He writes, "Fiction does not exist to present history or preach theology, but to give an author's impression of great truth. Novels accomplish for great ideas and events what paintings and landscapes do for mountains. They do not give us photographic realism, but the inner impressions of the heart. In this, they often present a greater truth than documentary history or accurate theology. They give us the feelings they produce. What makes good fiction is not its slavish attention to the facts, but its ability to accurately convey the heart. For this reason, fiction gives us insights that mere facts cannot—the inner contour of the Christian heart.

"The books mentioned below have changed lives by revealing great biblical truths. Sometimes, the truths they reveal hurt. Other times they make us laugh. Still other times, they come at us sideways through the veil of symbols and surreal images. But if we listen to what they are saying and meditate on them prayerfully, Christian fiction may deeply enrich our emotional lives and point our hearts to God" (**Fleming**).

*Arana, Nikki. *The Next Target*. Colorado Springs: David C. Cook, 2012.

> Winner of the ECPA's 2013 Christian Book Award for Fiction.

*Brooks, Geraldine. *Caleb's Crossing*. New York: Viking Adult, 2011.

> Winner of *Christianity Today's* 2012 Book Award for Fiction.

*Brown, Sharon Garlough. *An Extra Mile: A Story of Embracing God's Call*. Downers Grove: IVP, 2018.

> The conclusion to the popular Sensible Shoes series. Winner of *Christianity Today's* 2019 Book Award for Fiction.

+*Bunyan, John. *The Pilgrim's Progress*. London: Ponder, 1678; Reprint, Mount Vernon, NY: The Peter Pauper Press, n.d.

> First published in 1678, this classic of the Christian life describes in allegorical fashion the experiences of a believer from conversion to glorification. It is probably safe to say that except for the Bible, this is the most-beloved Christian book available in the English language. The great Victorian English preacher, Charles H. Spurgeon claimed in his autobiography that he had read this book at least 100 times. Quite an endorsement from what many consider to be the English-speaking world's best preacher! This book is a true religious classic that is considered one of the most significant works of religious fiction ever written. It has been translated into over 200 languages and has never been out of print. A Christian allegory, the book traces the journey of Christian, its everyman protagonist, from his hometown, the "city of destruction," to the "Celestial City" atop Mount Zion. The original title of the book, *The Pilgrim's Progress from This World to That Which is to Come* reflects that pilgrimage. Along the way, Christian is weighed down by the burden of the knowledge of his sin. It is possible to obtain a modern English language edition, which makes it more accessible to today's readers (Thomas, James H. *Pilgrim's Progress in*

Today's English. Chicago: Moody, 1964). There is also a book still in print by the great nineteenth century Scottish preacher, Alexander Whyte, that provides an outstanding exposition of the characters in Bunyan's classic work (Whyte, Alexander. *The Characters in Pilgrim's Progress*. Grand Rapids: Baker, 1976). My edition of *The Pilgrim's Progress* is an undated one from The Peter Pauper Press that has delightful woodcut illustrations. In whatever form you read this book, it is not to be missed!

*Chesterton, G. K. *The Father Brown Series*.

"Before there was Sayers, Lewis or Tolkein, there was G. K. Chesterton. He was an influence on all three. His detective is a priest, Father Brown, who solves mysteries in the hopes of seeing the criminals redeemed. Father Brown stories are not just mysteries, though. Every one is a morality play, exploring saints and sinners" **(Fleming)**.

*———. *The Man Who Was Thursday: A Nightmare*. Reprint, Whitefish, MT: Kessinger Publishing, 2010.

"G.K. Chesterton is probably best known today for his Father Brown series of detective stories. This is unfortunate since his more philosophical and theological books such as *Orthodoxy* and *The Everlasting Man* are among the most profound Christian writing of the Twentieth Century. A foray into Chesterton's writings soon convinces the reader that they are in the presence of brilliance. His book, *The Man Who Was Thursday*, is an example of this. It is hard to say what this book is about. It starts off like spy fiction, but then soon veers off into philosophy, metaphysics, and Christian allegory. This book won't be for every reader. Some of the loyal fans of Father Brown will be disappointed by his metaphysical musings. But those who like their fiction deep and philosophical will find much to appreciate here" **(Fleming)**.

!+*Dante Alighieri. *The Divine Comedy*. Illustrated by Umberto Romano. Garden City, NY: Doubleday & Company, 1947.

"Like Milton, *The Divine Comedy* is no easy read. It is a journey through hell (Inferno), purgatory (purgatory), and heaven (Paradiso). Dante's Inferno, the first volume, is the better known of the three. What surprises modern readers of Dante most is probably the wicked humor throughout the book. He does not hesitate to put contemporary politicians, cardinals, and even popes in hell, and devises some wicked tortures for them. But if you can make it through the first volume, go on to read the other two as well. His pictures of heaven are particularly moving" (**Fleming**).

*Dorr, Lawrence. *A Bearer of Divine Revelation*. Grand Rapids: Eerdmans, 2003.

A collection of fifteen stories that follow a central character through episodes that reflect the author's life experiences as a child in Hungary, his wartime experiences on the Russian front, deprivation and poverty, and the death of family and friends. The title story follows the protagonist as he struggles both spiritually and physically in the aftermath of World War II in Salzburg, Austria. Winner of *Christianity Today's* 2004 Book Award for Fiction.

+*Dostoevsky, Fyodor. *Crime and Punishment*. Translated by Constance Garnett. New York: Random House, 1956.

I first read this novel for an English class while an undergraduate at the University of Maryland and it immediately became my favorite novel of all time. First published in 1866 in installments in the literary magazine *The Russian Messenger,* this novel focuses on the inner turmoil and mental anguish of Raskolnikov, an impoverished student in Saint Petersburg who devises a plan to murder a pawnbroker for her money. He completes the deed with an axe and spends the rest of the novel dealing with the mental and spiritual consequences of his dastardly actions. The writing of this novel came after completion of Dostoevsky's ten years of exile in Siberia and is widely acclaimed as one of the masterpieces of world literature. Totally absorbing! Russian.

+*———. *Notes from Underground.* Translated by Boris Jakim. Grand Rapids: Eerdmans, 2009.

Another classic following the author's ten-year exile in Siberia, this novel is considered to be one of the first in the existential genre and is perhaps less accessible than *Crime and Punishment.* The book presents itself as the bitter ramblings of a retired unnamed civil servant living in Saint Petersburg. Dostoevsky challenges the pagan ideologies of his day such as nihilism and rational egoism as well as Western culture. Russian. Winner of *Christianity Today's* 2010 Book Award for Fiction.

*Douglas, Lloyd C. *The Robe.* Chicago: People's Book Club, 1942.

Written by a Lutheran and Congregational clergyman who struggled with orthodox Christian doctrine, this book nevertheless created a firestorm and became a bestseller drawing many to the Bible to investigate its claims. Featured in Petersen and Petersen's *100 Christian Books That Changed the Century.* The book inspired a film by the same name which was nominated for a Best Picture Academy Award.

*Fabry, Chris. *Almost Heaven.* Carol Stream, IL: Tyndale House, 2010.

Winner of the ECPA's 2011 Christian Book Award for Fiction.

*Hedlund, Jody. *Luther and Katharina.* Colorado Springs: WaterBrook, 2015.

The fictionalized story of Martin Luther and the nun, Katharina von Bora. Winner of the ECPA's 2016 Christian Book Award for Fiction.

*———. *Every Waking Moment.* Carol Stream, IL: Tyndale House, 2013.

Winner of *Christianity Today's* 2014 Award of Merit for Fiction.

+*Hugo, Victor. *Les Misérables.* Translated by Isabel Hapgood. Reprint, San Diego: Canterbury Classics, 2015.

> One of the great novels of the nineteenth century, this historical work was first published in 1862 and examines the themes of law and grace through the struggles of an ex-convict, Jean Valjean, as he experiences redemption. The subject of a 2012 major motion picture directed by Tobe Hooper as well as a major Broadway stage production. French.

> "If you haven't read this book, or at least seen one of the movies or musical adaptations of this novel, you should do yourself the favor of doing so immediately. *Les Misérables* is one of the most moving presentations of what selfless, sacrificial love looks like, of the victory of God's grace versus legalism, and what it means to absolutely love one's enemies and the poor" **(Fleming).**

Hurnard, Hannah. *Hind's Feet on High Places.* Old Tappan, NJ: Fleming H. Revell, 1973.

> An allegory of Christian faith which dramatizes the spiritual journey of Much-Afraid as she makes her way to the High Places. Beloved by many. Considered by others to be overwritten and overly spiritualized.

*James, Katherine. *Can You See Anything Now?* Orleans, MA: Paraclete Press, 2017.

> Winner of *Christianity Today's* 2018 Book Award for Fiction.

*James, Steven. *The Queen.* Grand Rapids: Revell, 2011.

> Winner of the ECPA's 2012 Christian Book Award for Fiction.

*Karon, Jan. *A Common Life: The Wedding Story.* New York: Viking, 2001.

> The sixth novel in the Mitford series which chronicles the wedding of Father Tim Kavanagh and Cynthia Coppersmith. Winner of *Christianity Today's* 2002 Book Award for Fiction.

———. *Home to Holly Springs.* New York: Viking, 2008.

> Winner of *Christianity Today's* 2008 Award of Merit for Fiction.

*———. *In This Mountain.* New York: Viking, 2003.

> The seventh novel in the author's Mitford series in which the Episcopal priest struggles during his retirement. Winner of *Christianity Today's* 2003 Book Award for Fiction.

*———. *A New Song.* New York: Viking, 1999.

> Winner of *Christianity Today's* 2000 Book Award for Fiction and the ECPA's Gold Medallion Book Award for Fiction..

*Kingsbury, Karen. *Oceans Apart.* Grand Rapids: Zondervan, 2004.

> Winner of the ECPA's 2005 Gold Medallion Book Award for Fiction.

+*L'Engle, Madeleine. *A Wrinkle in Time.* 1962; Reprint, New York: Square Fish, 2007.

> Winner of the prestigious Newbury Award for children's fiction, this science fiction classic is not as overtly "Christian" as the works of C. S. Lewis. With foreshadowing of *Star Trek* and elements of Orwell, this book is a real treat. Featured in Petersen and Petersen's *100 Christian Books That Changed the Century.*
>
> "Forget the film adaptations and go back to the novel, and you will see the roots of the book in the story of Christian redemption. A worthy read for young people" (**Fleming**).

*Lee, Tosca. *Iscariot: A Novel of Judas.* Brentwood, TN: Howard Books, 2013.

> Winner of ECPA's 2014 Christian Book Award for Fiction.

+*Lewis, C. S. *The Chronicles of Narnia*. Reprint, Scholastic Books, 1995.

> This boxed set paperback reprint edition contains all seven books of the series: *The Magician's Nephew; The Lion, the Witch and the Wardrobe; The Horse and His Boy; Prince Caspian; The Voyage of Dawn Treader; The Silver Chair;* and *The Last Battle.* Lewis was one of the intellectual giants of the twentieth century and a foremost Christian apologist. Originally published between 1950 and 1956, these seven fantasy novels are set in the fictional land of Narnia and appeal to adults as well as children with their talking animals and mythical beasts, and not-so-thinly disguised Christian themes. Basically, Lewis retold the Christ story in allegory form. A classic of children's literature! Featured in Petersen and Petersen's *100 Christian Books That Changed the Century.*
>
> "These books are an excellent way of introducing the message of the Gospel to children and are highly recommended. The otherworld approach makes them appropriate and accessible to unbelievers as well as believers" (**Fleming**).

———. *The Great Divorce*. Reprint, New York: HarperCollins, 2001.

> "In this short book, Lewis, arguably the most influential Christian apologist of the twentieth century, imagines a dream about a bus trip from hell to heaven. On the way, he and his fellow passengers must face up to the hard reality that human evil cannot merely be 'improved;' it must die a painful death as we follow the way of Christ to our ultimate destination. Readers will recognize the spiritual battles in their own lives or in the lives of people they have known—temptations such as power, lust, and (perhaps the most difficult) the disordered love of someone or something more than God. In Lewis' apologetic method, hell is always chosen by those who go there, rejecting God's gracious gift of heaven" (**Brafford**).

*Lewis, C. S. *The Perelandra Trilogy*. Reprint, New York: Simon & Schuster, 2011.

> *Perelandra* is the second book in what is also known as *The Space Trilogy*. The other two are *Out of the Silent Planet* and

That Hideous Strength. "Lewis' book is a rare example of science fiction with a Christian theme. Lewis' style is light on the science though, and heavy on the fantasy. He presents a model of the Solar System as being alive with life, all under the power of God. In the first book, Lewis' protagonist, Ransom, travels to Mars and meets a world of creatures who resemble what our world would be if it had not fallen. In the second book *Perelandra,* Ransom travels to Venus and becomes involved in a struggle with evil to prevent another fall into sin from happening by Venus' version of Adam and Eve.In the third book, Ransom on Earth becomes a messianic figure, fighting against emissaries of Satan who want to bring about the end times. Along the way, there are deep and profound insights into the nature of good, evil, and redemption. It is an exciting read, and well worth your time" **(Fleming).**

*Marshall, Catherine. *Christy.* 1967. Reprint, San Jose: Evergreen Farm, 2017.

A work of historical fiction by the widow of the late U.S. Senate chaplain and Presbyterian minister, Peter Marshall, that is set in the fictional Appalachian village of Cutter Gap, TN in 1912. It is based on the experiences of the author's mother, Christy Huddleson, who taught poor children in a similar impoverished community. Featured in Petersen and Petersen's *100 Christian Books That Changed the Century.*

*Martin, Charles. *When Crickets Cry.* Nashville: Thomas Nelson, 2006.

Winner of the ECPA's 2007 Christian Book Award for Fiction.

*Mazzarella, Nicole. *This Heavy Silence.* Orleans, MA: Paraclete, 2005.

Winner of *Christianity Today's* 2006 Book Award for Fiction.

*Meissner, Susan. *The Shape of Mercy.* Colorado Springs: WaterBrook, 2008.

Winner of the ECPA's 2009 Christian Book Award for Fiction.

*Miller, Walter M., Jr. *A Canticle for Leibowitz*. Reprint, New York: Bantam, 1964.

"This book, published in 1959, was one of the first books in the post-apocalyptic genre. It is set in a Catholic monastery in the American desert after a nuclear war has destroyed civilization. The story spans thousands of years of rebuilding civilization and the pivotal place the church has in preserving knowledge. Instead of seeing Christianity and the church as the enemy of reason and science, the church is portrayed as the greatest force in preserving knowledge for future generations. A thoughtful, moving portrayal of the role of faith as a beneficent organizing force in human development" (**Fleming**).

!+*Milton, John. *Paradise Lost*. Norton Critical Editions. 3rd revised edition. Edited by Gordon Teskey. New York: W. W. Norton & Company, 2004.

"Milton, the great blind poet of the 17th Century, produced his greatest work telling the story of the fall of Satan, the fall of Adam, and human redemption. It is written in blank verse, like Shakespeare. If you are a person who likes your reading to be simple and easy, don't bother with this book. But if you are the kind of person who likes to chew on a great classic, check this one out. The sheer beauty of the book will amaze you, and his insights into heaven and hell will inspire you" (**Fleming**).

Morris, Michael. *Man in the Blue Moon*. Carol Stream, IL: Tyndale, 2012.

Winner of *Christianity Today's* 2013 Award of Merit for Fiction.

*Nichols, Linda. *In Search of Eden*. Bloomington, MN: Bethany House, 2007.

Winner of the ECPA's 2008 Christian Book Award for Fiction.

*Parrish, Christa. *Watch Over Me.* Bloomington, MN: Bethany House, 2009.

> Winner of the ECPA's 2010 Christian Book Award for Fiction.

*Peretti, Frank. *The Oath.* Waco: Word, 1995.

> A town controlled by evil in the Pacific Northwest is the backdrop for this gripping novel. Winner of the ECPA's 1996 Gold Medallion Book Award for Fiction.

Rice, Anne. *Angel Time.* New York: Knopf, 2009.

> Winner of *Christianity Today's* 2009 Award of Merit for Fiction.

*Rivers, Francine. *The Last Sin Eater.* Carol Stream, IL: Tyndale House, 1998.

> Set in 1850s Appalachia, this novel tells the story of a community that believes in the myth of a human "sin eater." Winner of the ECPA's 1999 Gold Medallion Book Award for Fiction.

*Robinson, Marilynne. *Gilead: A Novel.* New York: Farrar, Straus, and Giroux, 2004.

> A highly acclaimed novel about three generations of a family from the Civil War to the 20th century. Winner of the 2004 Pulitzer Prize for the novel, the National Book Critics Award for Fiction, and *Christianity Today's* 2005 Book Award for Fiction.

*———. *Home: A Novel.* New York: Farrar, Straus, and Giroux, 2008.

> The follow-up to *Gilead,* which won the Pulitzer Prize. Winner of *Christianity Today's* 2009 Book Award for fiction.

*———. *Lila.* New York: Farrar, Straus, and Giroux, 2014.

> Winner of *Christianity Today's* 2015 Book Award for Fiction.

*Rosenberg, Joel. *The Ezekiel Option*. Carol Stream, IL: Tyndale, 2006.

> A political thriller with a Christian perspective. Winner of the ECPA's 2006 Christian Book Award for Fiction.

*Samson, Lisa. *Quaker Summer*. Nashville: Thomas Nelson, 2007.

> Winner of *Christianity Today's* 2008 Book Award for Fiction.

*———. *The Sky Beneath My Feet*. Nashville: Thomas, Nelson, 2013.

> Winner of *Christianity Today's* 2014 Book Award for Fiction.

*Sayers, Dorothy. *The Lord Peter Wimsey Series*

> "Dorothy Sayers belonged to one of the circles of writers that included C. S. Lewis and J. R. R. Tolkein. She wrote mysteries in the Agatha Christie mode. Her detective is a priest, Father Brown, who solves mysteries in the hopes of seeing the criminals redeemed. Father Brown stories are not just mysteries though. Every one is a morality play exploring saints and sinners" **(Fleming)**.

*Schaap, James Calvin. *Startling Joy: Seven Magical Stories of Christmas*. Revell, 2005.

> Utilizing seven motifs from the Christmas season (a gift, the baby, the pageant, the parties, the worship, the afterglow, the story), Schaap tells seven stories demonstrating how imperfect people can find grace and joy in an imperfect world particularly during the Christmas season. Winner of *Christianity Today's* 2006 Award of Merit for Fiction.

+Sheldon, Charles. *In His Steps*. Reprint, Revell, 1985.

> Originally published in 1899, this book's author was a Congregational church pastor in Topeka, KS. Although it is not particularly well-written, this classic was hugely influential and was included in William and Randy Petersen's *100 Christian Books That Changed the Century*. It poses the question, "What would Jesus do?" Though simplistic and idealistic in its

application, its basic premise was correct that the example of Jesus is our ethical guide. It is a work of fiction and deserves to be read by every thoughtful Christian. I read it decades ago and it greatly blessed my heart. As Petersen and Petersen put it so well, "Its simple message strikes home in any era."

*Singer, Randy. *The Advocate*. Carol Stream, IL: Tyndale, 2014.

Winner of the ECPA's 2015 Christian Book Award for Fiction.

*Smucker, Shawn. *Light from Distant Stars*. Ada, MI: Revell, 2019.

Winner of *Christianity Today's* 2020 Book Award for Fiction.

*Sproul, R. C. *Johnny Come Home*. Ventura, CA: Regal, 1984.

A particular favorite of mine, this book chronicles the contrasting lives of two best friends from high school. One becomes a down and out used car salesman who drinks too much and the other a nationally known minister. This study in contrasts is a touching tale, a metaphor of grace.

*Taylor, Daniel. *Death Comes for the Deconstructionist*. Eugene, OR: Slant, 2014.

Winner of *Christianity Today's* 2016 Book Award for Fiction.

*Thoene, Bodie. *In My Father's House*. Bloomington, MN: Bethany House, 1993.

Part of the Shiloh series. Winner of the ECPA's 1993 Gold Medallion Book Award for Fiction.

*———. *Say To This Mountain*. Bloomington, MN: Bethany House, 1993.

Part of the Shiloh series. Winner of the ECPA's 1994 Gold Medallion Book Award for Fiction.

*Thoene, Bodie, and Brock Thoene. *Munich Signature*. Bloomington, MN: Bethany House, 1990.

> This book is Book 3 of the Zion Covenant series. The plot unfolds with the Hitler's Third Reich as a backdrop. Winner of the ECPA's 1991 Gold Medallion Book Award for Fiction.

*———. *Only the River Runs Free*. Nashville: Thomas Nelson, 1997.

> This is Book 1 of the four-volume Galway Chronicles. The other volumes are *Of Men and Angels*, *Ashes of Remembrance*, and *All Rivers to the Sea*. Winner of the ECPA's 1998 Gold Medallion Book Award for Fiction.

*———. *The Twilight of Courage*. Nashville: Thomas Nelson, 1994.

> Several stories are intertwined with the backdrop of World War II in this gripping novel. Winner of the ECPA's 1995 Gold Medallion Book Award for Fiction.

*———. *Warsaw Requiem*. Bloomington, MN: Bethany House, 1991.

> The action begins in 1936 and tells the story of the courageous resistance against the spread of Nazi terrorism. Had Leon Uris been a Christian, this might have been the novel he would have written instead of *Mila 18*. Winner of the ECPA's 1992 Gold Medallion Book Award for Fiction.

+*Tolkien, J. R. R. *The Hobbit: or There and Back Again*. Houghton, Mifflin, and Harcourt, 1937; Reprint, 2012.

> Originally written as a bedtime story for his children, Tolkien's classic has delighted readers, young and old, for generations. "During his years as an Oxford professor, Tolkien published *The Hobbit* (1937) and completed *The Lord of the Rings* (1948). Together with related works published after his death by his son, Christopher, these books established Tolkien's reputation as the leading pioneer of modern or 'high' fantasy literature. *The Hobbit* takes place in Middle Earth, which has no apparent connection with our world other than a brief and humorous

allusion to the origin of golf. The story begins with Bilbo's inadvertent discovery of the One Ring. He would much prefer his comfortable home in the Shire to 'adventures,' but he joins one at the urging of Gandalf, the Wizard. Knowing almost nothing about the ring, he uses its powers of invisibility to assist a band of dwarves in their journey to recover stolen treasure from the great dragon Smaug. The story reaches a climax with the Battle of the Five Armies—two armies (men and elves) against one (dwarves) against two (goblins and wild wolves). There is no allegory, Christian or otherwise; however, the lines between good and evil are clearly drawn. Bilbo remains faithful to his sense of duty and honor, but his success merely sets the stage for a greater adventure by his nephew, Frodo, which follows in *The Lord of the Rings*. Both books are deeper, richer, and generally better than the movies released during 2001–2014, not least because the books have no distortion of the story by excessive computer-generated graphics. There are many published editions from which to choose. Readers should consider purchasing an edition with the best available maps of Middle Earth, which help in following the storyline" (**Brafford**).

+*———. *The Lord of the Rings*. 3 vols. New York: Harper Collins, 2001.

Originally written in stages between 1937 and 1949, this epic novel was originally intended to be a sequel for *The Hobbit*, but evolved into a much larger book published in three volumes in 1954 and 1955. The three volumes were titled *The Fellowship of the Ring*, *The Two Towers*, and *The Return of the King*.

"Tolkien was a friend of C. S. Lewis, and even played a key role in Lewis' conversion to Christianity. Tolkien and Lewis differed, though, in their approach to fiction. Tolkien's novels are not as allegorical as Lewis' writings, but chose a more subtle approach to weaving fantasy and Christianity. The power of Tolkien's writing is beyond question. His books have been an inspiration to generations of children and adults, not only through the books themselves, but through the movies the books inspired. As you read Tolkien, you can spot parallels to the Gospel in themes and values. Reading Tolkien is always rewarding, but reading Tolkien, knowing his connection to the Gospel, is even more rewarding" **(Fleming)**.

*Turner, Jamie Langston. *Winter Birds*. Bloomington, MN: Bethany House, 2006.

> Winner of *Christianity Today's* 2007 Award of Merit for Fiction.

*Wangerin, Walter, Jr. *The Book of God*. Grand Rapids: Zondervan, 1996.

> Using the novel format, the author writes about the panorama of biblical events from Abraham in the desert to Jesus teaching on a hillside. Winner of the ECPA's 1997 Gold Medallion Book Award for Fiction.

*———. *The Book of the Dun Cow*. New York: Harper & Row, 1987; Reprint, San Francisco: HarperOne, 2003.

*———. *The Book of Sorrows*. New York: Harper Collins, 1985.

> "Wangerin is one of the most profound Christian authors writing today. These two books are particularly moving and are two of the most human books about talking animals. Set in a barnyard where Chanticleer the rooster reigns, he is called to lead his fellow creatures in a battle against unspeakable evil. Wangerin's second book, *The Book of Sorrows*, deals with the aftermath of that battle and the problem of suffering. Beautiful and profound. The books will lead you to weeping" **(Fleming)**.

*———. *Paul: A Novel*. Grand Rapids: Zondervan, 2000.

> Historical fiction about the life of the Apostle Paul. Winner of *Christianity Today's* 2000 Book Award for Fiction and the ECPA's 2001 Gold Medallion Book Award for Fiction.

*Wilson, Douglas. *Evangellyfish*. Moscow, ID: Canon Press, 2012.

> A witty satire on contemporary Christian culture. Winner of *Christianity Today's* 2013 Book Award for Fiction.

Wolfe, Suzanne M. *The Confessions of X*. Nashville: Thomas Nelson, 2016.

> A well-written historical novel about Augustine of Hippo and the unnamed woman he loved and with whom he cohabited for thirteen years. Winner of *Christianity Today's* 2017 Book Award for Fiction.

*Wright, Vinita Hampton. *Dwelling Places*. San Francisco: Harper SanFrancisco, 2006.

> Winner of *Christianity Today's* 2007 Book Award for Fiction.

CHRISTIAN LIVING

*Collins, Gary R. *Beyond Easy Believism: How to Build a Christian Lifestyle*. Waco: Word, 1982.

> Many Christians adhere to what Collins labels "easy believism." They believe that to become a Christian, all that is needed is to walk down an aisle, say a little prayer, and then go on one's way. That may be an oversimplification. But it is not too far off the mark. Collins exposes such thinking as the heresy that it is. He says that easy believism is not demanding, not costly, socially acceptable, and self-centered among other things. He challenges believers to go beyond easy believism to the real thing.

*Colon, Christine A., and Bonnie E. Field. *Singled Out: Why Celibacy Must Be Reinvented in Today's Church*. Grand Rapids: Brazos, 2009.

> Winner of *Christianity Today's* 2010 Award of Merit for Christian Living.

*Grubbs, F. Michael. *Broken Chains: Freedom from Unwanted Habits and Addictions*. Kansas City, KS: The Lyndon Center, 2014.

> Christians are not immune from bad habits and addictions. This slender volume by a Christian Counselor and Coach at the Lyndon Center in Kansas City is step-by-step guide

to freedom from addiction and bad habits that is free from the technical jargon of similar works. From Addictiveness to Liberation to finally Living Free, this book helps the reader to jettison the destructive behaviors that are a part of the lives of so many believers. The chapters are brief and to-the-point with helpful Honest Questions Leading to Freedom at the end of each.

*Guiness, Os. *Time for Truth*. Grand Rapids: Baker, 2000.

Jesus taught that the truth will set us free. Unfortunately, an utter disregard for the truth, from the president down to the Wall Street broker to the pastor, has grave consequences for our character as Christians as well as for our society. This book argues that without truth there is no freedom. Winner of *Christianity Today's* 2001 Book Award for Apologetics/ Evangelism.

*Lindsell, Harold. *The World, the Flesh, and the Devil*. Washington, D. C.: Canon Press, 1973.

This book by the former Editor-Publisher of *Christianity Today* and professor of missions at Columbia Bible College, Northern Baptist Theological Seminary, and Fuller Theological Seminary deals with how to choose a lifestyle that brings glory to Jesus Christ. He argues that we are either allied with God or with the devil. He writes, "There can be no fence-sitters on this planet." He then describes what a Christian lifestyle looks like and what it doesn't look like. Of particular interest is a chapter that might anger some Christians titled "Things Not Prohibited." Challenging!

*McCracken, Brett. *Uncomfortable: The Awkward and Essential Challenge of Christian Community*. Wheaton: Crossway, 2017.

Many people seek a church fellowship that makes them comfortable or meets their needs. This book challenges readers to embrace the uncomfortable aspects of church community such as loving difficult people for the sake of the gospel and God's glory. As the title so aptly suggests, this is an uncomfortable book. Winner of the ECPA's 2018 book award for Christian Living.

*McMinn, Mark R. *Finding Our Way Home: Turning Back to What Matters Most.* San Francisco: Jossey-Bass, 2005.

In this intriguing book, the author sees the different aspects of home as a spiritual metaphor and our longing for home as representative of our deepest spiritual yearnings. Winner of *Christianity Today's* 2006 Award of Merit for Christian Living.

*Ortberg, John. *If You Want to Walk on Water, You've Got to Get Out of the Boat.* Grand Rapids: Zondervan, 2001.

The author, a popular Presbyterian pastor and conference speaker, urges believers to step outside their comfort zones in faith. Winner of *Christianity Today's* 2002 Book Award for Christian Living.

*Owens, Virginia Stem. *Caring for Mother: A Daughter's Long Goodbye.* Louisville: Westminster John Knox, 2007.

A touching account of caring for an elderly parent that deals with the issues of aging, dementia, and death. Winner of *Christianity Today's* 2008 Book Award for Christian Living.

*Packer, J. I. *Hot Tub Religion.* Wheaton, IL: Tyndale, 1987.

In this collection of thoughts and essays, Packer challenges the contemporary notion that the Christian life should be relaxing and laid-back and in no way demanding. Although written over thirty years ago, Packer's indictment of the self-absorbed hedonism that characterized much of the evangelical church scene back then is even more to the point today.

Peterson, Eugene H. *Subversive Spirituality.* Grand Rapids: Eerdmans, 1997.

A compendium of miscellaneous articles written by the author over a quarter century that reflect on overlooked aspects of the spiritual life. One of *Christianity Today's* best books of 1998.

*Piper, John. *Spectacular Sins*. Wheaton: Crossway, 2008.

> Winner of the ECPA's 2009 Christian Book Award in the Christian Life category.

*Schaeffer, Edith. *Common Sense Christian Living*. Nashville: Thomas Nelson, 1983.

> The author, wife of the late Francis Schaeffer and co-founder of the Christian community *L'Abri*, which is centered in Switzerland, helps believers make sense out of what is often a seemingly senseless world. In doing so, she deals with some of the central issues of the Christian life.

*Short, Robert L. *The Gospel According to Peanuts*. Richmond: John Knox, 1964.

> A funny and poignant handbook of the Christian faith illustrated with Charles M. Schulz's comic strip, *Peanuts*. Prophetic and perceptive! Who knew that reading the "funny papers" could be a theological exercise?

*Sider, Ronald J. *The Scandal of the Evangelical Conscience: Why Are Christians Living Just Like the Rest of the World?* Grand Rapids: Baker, 2005.

> The title of this unflinching book says it all. If Christians are called to be in the world, but not of the world, why are their attitudes and practices just like those of unbelievers? Sider has for decades been the conscience of evangelicalism. This book is hard-hitting and may offend you. A must read! Winner of *Christianity Today's* 2006 Book Award for Christian Living.

Swindoll, Charles R. *Living on the Ragged Edge: Coming to Terms with Reality*. Waco: Word, 1985.

> Using the ancient book of wisdom, Ecclesiastes, as a jumping off point, Swindoll demonstrates how Christians can discover joy, peace, and happiness in the eternal struggle to find pleasure in "life under the sun." The author, senior pastor of the

First Evangelical Free Church in Fullerton, CA, is a master communicator who has influenced millions worldwide.

*Ten Elshof, Gregg A. *I Told Me So: Self-Deception and the Christian Life.* Grand Rapids: Eerdmans, 2009.

> Winner of *Christianity Today's* 2010 Book Award for Christian Living.

White, John. *The Fight: to Know God's Word, to Share the Faith, to Communicate with God, to Know God's Will.* Downers Grove: IVP, 1978.

> This book deals with the basic areas of the Christian life with which believers wrestle throughout their lives. Faith, prayer, evangelism, temptation, guidance, holiness, relationships, and Bible study are some of the topics explored.

*———. *Flirting with the World: A Challenge to Loyalty.* Wheaton, IL: Harold Shaw, 1982.

> In this compelling book, the author lays bare the shameful truth that most Christians are not only in the world, but very much of it. He points out that our churches, like secular associations, are more concerned with fund-raising, beautiful buildings, large congregations, and comforting sermons than ministering to the outcasts of society and he concludes that Jesus would not be very comfortable in the average church today. A shocking indictment of the church that is just as relevant today as it was almost forty years ago!

*———. *The Golden Cow: Materialism in the Twentieth-Century.* Downers Grove: IVP, 1979.

> Although this book is now over forty years old, its message about materialism among modern Christians is as relevant today as it was when it was written.

*Winner, Lauren F. *Real Sex: The Naked Truth About Chastity.* Grand Rapids: Brazos, 2005.

> According to the author, the only real sexual relations that occur do so within the context of marriage. That which occurs outside of marriage is not sex at all, but faux sex, a distorted representation of it. This book is a frank and personal examination of a very misunderstood topic. Winner of *Christianity Today's* 2006 Award of Merit for Christian Living.

*Yancey, Philip. *The Bible Jesus Read.* Grand Rapids: Zondervan, 1999.

> Explores the writings of the Old Testament to assist Christians in knowing God better. Winner of *Christianity Today's* 2000 Book Award for Christian Living.

CHRISTIAN PREACHING (SERMONS)

At the urging of a friend, I have added this section. My personal taste tends towards classic works of sermon compilations. Reading the sermons of pulpit masters is a spiritual exercise that will pay rich dividends for the reader. Some of these books/sets may be out of print, but all should be obtainable either online or through used books stores. Take the time to get to know some of these great preachers and enjoy!

Blackwood, Andrew Watterson. *The Protestant Pulpit.* New York: Abingdon-Cokesbury, 1947.

> This compilation provides sermons from some of the best-known preachers from the Reformation to the time of publication. Part I contains sermons ranging from and including Martin Luther, John Bunyan, John Wesley, George Whitefield, Jonathan Edwards, Alexander Maclaren, Charles Spurgeon, D. L. Moody, and G. W. Truett. Part II includes sermons from A. J. Gossip ("But When Life Tumbles In, What Then?"), Clarence Macartney, and James Stewart. Some of the sermons can be safely bypassed, but some are absolute gems.

*Broadus, John A. *Favorite Sermons of John A. Broadus.* Edited by Vernon Latrelle Stanfield. New York: Harper & Brothers, 1959.

> Broadus' textbook, *Treatise on the Preparation and Delivery of Sermons,* was the "bible" for generations of seminary students. This book provides an example of Southern Baptist preaching from a bygone generation at its best.

+*Brooks, Phillips. *The Light of the World and Other Sermons.* New York: E. P. Dutton and Company, 1904.

> Phillips Brooks was known for much more than his classic hymn, *O, Little Town of Bethlehem.* He was a master sermon craftsman. Although far from an evangelical in his theology, his sermons are worth reading and still have much to say to us.

*Lloyd-Jones, D. Martyn. *Evangelistic Sermons at Aberavon.* Edinburgh: Banner of Truth, 1983.

> These twenty-one sermons were preached at Sandfields, Aberavon between the years 1927–38 during Jones' first ministry, years before his ascension to the pulpit at Westminster Chapel in London. These sermon manuscripts lay undiscovered in a box in the attic of Lloyd-Jones' home until they were discovered by Mrs. Lloyd-Jones in 1981, the year of his death. These sermons are examples of what Gospel preaching ought to be by one of the greatest masters of that craft. I have been blessed greatly by the preaching and writing ministry of Lloyd-Jones over the years.

+*Luther, Martin. *Sermons of Martin Luther.* 8 vols. Edited by John Nicholas Lenker; Translated by John Nicholas Lenker and others. Minneapolis: Lutherans in All Lands, 1904–09. Reprint, Grand Rapids: Baker, 1983.

> A set of remarkable sermons by the fiery individual who spearheaded the Protestant Reformation. In an age when most preachers were content simply to read the weekly Gospel and Epistle lessons or the sermon of another preacher, Luther prepared his own sermons through diligence and study and

prayer. He left behind a substantial legacy of his sermons, which he himself wrote out and prepared for the printer. These sermons, for which he is perhaps best known, were delivered mainly in the 1520s in his home church in Germany.

+*Maclaren, Alexander. *Expositions of Holy Scripture*. 17 vols. Reprint, Grand Rapids: Baker, 1974.

> Originally published in 1908 in twenty-five volumes, this compilation of Maclaren's sermons are a wonder to behold. Maclaren was workmanlike in his sermon preparation. He always began with the original languages (Hebrew and Greek) and let the text speak for itself. While other preachers may have used gimmicks in their preaching, Maclaren simply presented the truth of God's Word in such a way that his listeners could easily understand it. I began reading through this set of sermons while a young seminary student over forty years ago and was greatly blessed. Some-day, I hope to complete the set.

*Marshall, Peter. *John Doe, Disciple: Sermons for the Young in Spirit*. New York: McGraw-Hill, 1963

*———. *Mr. Jones, Meet the Master: Sermons and Prayers of Peter Marshall*. Edited by Catherine Marshall. Old Tappan, NJ: Revell, 1950.

> Peter Marshall is perhaps the best preacher I have ever heard. I wish I had heard the likes of Charles Spurgeon, Alexander Maclaren, Joseph Parker, Phillips Brooks, G. Campbell Morgan and so many others, but I am limited to reading their sermons. However, I did find, while a student in seminary back when the earth's crust was cooling, in my local library a 33 rpm recording containing two of Marshall's sermons, "The Trumpet of the Morning" and "Trial By Fire." Hearing them enthralled me by their power, passion, and eloquence. Immediately Peter Marshall became my preaching model. These two volumes, published posthumously, contain selected sermons and prayers of this popular Scottish preacher who became the pastor of the New York Avenue Presbyterian Church in

Washington, D.C., and later the U.S. Senate chaplain. I promise you that they will stir your soul.

+*Meyer, F. B. *Great Verses Through the Bible.* Reprint, Grand Rapids: Zondervan, 1966.

I hesitated to include this book because there are no sermons as such included. However, these brief devotions, or homilies, are so rich that I could not leave it out. Meyer, a protégé of D. L. Moody, was one of the towering religious figures of the late nineteenth/early twentieth century who was widely influential. This collection of brief devotional thoughts on some of the great verses of the Bible is an absolute gem! Highly recommended!

+*Morgan, G. Campbell. *Great Chapters of the Bible.* London: Marshall, Morgan, and Scott, 1963.

Morgan is one of my favorite preachers of all time. "Masterful addresses on forty-five chapters of the Bible" (Barber, 261).

+*———. *The Westminster Pulpit.* 10 vols. London: Pickering and Inglis, 1955–56; Reprint, Old Tappan, NJ: Fleming H. Revell, n.d.

Morgan was one of the greatest English-speaking preachers of the twentieth century and was known widely as the "prince of expositors." He was an itinerant preacher who pastored churches in the U.S. and his native England. He was best known for his longest pastorate, that of the Westminster Chapel in London from 1904–17 and 1938–43. When he resigned during World War II, the great D. Martyn Lloyd-Jones, his associate, succeeded him. His preaching on the Gospels soars to heights seldom seen. He will bless your heart. "Containing the cream of Morgan's exemplary expositions" (Barber, 261).

+*Spurgeon, Charles Haddon. *Treasury of the Bible.* 8 vols. Reprint, Grand Rapids: Baker, 1981.

This excellent set contains more than 2600 sermons preached at the Metropolitan Tabernacle in London in the 1800s.

Spurgeon was, and still is, considered by many to be the finest English-speaking preacher in history. He was a plain-spoken preacher and these sermons aim directly at the heart. There is nothing flowery about them, but they wield a powerful message. For those who want to read more of Spurgeon's preaching (as if 2600 sermons were not enough), check out the fifty-six-volume set, *The Metropolitan Tabernacle* (London: Passmore and Alabaster, 1863ff; Reprint, Pasadena, TX: Pilgrim). "An example of pastoral preaching at its best" (Barber, 61).

*Stewart, James S. *The Gates of New Life.* New York: Charles Scribner's Sons, 1940.

*———. *The Wind of the Spirit.* Nashville: Abingdon, 1969; Reprint, Grand Rapids: Baker, 1984.

James Stewart was a giant among preachers. He was a minister in the Church of Scotland who also taught New Testament Language, Literature, and Theology at the University of Edinburgh. In 1999, *Preaching Magazine* named him the best preacher of the twentieth century. The sermons in this book were originally preached in the 1930s at the North Morningside Church in Edinburgh and represent preaching at its finest. Stewart's sermons are "a beautiful blending of Bible doctrine, contemporary insights, and sensible applications to the needs of life" (Wiersbe, 213).

*Tozer, A. W. *The Tozer Pulpit.* 2 vols. Edited by Gerald B. Smith. Reprint, Camp Hill, PA: Christian Publications, 1967.

Tozer was the pastor of the Southside Alliance Church in Chicago from 1928 to 1959 and was widely known as both a twentieth-century prophet and evangelical mystic. Warren Wiersbe in *Walking with the Giants* described him as the "conscience of evangelicalism at large" (163). He was one of the towering Christian figures of the twentieth century and his voice deserves to be heard today. Reading these sermons will, as Wiersbe wrote, "prevent a generation arising that knows not Tozer" (163).

+*Whitefield, George. *Select Sermons of George Whitefield*. Carlisle, PA: Banner of Truth, 1958.

> This edition contains a foreward by the great British preacher, D. Martyn Lloyd-Jones, as well as a brief biographical sketch of Whitefield by J. C. Ryle, the first Anglican Bishop of Liverpool. Whitefield was widely considered the greatest preacher of the eighteenth-century and perhaps the key figure of the Great Awakening. He was also a personal hero of the faith to Charles Spurgeon, which is quite an endorsement in itself. These six sermons are exemplars of evangelical preaching at its very best.

*Wiersbe, Warren W., ed. Treasury of the World's Great Sermons. Grand Rapids: Kregel, 1977.

> This marvelous collection contains sermons from 123 of the world's greatest preachers ranging from the church fathers (Augustine, Basil, John Chrysostom) through the twentieth century (G. Campbell Morgan, James Stalker, George Adam Smith). I wish Wiersbe would issue a revised edition of this work including preachers from the latter part of the twentieth century and including the twenty-first.

DAILY DEVOTIONAL

There are a variety of daily devotional books for believers. There are daily devotional books for men, women, as well as for children and teens. There are also books for couples. There are devotionals for girlfriends and farmers and college students. It is not difficult to find a serviceable daily devotional guide if one looks. Many believers have a Bible in one hand and a daily devotional guide in the other during their devotional time. I have included two classic guides that I have personally used (Chambers and Spurgeon) over and over again, which have passed the test of time, and then two others, Piper and Wiersbe, which I have read at least twice. All four are excellent and I recommend them without hesitation. The other three devotionals have strong advocates as well.

*Carson, D. A. *For the Love of God: A Daily Companion for Discovering the Riches of God's Word*. Wheaton: Crossway, 1998.

> "The author is Emeritus Professor of NT at Trinity Evangelical Divinity School in Deerfield, IL and founder of The Gospel Coalition. The prolific writer of over fifty scholarly books and dozens of journal articles, Carson is also the General Editor of the *NIV Zondervan Study Bible*. This remarkable book is an amazing devotional adjunct to the 365 Bible reading plan of Robert Murray M'Cheyne, a nineteenth century Scottish minister. Each day includes readings from two OT chapters and two NT chapters. Over the course of a year, the Psalms and the NT are read twice, while the OT is read once. Each daily devotional corresponds to the Scripture selections to be read that day. Carson has the unique ability to provide in-depth understanding to link the OT and the NT in a way that brings insight and a renewed love and joy for the Word of God" (**Van Hook**).

+*Chambers, Oswald. *My Utmost for His Highest*. Edited by James Reimann. Grand Rapids: Discovery House, 1992.

> Originally published posthumously in 1933, this book was compiled by the author's wife from his preaching to students and soldiers. It has since become the best-selling devotional book of all time. It includes brief daily devotional readings for every day of the year. Heartwarming and insightful! This edition is an updated version into modern English. I have read some version of this book from cover-to-cover for about the past twenty years, always with great profit. Not to be missed! The original of this book is featured in Petersen and Petersen's *100 Christian Books That Changed the Century*.

+*Cowman, L. B. *Streams in the Desert*. Edited by James Reimann. Grand Rapids: Zondervan, 1997.

> Originally published in 1925, the author, Lettie Cowman, was a good friend of Oswald Chambers, the author of *My Utmost for His Highest*. This hugely influential devotional has continued to bless and inspire Christians for almost 100 years. This

edition is an updated version into modern English by the same man who did a similar treatment for Chambers' classic. The original of this book is featured in Petersen and Petersen's *100 Christian Books That Changed the Century*.

*Piper, John. *Taste and See: Savoring the Supremacy of God in All of Life*. Sisters, OR: Multnomah, 1999.

Although not actually a daily devotional, these 140 meditations are so rich and spot on that I felt it merited inclusion. From "The Exuberant Omnipotence of God" to "Lessons from a Lost Mastercard" to "What is the Christian Gospel?," your heart will be blessed and your faith strengthened. I am reading this book again this year (2020) along with my Oswald Chambers and my *New International Version*

+*Spurgeon, Charles. *Morning and Evening*. Reprint, Urichsville, OH: Barbour Books, 2018.

For more than 150 years, this daily devotional has been a favorite. Spurgeon was the pastor of the Metropolitan Tabernacle in London until his death in 1892. He has a wide following even today across denominational lines and has been known as the Prince of the Preachers. There is also a newer edition that has been revised and updated published by Crossway Books and edited by Alistair Begg.

*Wiersbe, Warren W., ed. *Giant Steps: Daily Devotions from Spiritual Giants of the Past*. Grand Rapids: Baker, 1981.

Like Piper's book, this book is not really a daily devotional, but rather fifty-two excerpts from the writings and sermons of some of the giants of the Christian faith. There is one devotional per week. The list of contributors is staggering from Charles Haddon Spurgeon, to Hudson Taylor, from A. W. Tozer to D. L. Moody, from John Bunyan to Thomas Manton; every devotional is guaranteed to warm your heart and challenge your spiritual walk.

*Young, Sarah. *Jesus Always: Embracing Joy in His Presence*. Nashville: Thomas Nelson, 2016.

> This book was the ECPA's 2018 Book of the Year winner. It is a 365-day daily devotional that focuses on the often-overlooked fruit of the Spirit, joy.

DEPRESSION

It would be nice if Christians were immune to the problem of depression, but we know that it is not so. Depression is like carbon monoxide. It is colorless, odorless, tasteless, and can be deadly. It has many causes. Two are particularly common. The first is high stress with little relief. This is often detectable until some form of collapse occurs. Anger toward self is another common cause. Christ-followers are not immune, but they have a healer and liberator. Following are a select list of books that deal with this problem.

Bloem, Steve. *The Pastoral Handbook of Mental Illness: A Gide for Training and Reference*. Grand Rapids: Kregel Ministry, 2018.

> This book is more for pastors and professional counselors, but it has some excellent reference material on depression and suicide.

*Haig, Matt. *Reasons to Stay Alive*. New York: Penguin, 2016.

> Written by some who has battled depression and suicidal thoughts, this book is an excellent insider's look at an insidious clinical disease. Helps give the reader perspective and suggestions in order to know what to say and when to say it.

*Lloyd-Jones, D. Martyn. *Spiritual Depression: Its Cause and Cure*. Grand Rapids: Eerdmans, 1972.

> Lloyd-Jones was a medical doctor as well as the pastor of Westminster Chapel in London for almost thirty years succeeding G. Campbell Morgan. He was arguably England's greatest preacher of the twentieth century and eminently qualified

to write about spiritual depression. This book is a collection of twenty-one sermons that were delivered at Westminster Chapel. The goal of every believer, according to Lloyd-Jones, should be to live an effective, healthy Christian life.

*White, John. *The Masks of Melancholy: A Christian Physician Looks at Depression & Suicide.* San Francisco: Harper & Row, 1982.

Written primarily for counselors and pastors who deal with depression and suicide, this book is very helpful in understanding issues such as Christianity and mental illness as well as how to cope with depression and suicide. The Glossary is particularly helpful.

*Wright, H. Norman. *The New Guide to Crisis & Trauma Counseling: What to Do and Say When It Matters Most!* Ventura, CA: Regal, 2003.

An excellent handbook for training lay ministers.

DISCIPLESHIP

!+*Bonhoeffer, Dietrich. *The Cost of Discipleship.* New York: Macmillan, 1948.

Originally published in German in 1937, this religious classic was written by a German theologian, who was executed by the Nazis just days before the concentration camp in which he was held was liberated by the Allies. He condemns cheap grace and calls for a radical discipleship. Groundbreaking in its day and still packs quite a punch. Bonhoeffer's writings are experiencing a resurgence in recent years. Featured in Petersen and Petersen's *100 Christian Books That Changed the Century.*

+*Bruce, A. B. *The Training of the Twelve.* Cosimo Classics, 1877; Reprint, Grand Rapids: Kregel, 2000.

"Bruce's book is a detailed analysis of Jesus' process of making disciples. It is the basis for much that has been written on discipleship today. A classic and a must-read" **(Fleming).**

DEVOTIONAL LITERATURE 199

"Unequalled in its field. Shows how Christ discipled and trained his disciples for the position of apostleship. A most rewarding study" (Barber, 212).

*Coleman, Robert. *The Master Plan of Evangelism*. Old Tappan, NJ: Revell, 1963.

"Coleman's book does a wonderful job of laying out the connections between discipleship and evangelism. To Coleman, they are all the same work of God. Coleman argues that God's plan for conquering the world is to build disciples who can build disciples, multiplying Christ's ministry in others. It is an approach that has proven effective over the years, especially in places resistant to the Gospel" **(Fleming)**.

*Eims, LeRoy. *The Lost Art of Disciple Making*. Grand Rapids: Zondervan, 1987.

"This book is another classic manual for disciple making. Eim's book is mainly aimed at making Christians into useful and productive church members and workers. While this is a worthy goal, it should not be seen as the end of Spiritual Formation, but only a stop along the way" **(Fleming)**.

*Piper, John. *What Jesus Demands from the World*. Wheaton: Crossway, 2006.

Winner of the ECPA's 2007 Christian Book Award in the Christian Life category, this volume by John Piper is a real jewel for those interested in becoming a disciple of Jesus. Written in an accessible and engaging style, Piper states without equivocation that our ultimate duty as Christians is absolute obedience to Christ's commands. A must read!

*Pope, Randy, with Kitti Murray, *Insourcing: Bringing Discipleship Back to the Local Church*. Grand Rapids: Zondervan, 2013.

Pope, a Presbyterian pastor in Atlanta, outlines a disciple-making process that has been proved to be effective for churches. Winner of *Christianity Today's* 2014 Award of Merit in The Church/Pastoral Leadership category.

*Rainer, Thomas, and Eric Geiger. *Simple Church: Returning to God's Process of Making Disciples*. Updated edition. Nashville: B & H, 2011.

> Originally published in 2006, this book focuses on how churches can actually make disciples. Since most churches do not actually disciple, but rather simply incorporate church attenders, this book is sorely needed. Winner of *Christianity Today's* 2007 Book Award in The Church/Pastoral Leadership category.

*White, John. *The Race: Discipleship for the Long Run*. Downers Grove: IVP, 1984.

> The author's contention is that the Christian life is not a sprint, nor is it a casual jog around the neighborhood. Rather, it is a lifelong race that requires perseverance, stamina, and strength. This book assists the believer in overcoming the obstacles along the way.

+*Willard, Dallas. The Divine Conspiracy: Rediscovering Our Hidden Life in God. New York, NY: HarperOne, 1997.

> This book is a modern classic of Christian discipleship. The late Willard, one of this generation's most compelling Christian thinkers and philosophers, argues for the relevance of God in every area of the believer's life. He observes that in today's Christian climate, it is possible to be a Christian without being a disciple of Jesus. This book is ground-breaking, insightful, accessible, and warm in spirit. This study was the magazine *Christianity Today's* 1999 Book of the Year.

*———. *The Great Omission: Reclaiming Jesus' Essential Teachings on Discipleship*. San Francisco: HarperSanFrancisco, 2006.

> Many have misunderstood Christ's Great Commission to be a call to make Christians, not disciples. In his inimitable way, Willard straightens out the fuzzy thinking of much of the

church. Winner of *Christianity Today's* 2007 Award of Merit for Christian Living.

*———. *Renovation of the Heart: Putting on the Character of Christ.* Colorado Springs: NavPress, 2002.

> This book is another modern classic of Christian discipleship. Willard compellingly outlines how believers can transform the mind, will, body, soul, and social dimension and move to the next level of Christlikeness. Any book by Dallas Willard is worth reading. Winner of *Christianity Today's* 2003 Book Award for Spirituality.

EVANGELISM

The great commission, in evangelical circles, has often been called "the great omission." Many believers don't share their faith because they don't know how to do it. They have never been discipled; they have never been taught. The following books provide the rationale and the motivation to do the work of evangelism. They also go a long way towards showing how to do it.

*Barna, George. *Evangelism That Works: How to Reach Changing Generations with the Unchanging Gospel.* Grand Rapids: Baker, 1995.

> Winner of the ECPA's 1995 Gold Medallion Award for Missions/Evangelism.

*Boa, Kenneth D., and Robert M. Bowman, Jr. *An Unchanging Faith in a Changing World: Understanding and Responding to Critical Issues that Christians Face Today.* Nashville: Thomas Nelson, 1998.

> Deals with eighteen important issues facing Christians today from the New Age Movement to Islam to the gay rights movement. Winner of the ECPA's 1998 Gold Medallion Book Award in the Missions/Evangelism category.

*Chan, Sam. *Evangelism in a Skeptical World: How to Make the Unbelievable News About Jesus More Believable.* Grand Rapids: Zondervan, 2018.

> A book that is as much about apologetics as it is about evangelism. A how-to manual for those involved in evangelism. Winner of *Christianity Today's* 2019 Book Award in the category Apologetics/Evangelism.

*Downs, Tim. *Finding Common Ground: How to Communicate with Those Outside the Christian Community . . . While We still Can.* Chicago: Moody, 1999.

> Explores how believers can communicate with unbelieving friends, neighbors, and coworkers in a way that won't appear to be intolerant, pushy, or judgmental. Helps Christians find common ground with unbelievers in practical and effective ways. Winner of the ECPA's 2000 Gold Medallion Book Award for Missions/Evangelism.

+*Kennedy, D. James. *Evangelism Explosion.* 4th edition. Wheaton, IL: Tyndale House, 1996.

> This seminal work explains the methodology that became the building blocks for the Coral Ridge Presbyterian Church in Ft. Lauderdale, FL helping it to grow from under 100 members to well over 6000. The methodology combines a conversational Gospel presentation with a lay-mentoring program that has worked miracles in countless churches.

+*Little, Paul. *How to Give Away Your Faith.* Revised edition. Downers Grove: IVP, 2008.

> This little book is a classic in teaching the art of personal evangelism. Originally published in 1966, it has helped thousands of Christians to be ambassadors for their faith. With humor and insight, Little walks the reader through the nuts and bolts of the Gospel presentation.

*Moore, Waylon B. *New Testament Follow-Up for Pastors and Laymen: How to Conserve, Mature, and Multiply the Converts.* Revised and enlarged edition. Grand Rapids: Eerdmans, 1963.

> The author believes that the number one problem the church faces is the problem of spiritual reproduction. People become saved and join a local church, but they never become disciples. They never grow up in the faith and they never reproduce themselves spiritually. This needed book examines New Testament principles of follow-up and then the practical applications of follow-up. Although this book is over a half century old, its message has never been needed as much as it is today.

+*Packer, J. I. *Evangelism and the Sovereignty of God.* Americanized edition. Downers Grove: IVP, 2012.

> "Why is it that Calvinists teach that salvation is a matter of God's grace and not our choice, yet so many of the great evangelists in the West have been Calvinists? Packer does a brilliant job of laying out how the Reformed faith and passionate evangelism are not incompatible. Whether or not the reader believes in predestination or free will, Packer's book will stimulate your thinking about the necessity of evangelism" **(Fleming)**. Reformed.

*Peel, William Carr, and Walt Larimore. *Going Public with Your Faith: Becoming a Spiritual Influence at Work.* Grand Rapids: Zondervan, 2004.

> The emphasis in this book is on what we are rather than what we do or say as a means of evangelism at work. It sets limits and outlines possibilities for workplace evangelism and explores how Christians can cultivate relationships. Winner of *Christianity Today's* 2004 Book Award for Apologetics/Evangelism.

*Pippert, Rebecca Manley. *Out of the Saltshaker and Into the World: Evangelism as a Way of Life*. Revised edition. Downers Grove: IVP, 1999.

> This revised and enlarged edition is an updated version of the original 1979 book, which revolutionized the way that evangelicals approach evangelism. It calls for what has come to be known as lifestyle evangelism. Practical and easy-to-read. Listed in Petersen and Petersen's *100 Christian Books That Changed the Century*.

*Strobel, Lee. *Inside the Mind of Unchurched Harry and Mary*. Grand Rapids: Zondervan, 1993.

> This book helps believers understand unbelievers and what motivates them. Strobel, a former atheist, offers practical strategies for building relationships with non-Christians. Winner of the ECPA's 1994 Gold Medallion Book Award for Missions/Evangelism.

*Warren, Rick. *The Purpose Driven Church: Growth Without Compromising Your Message & Mission*. Grand Rapids: Zondervan, 1995.

> This huge Christian best-seller was written by the pastor of Saddleback Church, the fastest-growing Baptist church in American history. This book shares pastor Rick Warren's five-part strategy for church growth: warmer through fellowship, deeper through discipleship, stronger through worship, broader through ministry, and larger through evangelism.

MARRIAGE AND FAMILY

*Arp, Dave, and Claudia Arp. *The Second Half of Marriage: Facing the Eight Challenges of Every Long-Term Marriage*. Grand Rapids: Zondervan, 1996.

> This book deals with how to create a marriage that is partner-focused rather than child-focused. How do couples survive

when the children leave the nest? Winner of the ECPA's 1997 Gold Medallion Book Award for Marriage.

*Arthur, Kay. *A Marriage Without Regrets*. Irvine, CA: Harvest House, 2000.

> A manual for Christian marriage. Winner of the ECPA's 2001 Gold Medallion Book Award in the Marriage category.

*Balswick, Jack O., and Judith K. Balswick. *A Model for Marriage: Covenant, Grace, Empowerment and Intimacy*. Downers Grove: IVP Academic, 2006.

> "The Balswicks have blessed readers with another wonderful textbook on marriage. With over thirty years of experience within the context of marital counseling, the book reflects that depth of understanding. With wonderful insights and theological sound writing, this 'model' provides great examples and directions. It is unashamedly Christian in its context and approach reminding the reader of God's original intentions for marriage. The book covers many practical issues also including communication and conflict resolution. This is an excellent resource for study and application" (**Baldwin**).

*———. *The Family: A Christian Perspective on the Contemporary Home*. 4th ed. Grand Rapids: Baker Academic, 2014.

> "Now in its fourth edition this classic perspective on the family remains the best text on the subject of the Christian family. I have used this text in most of my classes as a Pastoral Care Professor in the 3rd edition. I am welcoming an updated contemporary version to my list of required texts" (**Baldwin**).

Brandt, Henry R., and Kerry L. Skinner. *Marriage, God's Way*. Nashville: Broadman & Holman, 1999.

> "This is a dated, yet detailed reference work on Marriage. The Biblical references are worth the price of the book. The authors seek to present God's plan for marriage and show how any couple can enjoy a satisfying and richly rewarding marriage

by approaching the relationship with a Christian standard of love. It is written in a research style and can be used for research very effectively" (**Baldwin**).

*Chapman, Gary D. *The Five Love Languages: How to Express Heartfelt Commitment to Your Mate*. Chicago: Northfield, 2015.

"Gary Chapman, with over thirty years of applying his concept of 'five love languages' has a new approach to understanding these truths in a contemporary form. In the book he provides quizzes to help you discover your primary and secondary love languages. The five love languages are:

- Words of Affirmation: If this is your love language, you feel most cared for when your partner is open and expressive in telling you how wonderful they think you are, how much they appreciate you, etc.
- Acts of Service: This love language desires doing things that help you.
- Physical Touch: This love language is just as it sounds. A warm hug, a kiss, touch, and sexual intimacy make you feel most loved when this is your love language.
- Quality Time: This love language is about being together, fully present and engaged in the activity at hand, no matter how trivial.
- Giving and receiving Gifts: Your partner taking the time to give you a gift can make you feel appreciated.
  I use these concepts of Love Languages with every pre-marital and marital counseling couple. It always is a great help and always well received" (**Baldwin**).

*———. *Loving Solutions: Overcoming Barriers in Your Marriage*. Northfield, 1999.

Written for the vast majority of married couples whose marriages are not failing, but flawed. Winner of the ECPA's 1999 Gold Medallion Book Award in the Marriage category.

———. *The Marriage You've Always Wanted.* Chicago: Moody, 2009.

> This brief, easy to read book examines many of the problem areas that couples face in a marriage. The range of topics is as diverse as why a spouse will not change to the division of household tasks to in-law problems.

*Cloud, Henry, and John Townsend. *Boundaries in Marriage.* Grand Rapids: Zondervan, 1999.

> Helps spouses understand and respect their mate's needs, choices, and freedom so that they can give themselves freely and lovingly to one another. Winner of the ECPA's 2000 Gold Medallion Book Award for Marriage.

Conway, Jim. *Men in Mid Life Crisis.* Colorado Springs: David C. Cook, 1978.

> A helpful guide to assist men in dealing with an often-ignored issue in the Church.

*Crouch, Andy. *The Tech-Wise Family: Everyday Steps for Putting Technology in Its Proper Place.* Grand Rapids: Baker, 2017.

> Have you ever worried that technology has taken over your family? This book is an essential guide for putting technology in its place in the Christian home. A practical guidebook to helping the modern family navigate the perils of technology from computer to smartphone written by a concerned husband and father. Full of practical and down-to-earth advice for using technology and not letting it use us. Winner of *Christianity Today's* 2018 Book Award in the Christian Living/Discipleship category.

+*Dobson, James. *Dare to Discipline.* Wheaton: Tyndale House, 1970.

> This seminal work has undergone numerous reprintings and revisions since its initial 1970 publication. It has been a hugely popular work in the evangelical world in the US in the past five decades. Discipline as Dobson defines it is not limited

to punishment, but rather incorporates self-discipline and responsible living. In an age when the discipline of children has seemingly gone out of style, the author's message is sorely needed today. Featured in Petersen and Petersen's *100 Christian books That Changed the Century*.

*Eggerichs, Emerson. *Love & Respect: The Love She Most Desires; The Respect He Desperately Needs*. Nashville: Thomas Nelson, 2004.

This book examines the secret to couples meeting one another's deepest needs. Winner of the ECPA's 2005 Gold Medallion Book Award Winner in the Marriage category.

*Endicott, Irene. *Grandparenting Redefined: Guidance for Today's Changing Family*. Aglow Publications, 1992.

"The role of grandparent has changed over the years. At one time grandparents either lived in the same home or lived nearby. Now there are grandparents of the children of divorced parents, grandparents with grandchildren living far away, grandparents raising their grandchildren, grandparents with unsaved adult children, grandparents who have lost a grandchild to death as well as other scenarios. Included in this book are numerous illustrations and counsel from those who have endured these difficulties. While the book's statistics are outdated, both its biblical teachings and human relationship do not change. I recommend its use for classes, support groups, and for pastors, sermon ideas" (**Waterhouse**).

Hybels, Bill, and Lynne Hybels. *Fit to Be Tied: Making Marriage Last a Lifetime*. Grand Rapids: Zondervan, 1991.

The authors, the founding and former senior pastor of Willow Creek Community Church in South Barrington, IL and his wife, draw upon their own experiences to explore how to deal with the most common marital problems and avoid the most common pitfalls in a healthy marriage. Winner of the ECPA's 1992 Gold Medallion Book Award in the Marriage and Family category. The reason this book did not earn an * is that apparently Mr. Hybels failed to take his own advice in his own marriage.

*Keller, Timothy. *The Meaning of Marriage: Facing the Complexities of Commitment with the Wisdom of God*. Reprint, New York: Penguin, 2013.

Based on a sermon series by the noted Presbyterian pastor of Redeemer Presbyterian Church in Manhattan, this book critiques modern misconceptions about marriage such as that everyone has a soul mate and that romance is the most important part of a successful marriage. Keller instead shows what marriage should be according to Scripture.

*Kessler, Jay. *Family Forum*. Wheaton: Victor, 1984.

A very helpful book on how to live life in a family, with your spouse, with others, with yourself, without a spouse, in a broken world, in a permissive world, in a spiritual world, in a real world, and in a changing world. Based on his popular radio program of the same title, Jay Kessler, former President of Youth for Christ/USA and Chancellor and President Emeritus of Taylor University, utilizes a topical question and answer format to deal with just about any kind of question that a believer could face at least in the world of the 1980s.

*Kimmel, Tim. *Grace Based Parenting: Set Your Family Free*. Nashville: W Publishing Group, 2005.

This book rejects parenting styles that utilize rigid rules and checklists and embraces one that mirrors God's love. Winner of the ECPA's 2005 Gold Medallion Book Award in the Family and Parenting category.

LaHaye, Tim, and Beverly LaHaye. *The Act of Marriage: The Beauty of Sexual Love*. Grand Rapids: Zondervan, 1976.

This book is basically a "how to" handbook on the sexual aspect of marriage.

*McDowell, Josh. *The Father Connection: How You Can Make the Difference in Your Child's Self-Esteem and Sense of Purpose.* Nashville: B & H, 2008.

> An updated edition of the 1996 book that examines ten parenting qualities of fatherhood. Winner of the ECPA's 1997 Gold Medallion Book Award for Family and Parenting.

*Mehl, Ron. *Just in Case I Can't Be There: A Dad's Counsel to a Son or Daughter Leaving Home.* Portland, OR: Multnomah, 1999.

> A heart-to-heart talk that every father wants to have with his son or daughter about to leave home. Biblical counsel that is wise and practical. Winner of the ECPA's 2000 Gold Medallion Book Award for Family and Parenting.

Meier, Paul, and Richard Meier. *Family Foundations: How to Have a Happy Home.* Grand Rapids: Baker, 1981.

> This book examines seven factors essential for a spiritually and emotionally healthy home: a spiritual base, genuine love, gut-level communication, discipline, consistency, setting the example, and proper leadership roles.

*Moore, Russell. *The Storm-Tossed Family: How the Cross Reshapes the Home.* Nashville: B & H, 2018.

> In a tempest-tossed society, the home has been under attack. This book demonstrates both the good and bad sides of family relationships and how the Christ who calmed the storm-tossed sea can calm the waves threatening the family. Winner of *Christianity Today's* 2019 Award of Merit in the Christian Living/ Discipleship category.

*Ortlund, Ray. *Marriage and the Mystery of the Gospel.* Wheaton: Crossway, 2017.

> The author examines the institution of marriage throughout Scripture from Adam and Eve to the ultimate marriage in the Apocalypse of John. He believes that the transcendent vision

of God dignifies the imperfect marriages on earth as a display of the gospel. Winner of the ECPA's 2017 Christian Book Award in the Bible Study category.

*Penner, Clifford, and Joyce Penner. *Men and Sex*. Nashville: Thomas Nelson, 1997.

Reveals what every man should know about a woman and what every wife wishes her spouse knew. Winner of the ECPA's 1998 Gold Medallion Book Award in the Marriage category.

*Petersen, J. Allan. *The Myth of the Greener Grass*. Wheaton: Tyndale House, 1983.

An engaging and shocking look at adultery and marriage. In the almost forty years since the book was published, not much has changed except perhaps the rising incidence of STDs as a result of adultery. This is a "user friendly" read that will help couples to "affair proof" their marriages.

*Rainey, Dennis, and Barbara Rainey. *The Art of Parenting*. Bloomington, MN: Bethany House, 2018.

Based upon years of ministry and the experiences of raising six children, this book focuses on four crucial elements in the lives of children: relationships, character, identity, and mission. Winner of EPCA's 2019 Christian Book Award in the Christian Living category.

*———. *Building Your Mate's Self-Esteem*. Nashville: Thomas Nelson, 1995.

"Dennis and Barbara Rainey are co-founders of FamilyLife, a ministry of Cru. For decades they have conducted the well-known Weekend to Remember marriage seminars. *Building Your Mate's Self-Esteem* is at the heart of their own marriage and speaking ministry. The book is both practical and poignant. The author's share their own struggles and real-life solutions. This volume could easily be titled *Building a Marriage that Will Last a Lifetime*. It had a profound impact on my marriage and I presented a copy to each of my children on the occasion of their marriage" (**LeRoy**).

*Rosberg, Gary, and Barb Rosberg. *Divorce-Proof Your Marriage: 6 Secrets to a Forever Marriage.* Carol Stream, IL: Tyndale House, 2003.

> Outlines the threats to marriage and the key building blocks to counter those threats. The authors define the six facets of love—forgiving love, serving love, persevering love, guarding love, celebrating love, and renewing love. Has a companion workbook for couples and study groups. Winner of the ECPA's 2003 Gold Medallion Award.

*Schaeffer, Edith. *What is a Family?* Old Tappan, NJ: Fleming H. Revell, 1975.

> This book presents an optimistic view of family life. Drawing from her experiences as a wife, mother, and grandmother at L'Abri, the world-renowned Christian community in Switzerland, the author shares her insights gained as the wife of the brilliant theologian, Francis Schaeffer, mother to four children, and counselor and guide to the myriad of people who stopped at L'Abri in their quest for meaning in life. A side note: A few years ago, I sat at a lunch table with my late friend and colleague, the theologian, R. K. McGregor Wright, and his wife, Julia Castle, as he shared how his personal search led him to L'Abri as a young college student in the 1960s. My wife, Tess, and I sat enthralled as he shared his story of his encounter with the Schaeffers.

*Smalley, Gary, and John Trent. *The Two Sides of Love: What Strengthens Affection, Closeness, and Lasting Commitment?* Focus on the Family. Nashville: W Publishing Group, 1990.

> The authors argue that our personality type determines whether we are too hard or too soft in our relationships with loved ones. They explore four basic personality types and conclude that the key to stronger relationships is the ability to balance both sides of love. Winner of the ECPA's 1991 Gold Medallion Book Award in the Marriage and Family category.

*Sproul, R. C. *The Intimate Marriage: A Practical Guide to Building a Great Marriage*. Reprint, Wheaton: Tyndale House, 1986.

> In just over 120 pages, Sproul deftly and engagingly deals with six topics: communication in marriage, the roles of the spouses, problems in marriage, divorce, communication and sex, and the institution and sanctity of marriage. The author is sometimes profound and never dull.

*Swindoll, Charles R. *Strike the Original Match*. Portland, OR: Multnomah, 1980.

> Popular preacher and author Swindoll offers fresh, practical advice on rekindling and preserving the fire of marriage. All of his prescriptions are based on Scripture.

*Tripp, Paul David. *Parenting: The 14 Gospel Principles That Can Radically Change Your Family*. Wheaton: Crossway, 2017.

> Examines the fourteen gospel principles that can revolutionize the family—calling, grace, law, inability, identity, process, lost, authority, foolishness, character, false gods, control, rest, and mercy. Winner of the ECPA's 2017 Christian Book Award in the Christian Living category.

*Waterhouse, Steven. *Strength for His People: A Ministry for Families of the Mentally Ill*. Reprint, Amarillo: Westcliff Press, 2020.

> An excellent resource for Christian families of those who have severe mental illness. The author has served as the pastor of Westcliff Bible Church in Amarillo, TX since 1985, has a D.Min. from Dallas Theological Seminary, and was a student in many of my classes back in our seminary years. Originally published in 1994, this book examines in depth a biblical perspective on schizophrenia and touches also on the possibility of demon possession. Secondary applications of this book are in the areas of families dealing with physical disabilities, Alzheimer's disease, and mental retardation. Dispels misconceptions such as that schizophrenia is primarily a moral problem, not a medical problem and exposes the failure of churches in

responding to mental illness in their midst. A brief book that packs a punch and offers a lot of practical application and an excellent bibliography. Endorsed by the Christian Medical Society and NAMI (National Alliance on Mental Illness). May be downloaded without cost at www.webtheology.com.

White, Jerry, and Mary White. *The Christian in Mid Life: Biblical Guidelines and Inspiration for Men and Women Facing the Challenges of Mid-Life.* Colorado Springs: Navpress, 1980.

This helpful book enables Christians to navigate the dangers and opportunities of mid-life. Although many books on mid-life crises tend to deal with marriage and its challenges during this period, this volume also investigates how it affects singles as well as the overflow effects on children.

*White, John. *Parents in Pain: A Book of Comfort and Counsel.* Downers Grove: IVP, 1979.

This book is a how-to manual for parents of children with severe problems. The author is particularly adept at helping parents deal with feelings of guilt, inadequacy, frustration, and anger. Dated, but still helpful because its prescriptions are biblical.

*Wright, H. Norman. *Communication: Key to Your Marriage.* Ventura, CA: Regal, 1974.

The premise of this book is, as its title suggests, that communication is the key to a happy, vibrant marriage. It offers strategies for dealing with marital conflict as well as ways that spouses can build the self-esteem of their partners. Bethany House Publishers published an updated revised edition in 2012. When I was a pastor, I gave a copy of this book to every engaged couple who came to me for pre-marital counseling. "An important book" (Barber).

Yates, John, and Susan Yates. *What Really Matters at Home: Eight Elements for Building Character in Your Family.* Dallas: Word, 1992.

> This book helps parents build character in their families by communicating eight crucial elements: integrity, faith, a teachable spirit, a servant's heart, self-discipline, joy, compassion, and courage.

MISSIONS

+*Elliot, Elisabeth. *Through Gates of Splendor.* Rev. ed. Carol Stream, IL: Tyndale Momentum, 1981.

> "'He is no fool who gives what he cannot keep to gain what he cannot lose.' (Jim Elliot) For decades we have heard this prophetic quote by missionary, Jim Elliot. Author Elisabeth Elliot, Jim's wife and widow, gives us the full context of his famous words in this 1957 book. It is the moving account of the events leading up to the January 8, 1956 death of Jim and four other missionaries to the Auca tribe in Ecuador. The hand of God seems so near and so far as Elisabeth brings us to the sandy river beach where the five young men stepped out of the plane to share the gospel. However, on that beach, all five became martyrs. The shock and unspeakable pain of loss is overtaken by God's grace, love, forgiveness, and redemption. This missionary classic will challenge you to a deeper faith and fire your zeal for missions" (**LeRoy**). "One of the greatest missionary stories of this or any era" (Barber, 207).

+Jones, E. Stanley. *The Christ of the Indian Road.* Nashville: Abingdon, 1925.

> A ground-breaking book, controversial in its day, that helped to redefine foreign missions. Jones' main contribution to modern missions is that he saw missionary work as sharing Jesus Christ, not some westernized version of Christianity. Featured in Petersen and Petersen's *100 Christian Books That Changed the Century.*

*Long, Kathryn. *God in the Rainforest: A Tale of Martyrdom and Redemption in Amazonian Ecuador.* New York: Oxford University Press, 2019.

> This book examines the broad picture of the conversion of the Waorani people after the murder of five young missionaries in the jungle of Ecuador. The perspective of evangelicals who regarded their conversion as a *cause celebre* for the church is considered as is that of secular critics who made accusations of ethnocide. Winner of *Christianity Today's* 2020 Book Award in the History/Biography category.

*Moreau, A. Scott, ed. *Evangelical Dictionary of World Missions.* Grand Rapids: Baker, 2000.

> Winner of *Christianity Today's* 2001 Book Award for Missions/Global Affairs.

*Pocock, Michael, Gailyn Van Rheenen, and Douglas McConnell, eds. *The Changing Face of World Missions: Engaging Contemporary Issues and Trends.* Grand Rapids: Baker Academic, 2005.

> Examines the dramatic changes that have taken place in global society and the church and the implications for Christian missions in the twenty-first century. Written in a clear and easily understandable style suitable for both church leaders and the laity. Winner of *Christianity Today's* 2006 Award of Merit for Missions/Global Affairs.

*Smither, Edward. *Christian Mission: A Concise Global History.* Bellingham, WA: Lexham Press, 2019.

> A compact examination of Christian mission history from Christianity's beginnings to the present day. Winner of *Christianity Today's* 2020 Award of Merit in the Missions/Global Church category.

*Stearns, Bill, and Amy Stearns. *Catch the Vision 2000*. Bloomington, MN: Bethany House, 1991.

> Tells the exciting stories of how God is working in different parts of the globe from China to Korea to Soviet Central Asia. Shows practical ways for individuals and churches to "catch the vision" and become involved in this great work for God. Winner of the ECPA's 1992 Gold Medallion Book Award for Missions/Evangelism.

*Sunquist, Scott W. *Understanding Christian Mission: Participation in Suffering and Glory*. Grand Rapids: Baker Academic, 2013.

> Winner of *Christianity Today's* 2014 Book Award in the Missions/Global Affairs category.

+*Taylor, Frederick Howard, and G. Taylor. *Hudson Taylor's Spiritual Secret*. Reprint, Chicago: Moody, 1950.

> "Originally published in 1932, it is not trite to label this book as a missionary classic. The authors were the son and daughter-in-law of Hudson Taylor, pioneer missionary to China. Taylor's call to China was unmistakable. The challenges were beyond human resources and required complete dependence upon God. Taylor inspired generations of future missionaries with his total immersion approach into the foreign life and culture of China. Eventually, the trickle of results became a great flood as the founding of the China Inland Mission brought hundreds of missionaries to China. Though officially repressed today, Christians in China may number over 100 million" (**LeRoy**). "Deserves a place in every pastor's library" (Barber).

PRAYER

If reading God's Word is like eating for the Christ follower, then prayer is like breathing. Unfortunately, prayer is more discussed than actually practiced. What is even worse is that when it is practiced, it is often practiced incorrectly and selfishly. The following books will help you to get your prayer life on a firmer footing with God.

+*Baillie, John. *A Diary of Private Prayer*. Reprint, New York: Scribner's, 1977.

> Originally published in 1936, this classic work is a collection of daily prayers, morning and evening, for each day of the month. The language is couched in King James English, which is not too surprising considering the popularity of the KJV back in 1936. Featured in Petersen and Petersen's *100 Christian Books That Changed the Century*.

Berry, William, S. J. *Paying Attention to God*. Notre Dame, IN: Ave Maria, 1990.

> "I confess to a particular fondness for Barry's writings. He writes from a Roman Catholic perspective which may be off-putting for some Protestants, but readers may find, as I did, that this is an earthy, practical book on the need for honesty and openness in prayer. His advice goes deep into the life of inner companionship with God, and leads us to think of our God communication in exciting new ways. Where else can you find a chapter on the importance of getting mad at God?" **(Fleming)**

+*Bounds, Edward McKendrie. *Power Through Prayer*. 12th ed. London: Marshall, 1912; Reprint, Grand Rapids: Baker, 1972.

> Along with the author's *Purpose in Prayer*, these two books are two of the most powerful books on prayer ever published. They arose out of a life totally yielded to God. Originally published in 1907. Warren Wiersbe describes reading this book as akin to "opening a blast furnace." Highly recommended! "A book every pastor and Christian worker should read" (Barber 240). Featured in Petersen and Petersen's *100 Christian Books That Changed the Century*.

Eldredge, John. *Moving Mountains: Praying with Passion, Confidence, and Authority.* Nashville: Thomas Nelson, 2016.

> A practical primer on prayer by the director of Ransomed Heart. There is also an accompanying study guide, which divides the book's contents into eight sessions for use in groups or individually, as well as a DVD. We used this book along with the study guide and DVD in our Thursday evening Life Group comprised of members of our church and the reviews were mixed.

*Fleming, Bill Owen, Jr. *Prayer: The Adventure: A Six-Step Program for Developing the Habit of Prayer.* CreateSpace, 2013.

> In the church, there is a lot of talk about the necessity of prayer, but there is little practical direction on how to develop a disciplined prayer life. This book guides the reader through six aspects of prayer: meditation, praise, thanksgiving, confession/affirmation, petition, and practicing the presence. It was designed to be used as a guide for a six-week self or group study course on prayer. Fleming is a retired Presbyterian pastor who served numerous congregations in the Associate Presbyterian Church and is the former department head for Pastoral Studies at Charlotte Christian College and Theological Seminary. He also contributed numerous annotations for this book.

*Foster, Richard J. *Prayer: Finding the Heart's True Home.* San Francisco: HarperCollins, 1992.

> This helpful book explores the topic as the outgrowth of a "love relationship with the great God of the universe" (page 3). Foster, a Quaker, draws from many different faith traditions in this fine primer on prayer. There are three parts. Part I is Moving Inward: Seeking the Transformation We need; Part II is Moving Upward: Seeking the Intimacy We need; and Part III is Moving Outward: Seeking the Ministry We Need. Thoughtful and practical. "I found the selection on simple prayers to be particularly helpful" **(Fleming)**.

*———. *Sanctuary of the Soul: A Journey into Meditative Prayer.* Downers Grove: IVP, 2011.

"Meditative, or contemplative prayer is not for everyone. It is an advanced form of prayer which relies more on silence than words. Foster, coming from an evangelical Protestant background, provides a good introduction to one of the most mysterious and rewarding aspects of prayer" (**Fleming**).

*Jeremiah, David. *Prayer—The Great Adventure.* Sisters, OR: Multnomah, 1997.

The author believes that the first step in having a meaningful prayer life is a close relationship with God. Winner of the ECPA's 1998 Gold Medallion Book Award in the Christian Living category.

+*Murray, Andrew. *The Inner Chamber and The Inner Life.* Whitefish: Kessinger LLC, 2010.

This book is a companion volume to the author's *The Prayer-Life*. The author (1828–1917) was a South African pastor who was also a prolific devotional writer. His writings have blessed generations of believers. This edition of the two books is a facsimile reproduction of the original 1905 editions published together. *The Inner Chamber* is also available by itself in a 2009 edition published by the Christian Literature Crusade. These two books are classics on the devotional life of the Christian. "Strikes out against the feebleness of many Christians and their inability to resist the world, and emphasize the need for earnest prayer if the believer is to be fruitful in his service" (Barber, 239).

+*———. *The Prayer-Life.* London: Morgan and Scott, 1914; Reprint, Grand Rapids: Zondervan, n.d.

This book arose out of a series of messages that the author gave at a pastor's conference in South Africa in April 1912. The pastors, along with missionaries and students, had gathered to seek God's assistance and blessing over the condition of the church. Murray's messages helped to spark revival in South Africa over a century ago. They are still powerful today.

+*———. *With Christ in the School of Prayer.* Reprint, Westwood: Revell, 1953.

> Regrettably OP, this prayer classic can often be found secondhand. It can also be obtained through CreateSpace Independent Publishing Platform.

*Pratt, Jr., Richard L. *Pray with Your Eyes Open: Looking at God, Ourselves and Our Prayers.* Phillipsburg, NJ: Presbyterian & Reformed, 1987.

> A practical guide on how to improve the believer's prayer life.

*Shirer, Priscilla. *Fervent: A Woman's Battle Plan for Serious, Specific, and Strategic Prayer.* Nashville: B & H Books, 2015.

> As the subtitle of this book declares, its main audience is women. It begins with the premise that prayer is a weapon to be utilized in spiritual warfare and that women must learn how to pray more effectively. The book deals with ten strategies or areas of focus for women to consider when they pray: passion, focus, identity, family, past fears, purity, pressures, hurts, and relationship. Men will certainly find this material to be helpful too. Published in conjunction with the movie, *War Room,* which features the author in a leading role. Winner of the ECPA's 2016 Book of the Year.

*Sproul, R. C. *The Prayer of the Lord.* Orlando: Reformation Trust, 2009.

> A concise and insightful guide on both how to pray and how not to pray using the Lord's Prayer as a model. Sproul was a master teacher who is always interesting and readable.

Torrey, R. A. *How to Pray.* Reprint, Chicago: Moody, n.d.

> A reprint of the 1900 edition, this book gives practical pointers on the essential features of effective prayer. The author writes with clarity and insight.

*White, John. *Daring to Draw Near: People in Prayer.* Downers Grove: IVP, 1977.

> Examines the prayers of characters from the Bible and what they teach us about God and the world around us. The prayers of Abraham, Jacob, Moses, David, Daniel, Hannah, Job, Paul, and Jesus demonstrate that our modern struggles echo those of biblical times and are not unique.

+*Whyte, Alexander. *Lord, Teach Us to Pray.* Reprint, Grand Rapids: Baker, 1976.

> A classic study of prayer by the greatest Scottish preacher of the late nineteenth and early twentieth centuries, this book examines some of the great saints of the Bible and their examples of prayer. The prayers of such luminaries as Jacob, Moses, Job, Habakkuk, the Apostle Paul, and our Lord himself are placed under the microscope and surgically dissected. Then Whyte directs his attention to certain elements of prayer such as reverence, the costliness of prayer, pleading, concentration, and imagination in prayer. This study is profound, practical, and a delight to read.

*Yancey, Philip. *Prayer: Does It Make Any Difference?* Grand Rapids: Zondervan, 2006.

> Prayer is a mystery to some Christians and an exercise in futility to others. This book offers no easy answers to our questions about prayer. However, Yancey does argue that prayer is an essential component of our partnership with God and a window into knowing the mind of God. Winner of *Christianity Today's* 2007 Book Award for Christian Living.

SPIRITUAL DIRECTION AND FORMATION

"The term 'Spiritual Formation' in the Christian vocabulary refers to the ongoing process of conformity into the likeness of Christ. Though it is sometimes used synonymously with discipleship, Spiritual Formation is more inclusive, having to do with the development of Christian life, character, and emotions. It is more than learning facts and information, but involves growth into a Christlike nature. Spiritual Formation for a Christian is a lifelong process, whereas discipleship usually refers to the initial stages of spiritual development. In Protestant churches, the Spiritual Formation movement began in the 1980s and is usually associated with authors such as Dallas Willard and Richard Foster. Today it has gained a broad acceptance because of its emphasis on balancing heart, head, and actions, and because of its call to lifetime spiritual development.

"Along with Spiritual Formation is the growing practice of Spiritual Direction. Spiritual Direction is, as one author puts it, 'Two people meeting together in prayer to find what God is saying to one of them.' It is not counseling or giving advice, but the practice of discernment and prayer. Spiritual direction is not for everyone, but it is a valuable practice for many believers" **(Fleming)**.

Benner, David. *Sacred Companions: The Gifts of Spiritual Friendship and Direction.* Downers Grove: IVP, 2003.

> "This book lays out the general principles of Spiritual Direction and describes the work of a Spiritual Director. Benner has been an influential author in bringing Spiritual Direction to a Protestant evangelical audience" **(Fleming)**.

*Boa, Kenneth. *Conformed to His Image: A Biblical and Practical Approach to Spiritual Formation.* Grand Rapids: Zondervan, 2001.

> "Boa focuses on the diversity of spirituality in the Christian formation experience. He lists twelve different facets of spirituality and gives examples from church history of each. His thesis is that we need them all. A good, basic reader on appreciating the diversity of the Body of Christ" **(Fleming)**.

Crabb, Larry. *Soul Talk: The Language God Longs for us to Speak.* Brentwood, TN: Integrity Press, 2003.

> "Larry Crabb began his career as a Christian counselor and speaker. In recent years, though, he has become more involved in training and equipping Christians in Spiritual Direction. *Soul Talk* is a simple call to develop interpersonal relationships

that go deeper than superficial sharing and to develop relationships of mutual trust and spiritual strength, in which emotional and spiritual healing can happen" **(Fleming)**.

*Demarest, Bruce. *Seasons of the Soul*. Downers Grove: IVP, 2001.

"Demarest provides a pattern for Spiritual Formation and growth, which is very simple—initial orientation, painful disorientation, and joyful reorientation. What makes this book particularly helpful is his appendix 'Spiritual Journey Paradigms, classical and contemporary' comparing several paradigms of spiritual growth" **(Fleming)**.

*Ford, Paul F., ed. *Yours, Jack: Spiritual Direction from C. S. Lewis*. New York, NY: HarperOne, 2008.

C. S. Lewis was one of the towering intellectual figures of the twentieth century and perhaps the most influential Christian writer and apologist of his day. This book is an edited collection of his personal correspondence to friends and acquaintances spanning the years 1916 until his death in 1963. His original letters were always handwritten and signed "Yours, Jack." These letters give the reader a compelling look at the writer's view of the Christian life and deserve to be read and re-read.

*Hudson, Trevor. *Discovering Our Spiritual Identity: Practices for God's Beloved*. Downers Grove: IVP, 2010.

"What can we say about this wonderful book? Hudson sees the central issue for believers is to both know and feel that we are God's beloved children. Our spiritual identity does not come from what we think of ourselves, but from what God thinks of us. Each chapter includes spiritual practices, called 'holy experiments' to strengthen our acceptance of God's love for us and our love for God. Hudson's gentle, winsome style goes a long way towards helping us see ourselves as truly God's beloved" **(Fleming)**.

+*Lawrence, Brother. *The Practice of the Presence of God*. Reprint, Leyland Edwards, 2017.

> "This volume by a seventeenth century monk in a monastery in Paris is a must-read for anyone seeking a deeper connection to God. Lawrence's central idea is that God is with us everywhere, and can be found anywhere—in the kitchen or field as well as in the chapel on our knees. He practiced a moment-by-moment discipline of thankfulness, joy, and prayer. A foundational book in understanding the goal of spiritual formation" **(Fleming)**.

*MacDonald, Gordon. *Ordering Your Private World*. Expanded edition. Nashville: Thomas Nelson, 1985.

> This study by former president of Inter-Varsity Christian Fellowship helps the believer move from a state of physical and spiritual disorganization to a life that is more organized. The author deals with such topics as Use of Time, Wisdom and Knowledge, Spiritual Strength, and Restoration. MacDonald writes with clarity and insight.

*———. *Restoring Your Spiritual Passion*. Nashville: Thomas Nelson, 1986.

> This book, by a former pastor and internationally-known Christian leader and conference speaker who lost his spiritual passion and had an extramarital affair, explores how unhappiness and disillusionment manifest themselves in different ways, such as burn-out and depression. It gives a prescription for the unrest and disquiet, which is so much a part of modern life.

+*Packer, J. I. *Knowing God*. Downers Grove: IVP, 1973.

> Not yet fifty years old, this book is an acknowledged classic of the Christian life. In 2006, *Christianity Today* designated it as one of the top fifty books that have shaped evangelicals. In 1993, IVP published a 20th anniversary edition with a new preface by Packer as well as Americanized language and spelling. Personally, I prefer the original edition. In whatever form you encounter this book, it is not to be missed!

*Peterson, Eugene H. *Practice Resurrection: A Conversation on Growing Up in Christ*. Grand Rapids: Eerdmans, 2010.

> In this book, the author laments the failure of the American church to treat Christian maturity and character formation with urgency. Winner of *Christianity Today's* 2011 Book Award in the Spirituality category.

*Pink, Arthur W. *Spiritual Growth*. 3rd ed. Grand Rapids: Baker, 1996.

> A spiritual analysis of 1 Peter 3:18 which challenges believers to "grow in grace." "As with all of Pink's works, this one needs to be studied" (Barber).

Ryrie, Charles Caldwell. *Balancing the Christian Life*. Chicago: Moody, 1969.

> This book is a helpful guide to the Christian life organized into three parts. First, the author attempts to develop a theology of man and spirituality. He then develops some personal responsibilities of believers under the headings of sanctification, dedication, faithfulness, spiritual gifts, and money. Finally, he deals with such practical issues as being filled with the Spirit, temptation, legalism, Lordship salvation, and speaking in tongues. Dated, but still helpful.

*Scazzero, Peter. *Emotionally Healthy Spirituality*. Grand Rapids: Zondervan, 2006.

> "This popularly written book has been an introduction to Spiritual Formation for many Christians, and may be a good place to begin. Scazzaro is the pastor of New Life Fellowship in New York City and the author of many books. His title, 'emotionally healthy,' comes from the realization that he came to late in his ministry, that people cannot be spiritually healthy without the transformation of our emotional lives. Scazzero believes that this transformation of the heart occurs through the ministry of the Holy Spirit working in our lives through the development of spiritual exercises and disciplines" (**Fleming**).

*Schaeffer, Francis A. *True Spirituality.* Wheaton: Tyndale, 1971.

> This book began as a series of messages first preached in Huemoz, Switzerland, and led to the creation of L'Abri. Although more than sixty years old, these messages still retain their intellectual vibrancy and relevancy. Schaeffer was one of the true spiritual giants of the twentieth century as well as one of its leading intellectuals and still deserves to be heard and read. "Comes to grips with the problem of reality and the all-sufficiency of Christ, and presents the gospel as the only message to meet the needs of men and women today" (Barber, 221).

*Smith, James K. A. *You Are What You Love: The Spiritual Power of Habit.* Grand Rapids: Brazos, 2016.

> Christians are more than what they say they think and believe; they are in actuality more defined by what they practice and what they love. This book encourages believers to cultivate holy habits. Winner of *Christianity Today's* 2017 Award of Merit in the Spiritual Formation category.

*Swindoll, Charles R. *Growing Deep in the Christian Life.* Portland: Multnomah, 1986.

> This book by a popular preacher is a basic down-to-earth approach to spiritual growth in the Christian life. Swindoll has the rare gift of taking complex doctrines and making them easy to understand to the layperson. This book is no exception. He takes theological topics such as the Bible, God the Father, the Lord Jesus Christ, the Holy Spirit, human depravity, salvation, the return of Christ, the resurrection, and the body of Christ and presents them in such a way that the average person in the pew can understand them.

Thomas, Gary. *Sacred Pathways: Discover Your Soul's Path to God.* Grand Rapids: Zondervan, 1996.

> "Like Richard Foster, Thomas studies the many ways our souls seek God. He details nine approaches that people use and encourages us to seek Him in all ways, but to discover the ones

that most connect to us. At the end of each chapter, Thomas gives an inventory to help you discover your preferred path" **(Fleming)**.

+*Tozer, Aiden Wilson. *The Pursuit of God*. Harrisburg, PA: Christian Publications, 1948.

One of the greatest devotional works ever written! Tozer encourages Christians to spend time in the presence of God. Featured in Petersen and Petersen's *100 Christian Books That Changed the Century*.

*Warren, Tish Harrison. *Liturgy of the Ordinary: Sacred Practices in Everyday Life*. Downers Grove: IVP, 2016.

This book, in an engaging and non-preachy fashion, connects the humdrum and mundane of everyday life with our call to worship God. Beautifully written and conceived, this book is a delight to read. Winner of *Christianity Today's* 2018 Book Award in the Spiritual Formation category.

*Willard, Dallas. *The Divine Conspiracy*. New York: HarperCollins, 1998.

"Dallas Willard was probably the most influential voice in the Spiritual Formation movement until his death in 2013. He had a unique background as a Christian teacher, in that he was both a philosopher and a Southern Baptist minister. His work reveals keen exegetical insights into the Scriptures as well as deep philosophical insights. Although he wrote several influential books in this area, *The Divine Conspiracy* is considered his masterpiece. The structure of the book follows Jesus' Sermon on the Mount from Matthew 5–7. He uses this to discuss the Kingdom of God as a current reality on earth. Willard views the Kingdom as whenever people have yielded their lives to God's control. He describes the failings of the modern church, both liberal and conservative, as two forms of 'the Gospel of sin management,' not a life of obedience to God. Instead, he takes the Sermon on the Mount as the model of Christian obedience to God" **(Fleming)**.

SPIRITUAL DISCIPLINES

With the publication of Richard Foster's seminal book, *Celebration of Discipline*, in 1978 came a renaissance of interest in the classical spiritual disciplines of the Christian life. The Christian spiritual disciplines are not new; they go back almost 2000 years. They revolve around the reading, study, meditation, and memorization of Scripture along with prayer. There are others, but these constitute the core.

*Barton, Ruth Haley. *Invitation to Solitude and Silence: Experiencing God's Transforming Presence.* Expanded edition. Downers Grove: IVP, 2010.

> Originally published in 2004, this book deals with two underrated spiritual disciplines and how they can help us achieve greater intimacy with God. Winner of *Christianity Today's* 2005 Book Award for Spirituality.

*Bennett, Kyle David. *Practices of Love: Spiritual Disciplines for the Life of the World.* Grand Rapids: Brazos, 2017.

> The author's argument is that spiritual disciplines were not initially viewed as primarily a means to draw us closer to God (vertical relationship), but rather a means to draw us closer to one another (horizontal relationships). This element is mostly overlooked today in discussions of spiritual disciplines.

+*Chambers, Oswald. *Christian Disciplines.* Reprint, Grand Rapids: Chosen, 1985.

> This Christian classic concentrates on six major disciplines (or areas of concern) for the growing Christian: divine guidance, suffering, peril, prayer, loneliness, and patience. Chambers is always helpful in his observations and often profound.

+*Foster, Richard J. *Celebration of Discipline: The Path to Spiritual Growth.* San Francisco: Harper & Row, 1978.

> In this modern classic of the Christian life, Foster demonstrates how the practice of the three disciplines, inward, outward, and corporate, can lead the believer to a deeper inner life. He argues compellingly that there must be a renewal of

the classic spiritual disciplines: meditation, prayer, fasting, study, simplicity, solitude, submission, service, confession, worship, guidance, and celebration. Listed by Petersen and Petersen in their book, *100 Christian Books That Changed the Century.* "This book is one of the most influential books in the Spiritual Formation movement. It is a very human, non-legalistic approach to the development of spirituality through the development of godly habits. Foster's book has been much debated, discussed, and criticized over the years, but it has held up well, and retains its popularity today" **(Fleming)**.

*_____, and Gayle D. Beebe. *Longing for God: Seven Paths of Christian Devotion.* Downers Grove: IVP, 2009.

The authors introduce the reader to saints from the past who have known God deeply. Winner of *Christianity Today's* 2009 Book Award in the Spirituality category.

*Whitney, Donald S. *Spiritual Disciplines for the Christian Life.* Rev. ed. Carol Stream, IL: NavPress, 2014.

This edition is a revision of the 1991 book. "Whitney's book tackles the various spiritual disciplines with simple, straightforward writing, which is easily approachable to those who are not familiar with historical mysticism or Spiritual Formation writers. It is an excellent book for those who want some practical advice on the spiritual practices that draw us closer to God. His follow-up book, *Spiritual Disciplines for the Christian Church,* is also very helpful" **(Fleming)**.

*Willard, Dallas. *The Spirit of the Disciplines: Understanding How God Changes Lives.* New York: HarperOne, 1991.

Since the publication of Foster's *Celebration of Discipline,* there has been a renaissance of interest in spiritual disciplines. Willard stands at the forefront of spiritual formation movement and is always a delight to read. "Willard is a unique blend of preacher, mystic, and philosopher, who approaches the subject of spiritual formation in a way that is both biblically sound and philosophically deep. Along with his book, *The*

Divine Conspiracy, Willard's work has had a profound impact on church life today" (**Fleming**).

SPIRITUAL GUIDANCE

"Another aspect of Spiritual Formation is learning to discern and recognize the voice of God from other voices in our lives. This is a necessary skill to recognize God's will for our lives" (**Fleming**).

*Carey, Phillip. *Good News for Anxious Christians: 10 Practical Things You Don't Have to Do.* Grand Rapids: Brazos Press, 2010.

> "Don't let the title fool you; this is no 'feel good' book. Carey is not writing some light book about positive thinking. Instead, he writes for students in the Christian college where he teaches about the bondage of emotions in our lives. God, he argues, exists outside our minds and emotions, even when He is revealing Himself in the emotions. It is a welcome respite from people who wonder if they feel God enough or whether their inner feelings of call are for real. Carey argues that even when God speaks through feelings, He is not the feelings and encourages people to use their minds to assess what we feel God is saying to us. His chapter titles include: 'Why You Don't Have to Hear God's Voice in Your Heart,' 'Why You Don't Have to Experience Joy,' and 'Why Basing Faith on Experience Leads to a Post-Christian Future'" (**Fleming**).

*Friessen, Gary. *Decision Making and the Will of God: A Biblical Alternative to the Traditional View.* Portland: Multnomah, 1980.

> This is quite simply the best book I have ever seen about the subject of the will of God. When it came out in 1980, I was still a seminary student and trying to determine what God would have me do for ministry after I graduated. This book was like a breath of fresh air and quite liberating. I highly recommend it!

*Willard, Dallas. *Hearing God: Developing a Conversational Relationship with God.* Downers Grove: IVP, 2012.

> "Once again, Willard comes to the rescue. This book was originally released under the title, *In Search of Guidance,* but was later revised and expanded by the author. Willard introduces the reader to aspects of discernment that go back to the desert Fathers of the fourth century, but never abandons his firm grounding in biblical truth. A very useful and practical book" (**Fleming**).

WORSHIP

Carson, Herbert M. *Hallelujah!* Hertfordshire, England: Evangelical Press, 1980.

> This book defines exactly what worship is drawing from the Old Testament and New Testament as well as the Trinitarian structure. The author discusses such elements of worship as the sermon, the collection, the Lord's Supper and baptism, and the response of the congregation. Interesting and provocative!

*Chapell, Bryan. *Christ-Centered Worship: Letting the Gospel Shape Our Practice.* Grand Rapids: Baker Academic, 2009.

> This book attempts to go beyond the debate over traditional or contemporary worship to explore the historical flow of worship liturgy and how it relates to the Gospel. It emphasizes that what is important in worship is substance, not style. Reformed.

Jeremiah, David. *My Heart's Desire: Living Every Moment in the Wonder of Worship.* Nashville: Integrity, 2002.

> This book is a plea by a popular radio preacher and pastor to experience worship and passion for God every moment of life. Jeremiah is always interesting and biblically-based.

*Kidd, Reggie. *With One Voice: Discovering Christ's Song in Our Worship.* Grand Rapids: Baker, 2005.

> "This book focuses on the role music has in worship, focusing on the Psalms of David. What makes this book stand out is that the author is a musician with a broad appreciation of musical styles and a vibrant heart for worship. It is a good study for those who are interested in deepening their appreciation for music in worship." **(Fleming)**

*MacArthur, Jr., John. *The Ultimate Priority: John MacArthur, Jr. On Worship.* Chicago: Moody, 1983.

> This is another fine book by a popular radio preacher and pastor on the importance of worship. Much more detailed than that of David Jeremiah, the emphasis of this work is the biblical teaching about worship. The author argues for a fresh understanding of what worship is.

+*Tozer, A. W. *Whatever Happened to Worship?* Edited by Gerald B. Smith. Camp Hill, PA: Christian Publications, 1985.

> This is the next book that Tozer intended to write prior to his death in 1963. His oft-expressed belief that "worship acceptable to God is the missing crown jewel in evangelical Christianity" led to his desire to write a book on worship. This book is the result of a series of sermons that Tozer preached from his pulpit at the Avenue Road Church in Toronto in 1962. Tozer has been called a twentieth century prophet as well as mystic. He condemned much of modern worship as simply entertainment and called for a return to true, biblical worship. Tozer needs to be read and heeded today. His voice is sorely missed!

*Webber, Robert. *Worship is a Verb: Celebrating God's Mighty Deeds of Salvation.* 2nd ed. Peabody, MA: Hendrickson, 2004.

> "There are literally hundreds of books written about worship in the church. Most of them may be safely ignored. They are written from every conceivable slant from free worship to liturgy. However, Webber's works, not only in this volume but

in his following *Ancient-Future* series of books, ought not be ignored. Webber applies a rigorously biblical approach to worship without falling into the trap of grumpiness either towards traditional or contemporary worship. His books have sparked a renewed interest in liturgical worship in many Protestant and evangelical churches, as he makes a case for the use of ritual and liturgy. Whether or not a person agrees with Webber's conclusions about the value of liturgy, he challenges us to examine the theological foundations of what we do in worship, and to think of fresh ways of presenting deep theological and psychological truths" **(Fleming)**.

*Wilson, Jonathan R. *Why Church Matters: Worship, Ministry, and Mission in Practice*. Grand Rapids: Brazos, 2007.

Examines the question: What is it we are called to do as a church? The author believes that the practices of Christians are centered on gathered worship. Winner of *Christianity Today's* 2007 Award of Merit in The Church/Pastoral Leadership category.

5

Theological Topics and Church History

ANGELS AND DEMONS: SPIRITUAL WARFARE

Misinformation about angels abounds even among Christ followers. Depictions of angels in movies such as *It's a Wonderful Life* and television shows such as *Touched by an Angel* have fueled misconceptions about who angels are and what they do. The term "angel" is simply a transliteration of the New Testament Greek word *angelos*, which means "messenger." Angels do not fly around with wings and halos over their heads. Also, we do not receive wings and halos when we die and we don't sit around on clouds all day playing harps. Where these common errors came from, I have no idea. What I do know is that ignorance about angels is pervasive. Fact: We do not become angels when we die and go to heaven. Fact: There are good angels and there are evil angels. Fact: There is an invisible war going on right now between the forces of good and the forces of evil and angels are the foot soldiers. The following books will help you make sense of this topic.

*Barnhouse, Donald Grey. *The Invisible War: The Panorama of the Continuing Conflict Between Good & Evil*. Grand Rapids: Ministry Resources Library, 1965.

> A detailed study of the continuing conflict between the forces of good and evil in the spiritual realm.

DeHaan, Richard W. *Satan, Satanism, and Witchcraft*. Grand Rapids: Zondervan, 1972.

> A very brief study which begins with the fall of Satan and his present activity and ends with three of the manifestations in the world today: spiritism, fortune telling, and witchcraft.

*Dickason, C. Fred. *Angels Elect and Evil*. A Handbook of Bible Doctrine. Chicago: Moody, 1975.

> This helpful guide is divided into two sections. Part 1 deals with The Angels of God and Part 2 Satan and Demons. In Part 1 the author deals with the existence, origin, names, classification, and ministry of angels as well as our relationship to them. Part 2 examines the personality, names, original state and fall, and the present power and activity of Satan and the demons. Very helpful.

Graham, Billy. *Angels: God's Secret Agents*. Reprint ed., New York: Pocket Books, 1977.

> A popular treatment of the subject. Deals mainly with good angels and their ministries. There is one chapter titled "Lucifer and the Angelic Rebellion."

+*Gurnall, William. *The Christian in Complete Armour: A Treatise of the Saints' War Against the Devil*. Glasgow: Blackie & Son, 1864; Reprint, Edinburgh: Banner of Truth, 1964.

> First published in three volumes between 1662 and 1665, this able and exhaustive exposition of spiritual warfare is a real treat for those who enjoy reading the Puritans. At 600 pages, it

is not a quick read, but it will reward those who wish to mine its riches. A major Puritan classic!

*Unger, Merrill F. *Biblical Demonology: A Study of the Spiritual Forces Behind the Present World Unrest.* Wheaton, IL: Scripture Press, 1952.

> An exceptional study of demonic forces in the Bible and how they are behind today's interest in the occult. Unger was a noted Old Testament scholar at Dallas Theological Seminary. This book is almost seventy years old, but just as timely as when it was published in 1952.

APOLOGETICS

Apologetics is a theological discipline that deals with the defense of the Christian faith. Because there are so many attacks against the Christian faith and the authority of Scripture today, it is important for every believer to be an apologist for the faith. The first Christian apologist was likely the Apostle Paul when he gave his sermon to the Athenians on Mars Hill in Acts 17. Apologetics has a wide variety of forms including historical and legal evidentialism, the defense of miracles, and creationist apologetics.

!*Collins, Francis S. *The Language of God: A Scientist Presents Evidence for Belief.* New York: Free Press, 2006.

> This provocative book was *Christianity Today* magazine's Book of the Year in the category of Apologetics and Evangelism in 2007. Collins is head of the Human Genome Project and a world-respected scientist. In this book, he answers the question of whether it is possible to achieve harmony between a scientific and a spiritual worldview. He traces his own spiritual pilgrimage from atheism to faith and then examines modern science to demonstrate how it fits together with belief in God and the Bible. A must read!

*Evans, C. Stephen. *Why Christian Faith Still Makes Sense: A Response to Contemporary Challenges*. Grand Rapids: Baker Academic, 2015.

> An intellectual, yet accessible, response to the challenges of modern skeptics who say that Christian faith is not reasonable. The author is a prominent Christian philosopher who serves as University Professor of Humanities at Baylor University.

*Geisler, Norman L., and Frank Turek. *I Don't Have Enough Faith to be an Atheist*. Wheaton, IL: Crossway, 2004.

> "This work is perhaps one of the best and most accessible apologetics books in print today. Geisler and Turek present the classical apologetic approach from the ground up. The classical approach to apologetics combines classical arguments for God's existence (the cosmological argument, the teleological argument, and the moral argument) with the evidential/historical approach. The book is arranged around twelve main apologetics points, which can be summarized into five basic questions: Does truth exist? Does God exist? Are miracles possible? Is the New Testament historically reliable? and, Did Jesus rise from the dead? The book is relentlessly methodical as it gives numerous examples from reason, science, and history to support its claims. Presents a comprehensive case for Christianity beginning with the existence of truth, and ending with the resurrection of Christ and the reliability of the Bible" **(Wright)**.

*Keller, Timothy. *Making Sense of God: An Invitation to the Skeptical*. Viking, 2016.

> In an age of skepticism, New York Presbyterian pastor Tim Keller is a sure guide through the maze of secular values (freedom, individuality, justice, community, rationality, personal meaning, human rights). He concludes that it is not only reasonable to believe in God, it is also reasonable to believe in Christianity. Winner of *Christianity Today's* 2017 Book Award in the Apologetics/Evangelism category.

*———. *The Reason for God: Belief in an Age of Skepticism*. New York: Penguin/Dutton, 2008.

> Winner of *Christianity Today's* 2009 Book Award for Apologetics/Evangelism.

+*Lewis, C. S. *Mere Christianity*. New York: Macmillan, 1944.

> This book is a classic defense of Christianity and Christian behavior by arguably the foremost apologist of the twentieth century. C. S. Lewis, who taught at both Oxford and Cambridge Universities, wrote for the educated layperson as well as seminary student. This brilliant work is highly recommended and not to be missed! Featured in Petersen and Petersen's *100 Christian Books That Changed the Century*.

+*Little, Paul F. *Know Why You Believe*. Fourth edition. Edited by Marie Little. Downers Grove: InterVarsity, 2000.

> Originally published in 1967, this book was designed specifically for college students. It is a readable and user-friendly guide that has helped thousands to make sense of their faith in Christ. Still packs a wallop! Featured in Petersen and Petersen's *100 Christian Books That Changed the Century*.

*McDowell, Josh, and Sean McDowell. *Evidence That Demands a Verdict: Life-Changing Truth for a Skeptical World*. Nashville: Thomas Nelson, 2017.

> This book is a completely revised and updated treatment of Christian evidences. The original 1972 volume by Josh McDowell was hugely influential in my life when I was a college student bordering on agnosticism. This complete reworking of that resource updates it for a new generation. Particularly helpful for high school and college students, but will be appreciated by all. The original 1972 book was featured in Petersen and Petersen's *100 Christian Books That Changed the Century*. This revision was the ECPA's 2019 Christian Book Award for Bible Reference Works.

McDowell, Josh, and Bill Wilson. *He Walked Among Us: Evidence for the Historical Jesus.* Nashville: Thomas Nelson, 1993.

> This book is a popular study of the historical evidence for the existence of Jesus. Written in an engaging, readable style, the authors examine the New Testament writings as well as those of the early Church leaders, martyrs, and ancient rabbis along with historical geography and archaeology to prove the historicity of Jesus of Nazareth. They evaluate the teachings of liberal scholarship such as higher criticism and find their arguments lacking.

+*Morison, Frank. *Who Moved the Stone?* London: Faber and Faber, 1958.

> First published in 1930, this book was written by the attorney Albert Henry Ross under a pseudonym to debunk the scriptural accounts of Jesus' resurrection as fantasy. After investigating the facts, Ross concluded that the Gospel accounts were credible and led to his conversion. The result: this book, which has been used as an apologetic for the Christian faith by college students and laypersons for generations. Featured in Petersen and Petersen's *100 Christian Books That Changed the Century.*

*Strobel, Lee. *The Case for Christ.* Grand Rapids: Zondervan, 1998.

> "Strobel, a reporter, has done a terrific job of laying out the case for why we believe Christ is the Son of God. His book has done for this generation what C. S. Lewis and Josh McDowell did for previous generations—set down a popular, timely argument for the deity of Christ and the veracity of Scripture" **(Fleming).**

*Wallace, J. Warner. *Cold Case Christianity.* Colorado Springs: David C. Cook, 2013.

> "This is an excellent book to give to skeptics and/or introduce laymen to Christian apologetics. J. Warner Wallace is a retired cold-case homicide detective from CA, who utilizes his forensic research skills (think CSI) to investigate the claims of the

resurrection of Christ as it is recorded in the New Testament. The book is very well organized, the arguments are easy to follow and it contains numerous, helpful illustrations and charts. Wallace follows and 'interrogates' all relevant leads and sources, leaving no stone unturned for clues, including the four Gospel writers, contemporary historical accounts, and the early Church fathers" **(Wright).**

*———. *God's Crime Scene*. Colorado Springs: David C. Cook, 2015.

"*God's Crime Scene* is Wallace's second book in which he utilizes his forensic research skills as a cold-case homicide detective. In Wallace's first book, *Cold Case Christianity,* he investigates the claims of the resurrection of Christ. In *God's Crime Scene* he investigates the universe (on the small and large scale) and the evidence *for* and *against* a Creator. In his research, Wallace utilizes his forensic research skills to uncover compelling scientific evidence. This book would be an excellent introduction to two of the most convincing arguments in contemporary Christian apologetics: the argument from design (the teleological argument), and the argument from the beginning of the universe (the cosmological argument)" **(Wright).**

*Witherington, Ben III. *What Have They Done With Jesus?: Beyond Strange Theories and Bad History—Why We Can Trust the Bible*. San Francisco: HarperCollins, 2006.

"An engaging and sometimes humorous response to claims by modern writers, widely reported in popular media, that Gnostic documents from the second century and later have undermined the historical reliability of the biblical gospels and given us a better picture of Jesus. Witherington, a professor of NT at Asbury Theological Seminary in Kentucky, examines the biblical accounts of eyewitnesses to Jesus' life, ministry, death, and resurrection—the women (Joanna, Mary Magdalene, and Mary the mother of Jesus), and the brothers of Jesus (James and Jude)—as well as Paul. He argues that their first-hand knowledge and experience is preserved in the gospels and Acts. This book complements the technical work of Richard Bauckham (*Jesus and the Eyewitnesses*) along the same lines, while being more suitable for preaching and study by lay readers" (**Brafford**). Note: Bill Brafford was Ben Witherington's college roommate at the University of NC at Chapel Hill.

ATONEMENT

The atonement is one of the central doctrines of the Christian faith. What Jesus accomplished on the cross is of no minor consequence. According to the *New Dictionary of Theology,* "The atonement is critical; it is the central doctrine of Christianity" (54). One of the great questions that arises out of this doctrine is what is the extent of the atonement? In other words, for whom did Christ die? In the history of the Christian church, there have been two answers. Christ died for everyone or he died for only the elect. Two of the following books attempt to give an answer from a Reformed perspective.

*Kuiper, R. B. *For Whom Did Christ Die? A Study of the Divine Design of the Atonement.* Grand Rapids: Baker, 1959.

> The author taught theology at Westminster Theological Seminary for twenty years and served as president for seven years at Calvin Theological Seminary. This brief study of 100 pages argues for the Calvinistic position of limited, or particular, atonement. Reformed.

!*Murray, John. *Redemption—Accomplished and Applied.* Grand Rapids: Eerdmans, 1955.

> A classic argument by the longtime professor of systematic theology at Westminster Theological Seminary for limited, or what the author calls definite, atonement. That is the substance of Part I of the book. Part II examines the *ordo salutis* (order of salvation). It includes effectual calling, regeneration, faith and repentance, justification, adoption, sanctification, perseverance, union with Christ, and glorification. This book was extremely helpful to me about forty years ago when I

was preparing for ordination in the Presbyterian Church in America. Not the easiest reading. Reformed.

!*Treat, Jeremy R. *The Crucified King: Atonement and Kingdom in Biblical and Systematic Theology.* Grand Rapids: Zondervan, 2014.

> This book expounds the doctrine of two of the seminal themes presented in Scripture and demonstrates the relationship between the two. Kingdom and atonement are often presented in the church as almost mutually exclusive constructs. This work beautifully interweaves the two.

BIBLICAL INTERPRETATION (HERMENEUTICS)

Hermeneutics is the technical name for the science of biblical interpretation. Traditionally, this has meant the study of rules and principles for interpreting biblical texts. Of course, the major component that must not be overlooked is the illuminating ministry of the Holy Spirit when we study God's Word. One can read all of the books available on how to study the Bible, but without the ministry of the Holy Spirit, the message of Scripture would be superficial at best.

*Fee, Gordon D., and Douglas Stuart. *How to Read the Bible for All Its Worth.* 4th ed. Grand Rapids: Zondervan, 2014.

> This book is an indispensable tool for Bible study useful to everyone from the layperson to the scholar. Of particular value in this new edition is the updated list of recommended commentaries. Highly recommended!

*McKnight, Scot. *The Blue Parakeet: Rethinking How You Read the Bible.* Grand Rapids: Zondervan, 2008.

> Beginning with the premise that the Bible is essentially story and that it is not just a book for theologians and scholars to debate *ad infinitum*, McKnight has written a creative and eminently readable book that makes hermeneutics understandable to the average person. A lot of fun to read! Now available in a second edition as of 2018.

*McQuilkin, Robertson. *Understanding and Applying the Bible*. Revised and expanded. Chicago: Moody, 2009.

> This book by the president emeritus of Columbia International University is an excellent resource suitable for a textbook on both the undergraduate and graduate levels. Readable and informative!

*Sproul, R. C. *Knowing Scripture*. Downers Grove: InterVarsity, 1977.

> A very helpful book that would benefit anyone approaching the study of the Bible for the first time as well as seasoned students. Sproul is a master of breaking down complex ideas and making them accessible to laypersons. This book works on a number of levels. Highly recommended!

*Stein, Robert H. *A Basic Guide to Interpreting the Bible: Playing by the Rules*. 2nd ed. Grand Rapids: Baker Academic, 2011.

> This book is one of those rare volumes that can serve as a textbook for both graduate and undergraduate students. It is accessible enough for lay audiences, too. Takes a difficult subject and simplifies it.

Virkler, Henry A. *Hermeneutics: Principles and Processes of Biblical Interpretation*. Grand Rapids: Baker, 1981.

> This volume is interesting and readable and suitable as an undergraduate textbook. Virkler advocates a five-step hermeneutical method suitable for all genres of biblical literature: historical-cultural analysis, lexical-syntactical analysis, theological analysis, genre identification and analysis, and application. Very user friendly.

Zuck, Roy B. *Basic Bible Interpretation: A Practical Guide to Discovering Biblical Truth*. Wheaton, IL: Victor, 1991.

> This volume is one of the many hermeneutics textbooks that have been published in recent decades. At the time of publication, Zuck, was the Vice President of Academic Affairs and

professor of Bible Exposition at Dallas Theological Seminary. He has written a book that is informative, easy-to-read, and very user-friendly. His chapters on bridging the cultural gap, the literary gap, and the grammatical gap are particularly helpful. He argues for a three-fold pattern of biblical hermeneutics that includes observation, interpretation, and application.

BIBLICAL THEOLOGY

The term "biblical theology" was first used in the mid-seventeenth century. "It was intended to refer to a theology based on the Bible, as distinct from a theology which consisted largely of philosophical ideas and religious traditions" (*New Dictionary of Theology*, 96). There is a section on Systematic Theology later in this chapter. Suffice to say that systematic theology and biblical theology are two different ways of arranging the teaching of the Bible. Systematic theology seeks to systematize the entire biblical teaching on certain doctrines, whereas biblical theology attempts to understand the progressive unfolding of God's revelation throughout history. I hesitated to include this section because there are no lightweight books that I know of on this subject. Much of the following is pretty heavy reading, but I include them for those who are interested in the topic.

!*Goldingay, John. *Old Testament Theology*. 3 vols. Downers Grove: IVP Academic, 2003, 2006, 2009.

> This magisterial and comprehensive resource is probably the most complete work available on the subject. It's three volumes were published three years apart. Volume 1 is titled *Israel's Gospel,* Volume 2 *Israel's Faith,* and Volume 3 *Israel's Life.* Each volume is at least 800 pages, so the reader can be assured this is not the equivalent of reading a *Reader's Digest* condensed version. But it can be a daunting task for the uncommitted. Volume 1 was the ECPA's 2004 Gold Medallion Book Award winner in the Theology/Doctrine category. Between these three volumes and the equally impressive one by Waltke, the Old Testament is well-covered.

!*Payne, J. Barton. *The Theology of the Older Testament*. Grand Rapids: Zondervan, 1962.

> An older work that is much more condensed than those of Waltke and Goldingay. This was my seminary textbook. "An impressive work" (Barber, 84).

*Robertson, O. Palmer. *The Christ of the Covenants*. Phillipsburg, NJ: Presbyterian and Reformed, 1980.

> This important study of the covenantal structure of Scripture, by a former professor of Old Testament at Westminster Theological Seminary and Covenant Theological Seminary, ably presents the Reformed understanding of covenant theology, but with an emphasis on the overarching theme of all the covenants, Jesus Christ. Very accessible! Reformed.

!*Schreiner, Thomas R. *New Testament Theology: Magnifying God in Christ*. Grand Rapids: Baker Academic, 2008.

> This excellent resource focuses on two overarching themes. First, the unity of redemptive history and the kingdom of God. Schreiner argues that the kingdom has come, but remains unfulfilled. Second, the goal of the kingdom through the work of Christ and the presence of the Holy Spirit. He applies these themes to the lives of believers and the ministry of the community of faith. Schreiner is a top-notch Baptist New Testament scholar who teaches at the Southern Baptist Theological Seminary in Louisville, KY.

!*Thielman, Frank. *Theology of the New Testament: A Canonical and Synthetic Approach*. Grand Rapids: Zondervan, 2005.

> A fine work that vies with Schreiner for pride of place among modern New Testament theologies. Between this book and that of Schreiner, the New Testament is well-covered. Reformed.

!*Waltke, Bruce K. *An Old Testament Theology: An Exegetical and Thematic Approach.* Grand Rapids: Zondervan, 2007.

At almost 1000 pages, this work vies with that of Goldingay for supremacy. A challenging read. Winner of the EPCA's 2008 Christian Book Award in the Bible Reference & Study category.

*Zuck, Roy B., ed. *A Biblical Theology of the New Testament.* Chicago: Moody, 1994.

*_____, ed. *A Biblical Theology of the Old Testament.* Chicago: Moody, 1991.

These two books were written by the faculty of the Dallas Theological Seminary. The esteemed scholars, Eugene H. Merrill (Old Testament) and Darrell Bock (New Testament), were the contributing editors and are tops in their respective fields. The goal of each volume is to examine "divine revelation as it appears chronologically in the canon, allowing you to witness God's truth unfold through the centuries" (from the back cover). Dispensational.

CALVINISM AND WESLEYAN THEOLOGY

John Calvin is generally regarded as the one who systematized the doctrines of the Reformation. He was both a scholar and a pastor. Although his doctrines have not always been popular and have oftentimes been misrepresented, his influence has been widespread. Presbyterian and Reformed churches look to Calvin as the founder of their biblical-theological doctrinal position. Wesleyan Theology, named after the father of Methodism, John Wesley, is also often referred to as Wesleyan-Arminian Theology or Methodist Theology. Wesleyan Theology, like Calvinism basically covenantal in its theology, was primarily a reaction to Calvinistic Theology and emphasized an Arminian perspective on soteriology (the doctrine of salvation) as opposed to the Calvinist emphasis on predestination.

*Battles, Ford Lewis. *Analysis of the Institutes of the Christian Religion of John Calvin.* Grand Rapids: Baker, 1980.

> A detailed outline of the text of the *Institutes* as Calvin wrote it. Each section of the book is concisely organized into its salient points. Much more detailed than Lane's brief guide.

!+*Calvin, John. *Institutes of the Christian Religion.* 2 vols. The Library of Christian Classics Volume XX. Edited by John T. McNeill. Translated by Ford Lewis Battles. Philadelphia: Westminster, 1960.

> This book is widely regarded as one of the masterworks of Protestant theology and hugely influential. It systematized the theology of the Reformation. First published in Latin in 1536 and in his native French in 1541, the *Institutes* was written as an introductory textbook on Protestantism (a sort of *Protestantism for Dummies*) and covered a broad range of theological topics. Today's readers will find it challenging, but rewarding for those who persevere. Warning: This is not a breezy summer beach read!

*Coppes, Leonard J. *Are Five Points Enough? Ten Points of Calvinism.* Manassas, VA: Reformation Educational Foundation, 1980.

> When people talk about the five points of Calvinism, they often use the TULIP acrostic: total depravity, unconditional election, limited atonement, irresistible grace, and perseverance of the saints. In this provocative book, the author attempts to demonstrate the breadth of Calvinism.

*Greathouse, William M., and H. Ray Dunning. *An Introduction to Wesleyan Theology.* Rev. ed. Kansas City: Beacon Hill Press, 1989.

> An overview of Wesleyan theology that includes the thoughts of other Wesleyan theologians such as Adam Clarke.

*Harper, Steve. *The Way to Heaven: The Gospel According to John Wesley.* 2nd ed. Grand Rapids: Zondervan, 2003.

> This book is a twentieth anniversary revision which attempts to capture the message of John Wesley for a twenty-first century audience. The language is clear and accessible.

*Hunt, Dave, and James White. *Debating Calvinism: Five Points, Two Views.* Sisters, OR: Multnomah, 2004.

> Calvinism has been a topic of intense debate ever since John Calvin wrote his *Institutes* almost 500 years ago. This volume explores the topic in a lively debate in book format with points, response, and final remarks on each subject by both debaters. Answers the most frequently asked questions about Calvinism. If you want to understand the reasons for and against the doctrine, this is the book for you.

*Lane, Anthony N. S. *A Reader's Guide to Calvin's Institutes.* Grand Rapids: Baker Academic, 2009.

> A condensed, streamlined introduction to the major tenets of Calvin's theology in less than 200 pages. A *Cliffs Notes* version of Calvin's *Institutes*. Lane is professor of historical theology at the London School of Theology and a top Calvin scholar.

*Tuttle, Robert G., Jr. *Sanctity without Starch: A Layperson's Guide to a Wesleyan Theology of Grace.* First Fruits Press, 2016.

> Focuses on Wesley's doctrine of grace.

*Walls, Jerry L., and Joseph R. Dongell. *Why I Am Not a Calvinist.* Downers Grove: IVP, 2004.

> A work of deep insight with an irenic spirit by two professors at Asbury Theological Seminary in Wilmore, KY.

CHRISTIAN DOCTRINE

Christian doctrine, or systematic theology as the scholars usually refer to it, often has a bad reputation in the church at large. In fact, decades ago, systematic theology was even called "dogmatics" or "dogmatic theology." That may make you smile as you remember someone who was very dogmatic in his theology. Systematic theology is often defined as simply "an attempt to reduce religious truth to an organized system" (*Evangelical Dictionary of Theology*, 1064). In fact, the words "theology" and "doctrine" do not occur anywhere in the Bible. Christian doctrine, or systematic theology, is simply a way that theologians use to order God's truth in a way that makes sense. Although many in the church tend to think that the words "doctrine" and "theology" are synonyms for boredom, Christians need to know what they believe and why they believe it. The following books will help you to understand the whys and wherefores of your beliefs.

*Boice, James Montgomery. *Foundations of the Christian Faith*. 4 vols. Downers Grove: IVP, 1978–81.

> A comprehensive and readable theology of the Christian faith ideal for laity by a Presbyterian pastor. Volume I is titled *The Sovereign God*, Volume II *God the Redeemer*, Volume III *Awakening to God*, and Volume IV *God & History*. A one-volume hardcover revised edition was published in 1986. Boice is always very readable and down-to-earth.

Chafer, Lewis Sperry. *Systematic Theology*. 8 vols. Dallas: Dallas Seminary Press, 1947.

> Quite dated now, this set has been for decades the standard systematic theology from a dispensational perspective. The author was the founder and first president of Dallas Theological Seminary and editor of *Bibliotheca Sacra* for over ten years. This set was my first systematic theology and my introduction to Christian doctrine as a first-year seminary student. I read all eight volumes cover to cover back in the 1970s and found Chafer's writings to be very readable and clear. "A comprehensive manual of Christian doctrine. Remarkable for its clarity, brevity, and accuracy" (Barber, 189).

*Kennedy, D. James. *Truths That Transform: Christian Doctrines for Your Life Today.* Old Tappan, NJ: Fleming H. Revell, 1974.

> A brief book that presents in capsule form and plain language sixteen fundamental doctrines of the Christian faith: the sovereignty of God, free will, predestination effectual calling, repentance, faith justification, sanctification, adoption, assurance, and good works among others. Kennedy is the author of *Evangelism Explosion* and was for many years the senior pastor of the Coral Ridge Presbyterian Church in Fort Lauderdale, FL until his death in 2007. Reformed.

!*Schaeffer, Francis A. *The Complete Works of Francis A. Schaeffer: A Christian Worldview.* 5 vols. Westchester: Crossway, 1982.

> This collection contains all of the twenty-one books written by Schaeffer between 1968 and 1981. Volume One is titled "A Christian View of Philosophy and Culture," Volume Two is "A Christian View of the Bible as Truth," Volume Three is "A Christian View of Spirituality," Volume Four is "A Christian View of the Church," and Volume Five is "A Christian View of the West." Schaeffer was one of the most influential evangelical voices of the twentieth century and deserves to be read today. Not to be missed! Reformed.

Shannon, Ellen C. *A Layman's Guide to Christian Terms.* New York: A. S. Barnes and Company, 1969.

> From "abba" to "Zwingli," this helpful volume is a practical guide to hundreds of theological terms, names, and places. Although now more than fifty years old, it is a handy book to have on your shelf. I wish somebody would update it.

*Swindoll, Charles R. *Growing Deep in the Christian Life.* Portland, OR: Multnomah, 1986.

> This book, by a well-known Evangelical Free Church pastor who was for many years serving in Fullerton, CA, is as close to an *Idiots Guide to Christian Doctrine* as I have ever seen. Swindoll has the rare gift of taking complex Christian truth,

breaking it down, and making it come alive. This excellent book explains Christian doctrines under ten major categories: the Bible, God the Father, the Lord Jesus Christ, the Holy Spirit, the depravity of humanity, salvation, the return of Christ, resurrection, the body of Christ, and the family of God. While I do not agree with all of Swindoll's conclusions, I heartily recommend this volume to you.

!*Thiselton, Anthony C. *Systematic Theology.* Grand Rapids: Eerdmans, 2015.

This important new work, by a professor emeritus of Christian theology at the University of Nottingham, England, is an accessible and readable introduction to Christian theology that is designed for students and pastors, rather than professional theologians, but is accessible to motivated laypersons. Thistelton does not approach theology as an abstract system as so many theologians do, but rather sees theology as a living, organic whole. This book, as well as the author's *The Thistelton Companion to Christian Theology,* constitutes the capstone of a more than half century of teaching and research. Both books are affordable and highly recommended.

* ———. *The Thiselton Companion to Christian Theology.* Grand Rapids: Eerdmans, 2015.

See my review of the author's *Systematic Theology* above. This book, building upon and drawing from the author's earlier work *Concise Encyclopedia of the Philosophy of Religion,* is an encyclopedia of Christian theology including just over 600 articles ranging from A—Z, from *Abba* to *Zwingli.* Unlike most encyclopedias, this volume was written by one author, rather than having multiple contributors. The articles are well-written and interesting.

*Treier, Daniel J., and Walter A. Elwell, Eds. *Evangelical Dictionary of Theology*. 3rd ed. Grand Rapids: Baker, 2017.

> First published in 1984, this latest edition is a valuable resource that provides articles on topics ranging from A-Z, from "Abaddon" to Zwingli.

CHURCH HISTORY

There is an oft-repeated saying about history attributed to the American philosopher George Santayana that "he who forgets history is doomed to repeat it." The late American church historian, Bruce Shelley, once wrote, "Many Christians today suffer from historical amnesia. The time between the apostles and their own day is one giant blank" (*Church History in Plain Language*, 9). The Old Testament is replete with timely reminders for the Israelites to remember their own past. As a consequence of their own failure to do just that, the Israelites again and again fell into the sin of idolatry and failure to obey the Law of God. The same is true of Christians today. If we forget our own history, not just that of the Israelites in the Old Testament, but that of the Church since the time of the apostles, we become vulnerable to false religions and cults. The following books will help you keep today's Christian Church in perspective and to remember what came before us.

*Douglas, J. D. *The New International Dictionary of the Christian Church*. Revised edition. Grand Rapids: Zondervan, 1978.

> At well over 1000 pages, this massive work contains 4800 articles written by 180 Protestant scholars. It truly is a magnificent achievement and full of useful information. However, at forty years of age, it needs to be updated.

Early, Joseph Jr. *A History of Christianity: An Introductory Survey*. Nashville: B & H Academic, 2015.

> An easy-to-read survey that focuses on the key events, people, theological developments, and conflicts of Christianity's 2000-year history. Excellent for laypersons and undergraduate students.

+*Forbush, William Byron, ed. *Fox's Book of Martyrs: A History of the Lives, Sufferings, and Triumphant Deaths of the Early Christian and the Protestant Martyrs.* New York: Holt, Rinehart and Winston, 1926; Reprint, Grand Rapids: Zondervan, 1964.

> Popularly known as *Foxe's Book of Martyrs* by the Protestant English historian John Foxe, this book was first published under the title *Acts and Monuments* in 1563. It is an account of the early Christian martyrs including an account of the persecutions of the Roman Catholic Church against Protestants. It has been profoundly influential!

*Hannah, John D. *Invitation to Church History.* Invitation to Theological Studies. 2 vols. Grand Rapids: Kregel, 2019.

> This inviting two-volume set "walks readers through the story of God's people from Christ to the contemporary church around the world." The first volume subtitled *American* covers American church history beginning with the Pilgrims and ending with the contemporary American church scene. The second volume subtitled *World* does the same thing but with a global perspective beginning with Jesus Christ. Beautifully photographed with numerous diagrams that are very helpful in clarifying complex information.

*Hill, Jonathan. *Zondervan Handbook to the History of Christianity.* Oxford: Lion Hudson, 2007.

> This volume is an excellent "bird's eye" look at Christian history. At 560 pages, it is highly selective offering forty-two feature articles.

*Shelley, Bruce L. *Church History in Plain Language.* Waco: Word, 1982.

> This book is the author's attempt to simplify the story of Church history. He divides Church history into eight ages. If there is a weakness, it is that he devotes more than half the book to the period ranging from the Reformation until 1980. Engagingly written and fun to read! Written for laymen.

Vos, Howard F. *An Introduction to Church History.* Revised edition. Chicago: Moody, 1984.

> An easy-to-read introduction particularly helpful for college students and laypersons.

CULTS AND RELIGIONS

We live in an age in which terms such as "diversity," "inclusion," and "multiculturalism" have become household words and ideals towards which we should aspire according to some in our culture. But no matter what the current buzzwords are from decade to decade, the result is the same: The teaching that all religions are equally valid and that truth is a subjective concept. Some even claim that all religions are basically the same and that they all bring us to the same destination in the end. Christians serve the Christ who claimed to be "the way, the truth, and the life." If this is true, then the prophets of our culture are in error and not to be believed. How are Christ followers today to arm themselves so that they do not fall prey to the multitudinous cults and religions clamoring for their attention? The following books should prove to be quite useful in unmasking the many false religions that are encountered in our changing world. Please remember that God does not change.

*Bloesch, Donald G. *Faith & Its Counterfeits.* Downers Grove: IVP, 1981.

> Although false religions are an obvious threat to the Christian faith, this helpful book deals with some of the counterfeits hiding within the confines of the church itself. It examines six of them: Legalism, Formalism, Humanitarianism, Enthusiasm, Eclecticism, and Heroism. Some of us may feel a bit uncomfortable as we look into the mirror that Bloesch provides.

*Boettner, Loraine. *Roman Catholicism.* Philadelphia: Presbyterian and Reformed, 1962.

> This book was published in 1962, the same year that Pope John XXIII opened the Second Vatican Council. Although much has changed in the Roman Catholic Church since in the intervening years, much has not. This perceptive evaluation of

Roman Catholic doctrine is as valuable today as it was upon publication almost sixty years ago. If you want to know which issues still separate Protestants from Roman Catholics, this book is a must-read!

*Carey, George. *A Tale of Two Churches: Can Protestants & Catholics Get Together?* Downers Grove: IVP, 1965.

This book by the former Archbishop of Canterbury examines the issues that have divided Protestants from Roman Catholics over the past 500 years and attempts to answer several questions. What issues still separate us? What can we learn from one another? Can this breach be healed? My opinion is that I am not optimistic. J. I. Packer wrote the Foreward. Irenic in tone, but uncompromising.

+*Martin, Walter R. *The Kingdom of the Cults.* Grand Rapids: Zondervan, 1965.

A groundbreaking work that upon its publication in 1965 superseded all works of its kind on the subject. Its most lengthy chapter is on Seventh-day Adventism, which he concluded was not a cult after all. The most significant work of the twentieth century on the subject. Featured in Petersen and Petersen's *100 Christian Books That Changed the Century.*

*Nichols, Larry A., George A. Mather, and Alvin J. Schmidt, eds. *Encyclopedic Dictionary of Cults, Sects, and World Religions.* Revised and updated edition. Grand Rapids: Zondervan, 2006.

A most comprehensive and significant reference tool. Includes updated information on Islam and its global impact.

*Rhodes, Ron. *The Challenge of the Cults and New Religions.* Grand Rapids: Zondervan, 2001.

A significant resource that is more timely than the work by Martin. Has a foreword by Lee Strobel.

*Ridenour, Fritz, ed. *So, What's the Difference: A Biblical Comparison of Orthodox Christianity with Major Religions and Major Cults*. Glendale, CA: Regal, 1967.

> I included this book which I read over fifty years ago in my high school Sunday School class on cults and religions. It was eye-opening and very informative. It was also easy-to-read and user friendly. I recommend it to both high schoolers and adults looking for a simple guide to certain religions and cults. Its focus is a bit narrow and many religions are not covered, but those the book does cover, it does well. Section I examines Roman Catholicism and Section II the major religions of the world: Judaism, Islam, Hinduism, and Buddhism. Section III covers major cults such as Unitarianism, Jehovah's Witnesses, Christian Science, and Mormonism.

ETHICS

Ethics describes "the inquiry into man's moral nature so as to discover what are his responsibilities and the means by which he may fulfill them. Ethics shares with certain other human enterprises the quest for truth, but is distinct in its concern for what man ought to do in the light of the truth uncovered. It is not simply descriptive, but prescriptive in character" (*Evangelical Dictionary of Theology*, 375). Ethics has to do with what we should do in different situations and how we should behave. Intimately intertwined with ethics is character. Someone has defined character as how we behave when nobody is watching.

*Davis, John Jefferson. *Evangelical Ethics: Issues Facing the Church Today*. 3rd ed. Phillipsburg, NJ: Presbyterian and Reformed, 2004.

> Since its initial publication in 1985, this helpful book has served the evangelical world as a good basic textbook in Christian ethics. It included chapters on contraception, reproductive technologies, divorce and remarriage, homosexuality, abortion, infanticide and euthanasia, capital punishment, civil disobedience and revolution, and war and peace. For the most part, those topics remain important ones for conversation

today. However, with medical research and technology advancing at a rapid pace, this book was in great need of an infusion particularly in the area of bio-technology. This third edition does just that by including chapters on genetic engineering and environmental ethics, two areas of concern crying out for evangelical reflection.

*Harrison, R. K. *Encyclopedia of Biblical and Christian Ethics.* Nashville: Thomas Nelson, 1987.

This book is a must for Christians who are concerned with ethical issues. It is not only descriptive, but also prescriptive, in that it provides guidelines for behavior. There are two helpful indexes at the back of the book that give this volume added value as a reference tool. A Personalities Index helps readers locate all articles that mention specific persons or ethical thinkers, such as Thomas Aquinas or Aristotle. There is also a Scripture Index that should provide assistance to preachers and teachers. The list of contributors is impressive.

*Sproul, R. C. *Ethics and the Christian: Right and Wrong in Today's World.* Wheaton, IL: Tyndale House, 1983.

This handy little volume is a brief overview of Christian ethics written primarily for the layperson. Sproul, as always, is engaging and informative.

GENDER AND SEXUALITY

Over the past fifty plus years since the social ferment of the 1960s, the church has been bombarded by matters of sexuality and gender. At the forefront of the debates have been the issues of women's ordination, homosexuality, and gender identity. The following books will help Christians understand the biblical positions and illuminate their own understanding.

*Beilby, James K., and Paul Rhodes Eddy, eds. *Understanding Transgender Identities: Four Views*. Grand Rapids: Baker Academic, 2019.

> In recent years, much of the attention given to the sexuality debate has shifted to transgender experience. This enlightening book presents four essays by different scholars as well as rejoinders by each on a subject that is quite confusing to many Christians. My careful reading of the book led me to conclude that the subject is much more nuanced than first assumed. A must read if you want to understand transgender experiences and identities.

*Grudem, Wayne. *Evangelical Feminism & Biblical Truth*. Sisters, OR: Multnomah, 2004.

> This book at almost 800 pages of text is the most comprehensive examination available for discovering a biblical view of manhood and womanhood in the church and the Christian family. It analyzes more than 100 disputed questions. Takes a complementarian view in that the author believes that men and women are "equal in value and personhood, but different in roles in marriage and the church" (Preface, 17).

*Hassey, Janette. *No Time for Silence*. Grand Rapids: Academie Books, 1986.

> A careful and well-documented examination of the advocacy of women's ministries by evangelicals between 1880 and 1930. This book attempts to answer why so many evangelical groups who used women as pastors and teachers during that period now prohibit or discourage such ministry.

!*Köstenberger, Andreas J., and Thomas R. Schreiner, eds. *Women in the Church: An Analysis and Application of 1 Timothy 2:9–15*. Second edition. Grand Rapids: Baker Academic, 2005.

> A collection of six integrated essays addressing the important issue of the ministry of women in the Christian church. The seminal text for limiting the woman's role in church ministry, 1 Timothy 2:9–15, is examined in depth. The editors are

highly respected Baptist New Testament professors who each contribute an essay. Challenging!

*Piper, John, and Wayne Grudem. *50 Crucial Questions: An Overview of Central Concerns about Manhood and Womanhood*. Wheaton, IL: Crossway, 2016.

> The authors respond to fifty questions that are often asked in relation to biblical manhood and womanhood. Takes a complementarian view.

Ryrie, Charles Caldwell. *The Role of Women in the Church*. Chicago: Moody, 1970.

> Originally published in 1958 as *The Place of Women in the Church*, this book is a biblical and historical study of the position of women in the church by the former professor of systematic theology and dean of doctoral studies for many years at Dallas Theological Seminary. Ryrie represents the traditional view of much of the church up until about 1960. "One of the most definitive and reliable treatments available" (Barber, 317).

*Sprinkle, Preston, *People to Be Loved: Why Homosexuality Is Not Just an Issue*. Grand Rapids: Zondervan Academic, 2015.

> Christians who are confused by the debate over homosexuality will find this book to be enlightening as well as challenging. The author urges readers to consider what the Bible says about homosexuality and how we should approach it in the church in light of scriptural teaching. In plain language Sprinkle examines some of the difficult questions that often arise from the current debate. How should the church deal with people struggling with homosexuality? Is homosexuality a product of biological or societal factors, or both? How should Christians deal with some of the larger cultural issues such as homosexual marriage, "gay" pride, and intolerance towards LGBT? Where does Christian love and grace enter into the picture?

*_____, ed. *Two Views on Homosexuality, the Bible, and the Church*. Grand Rapids: Zondervan Academic, 2016.

> This book examines two views on homosexuality: the traditional view and the affirming view. There are four essays presented by four different scholars with robust interaction and debate. This book is a constructive dialogue between writers who disagree substantially on major ethical and theological issues, yet who maintain an irenic spirit throughout. If you want to understand what the major points of contention are in the homosexuality debate, this is the book for you.

*Tucker, Ruth A., and Walter Liefeld. *Daughters of the Church: Woman and Ministry from New Testament Times to the Present*. Grand Rapids: Academie Books, 1987.

> This book attempts to restore a balance to the history that has tended to downplay the contributions of women in the church.

*Westfall, Cynthia Long. *Paul and Gender: Reclaiming the Apostle's Vision for Men and Women in Christ*. Grand Rapids: Baker Academic, 2016.

> Winner of *Christianity Today*'s 2018 Award of Merit in the Biblical Studies category.

THE GODHEAD (TRINITY)

The term "Trinity" is not found in Scripture and thus is not a biblical term. However, it has been for centuries a convenient designation for the concept of one God in three persons, which is certainly a biblical description of the nature of God.

!+*Augustine, *The Trinity*. Works of Saint Augustine: A Translation for the 21st Century. Second edition. New City Press, 2012.

> Probably the most influential (and most misunderstood) work on the Trinity, this book is not an easy read, but the rendering into 21st century English is most helpful. A combination of

philosophical and theological concepts written with a pastor's heart for his people.

+*Bickersteth, Edward Henry. *The Trinity*. Reprint, Grand Rapids: Kregel, 1976.

This important study was originally published as *The Rock of Ages; or, Three Persons but One God* in 1859. It clarifies the true nature of the Trinity and clears up misconceptions.

*Erickson, Millard J. *Making Sense of the Trinity*. Grand Rapids: Baker, 2000.

This book attempts to establish the biblical foundation of the doctrine of the Trinity. It also tries to demonstrate the logical nature of the doctrine and its importance.

!+*Owen, John. *Communion with the Triune God*. Reprint, Crossway: Wheaton, IL, 2007.

A Puritan classic, this book draws upon Paul's benediction in 2 Cor. 13:14 in which Owen calls upon believers to rest in the love of the Father through the grace of the Son in the fellowship of the Holy Spirit. He argues that since God has revealed himself as three persons in eternal communion with one another, this understanding should have a profound impact on the believer's fellowship with God. Not an easy read.

Pink, Arthur W. *Gleanings in the Godhead*. Chicago: Moody, 1975.

This book focuses on God the Father and God the Son. As always, Pink's insights are warm and edifying. Particularly helpful for laypersons.

*Reeves, Michael. *Delighting in the Trinity: An Introduction to Christian Faith*. Downers Grove: IVP Academic, 2012.

A lively, pleasurable, and easy-to-read book that examines the role of the Trinity in the life of the Christian with clarity and wit. It is orthodox, rooted in sound scholarship, but not overwhelming and it even has pictures. Highly recommended!

*Ware, Bruce A. *Father, Son, & Holy Spirit: Relationships, Roles, & Relevance*. Wheaton: Crossway, 2005.

> This study is a very readable and user-friendly guide to the Trinity and the roles and relationships within it. Ideal for laypersons and undergraduates.

THE GODHEAD: GOD THE FATHER

!+*Charnock, Stephen. *The Existence and Attributes of God*. Reprint, Minneapolis: Klock & Klock, 1977.

> Originally published in 1797, this Puritan gem at just over 800 pages is the definitive exposition on the subject. Although the Puritans are often known as much for being longwinded as for their piety, this weighty work should be read and meditated upon. Very scholarly treatment.

+*Packer, J. I. *Knowing God*. London: Hodder and Stoughton, 1973.

> A true modern classic in every sense of the word, this book needs to be read and reread even now almost a half century after its initial publication. In his Foreword, Packer states his rationale for the book, "The conviction behind the book is that ignorance of God—ignorance both of his ways and of the practice of communion with him—lies at the root of much of the church's weakness today." His remedy to this sad state of affairs is found wonderfully laid out in three sections. First, he elucidates the blessings and benefits of knowing God. Second, he reveals just who God is. Finally, he unpacks the impact these truths should have on us. A must read! Featured in Petersen and Petersen's *100 Christian Books That Changed the Century*.

Pink, Arthur W. *The Attributes of God*. Reprint, Grand Rapids: Baker, 1975.

> A brief book that examines in seventeen short chapters seventeen attributes of God.

*Sproul, R. C. *The Holiness of God*. Revised and expanded. Orlando: Ligonier Ministries, 2010.

> Perhaps the most important attribute of God is his holiness. Certainly, it is central to his character. In this book, a master teacher paints an awe-inspiring picture of a holy God and how believers need to be holy as he is holy. Reformed.

*Tozer, A. W. *The Knowledge of the Holy: The Attributes of God*. New York: Harper, 1961.

> Tozer's writings are like an arrow shot into the heart of man. This book is no exception. "The finest modern devotional treatment of the attributes of God" (Wiersbe, 164).

THE GODHEAD: GOD THE SON

The technical term for the study of the person and nature of Jesus Christ is Christology. It also often includes the work of Christ, which many theologians classify under the doctrines of salvation (soteriology). However, for the purposes of this book, I am including works on his life here on earth and related topics. Following are some of my favorite volumes from my personal library.

!+*Andrews, Samuel J. *Life of Our Lord upon the Earth*. New York: Scribner, 1906; Reprint, Minneapolis: James Family, 1978.

> Originally published in 1862, this book is a massive, scholarly study of the life of the Lord Jesus Christ that has stood the test of time and is a true classic. An absolute jewel!

!*Berkouwer, G. C. *The Person of Christ*. Translated by John Vriend. Grand Rapids: Eerdmans, 1954.

> I am including these two books by Berkouwer for those with a scholarly bent, but these works are not for the faint of heart. This study is a classic work by the late professor of systematic theology at the Free University of Amsterdam, written "by a theologian's theologian" (Barber, 205). Examines the

ecumenical councils and confessions as well as the nature, unity, and sinlessness of Christ. Reformed.

!*———. *The Work of Christ.* Translated by Cornelius Lambregtse. Grand Rapids: Eerdmans, 1965.

This study followed the author's book on the person of Christ. He examines in detail Christ's birth, suffering, resurrection, ascension, and second advent among other topics. Reformed.

*Erickson, Millard J. *The Word Became Flesh—A Contemporary Incarnational Christology.* Grand Rapids: Baker, 1991.

An interesting study of the person of Jesus Christ that is stimulating enough for scholars, yet accessible for laity. Winner of The ECPA's 1992 Gold Medallion Book Award for Theology/Doctrine.

+*Farrar, Frederic W. *The Life of Christ.* New York: E. P. Dutton, n.d.; Reprint, Minneapolis: Klock & Klock, 1982.

A brilliant and heart-warming treatment of the life of Jesus by the former minister of London's famous Westminster Abbey and later Dean of Canterbury. A true classic!

!*Foster, Rupert Clinton. *Studies in the Life of Christ.* Reprint, Grand Rapids: Baker, 1971.

This massive study was originally published in four volumes over a roughly thirty-year period ending in 1968. It covers the entire period of the life of Christ. The book is well-written and a particular delight to read. "A scholarly study that rivals Edersheim for thoroughness and informative background" (Barber, 209).

+*Machen, John Gresham. *The Virgin Birth of Christ.* Reprint, Grand Rapids: Baker, 1967.

First published in 1930, this volume is a classic defense of the supernatural birth of Jesus Christ. Machen was a brilliant New

Testament scholar and theologian, and this book is one of his seminal works.

+*Morgan, G. Campbell. *The Crises of the Christ*. Old Tappan, NJ: Fleming H. Revell, 1936.

A classic study of the birth, baptism, temptation, transfiguration, crucifixion, resurrection, and ascension of Jesus Christ. "Should be read at frequent intervals" (Barber, 212).

!+*Owen, John. *The Glory of Christ*. Reprint, Chicago: Moody, 1949.

I would be remiss if I did not include at least one Puritan work in this section. Owen was perhaps the greatest of the Puritans and this work was his last. "No one can read this treatise and remain unmoved" (Barber, 205).

+*Stalker, James. *The Life of Jesus Christ*. Reprint, Grand Rapids: Zondervan, 1983.

Stalker, who lived from 1848–1927, was for many years a pastor in the Free Church in Scotland. This classic biography, first published in 1880, is one that has stood the test of time. Heartwarming and doctrinally sound.

+*———. *The Trial and Death of Jesus Christ*. Reprint, Grand Rapids: Academie Books, 1983.

Of utmost value are his treatment of the seven words from the cross. "An exceptional work" (Barber, 214).

*Stott, John R. W. *Christ the Controversialist*. Downers Grove: IVP, 1970.

Wherever Jesus walked upon this earth, he was a controversial figure confronting the Jewish religious establishment of his day by mingling with prostitutes and other social outcasts and showing insensitivity to the religious traditions of the Pharisees and Sadducees. This book examines the implications of his discussions with the people he encountered and how they touched on questions of morality, worship, authority, and social responsibility. "Brilliant, informative" (Barber, 260).

Walvoord, John F. *Jesus Christ Our Lord*. Chicago: Moody, 1969.

> This study is now fairly dated, but still a good introduction to the subject of Christology for undergraduates and laity. "Scholarly, evangelical presentation of Christology. A valuable work" (Barber, 206).

+*Whyte, Alexander. *The Walk, Conversation, and Character of Jesus Christ Our Lord*. Edinburgh: 1905, Reprint, Grand Rapids: Baker, 1975.

> A classic study by one of the giants of the Scottish pulpit. Not to be missed!

THE GODHEAD: GOD THE HOLY SPIRIT

The technical term often used by theologians for the doctrines of the Holy Spirit is pneumatology (*pneuma*=spirit).

Evans, Tony. *The Promise: Experiencing God's Greatest Gift the Holy Spirit*. Chicago: Moody, 1996.

> The author addresses biblically and practically some of the issues surrounding the doctrine of the Holy Spirit. Evans contends that it is impossible to live the Christian life unless one is "plugged in" to the Holy Spirit.

!*Ferguson, Sinclair B. *The Holy Spirit*. Contours of Christian Theology. Downers Grove: IVP, 1997.

> This excellent work, by a noted Presbyterian pastor and theologian, is a capable exposition of the Reformed understanding of the person and work of the Holy Spirit. It is well-written and readable on several levels, scholar, pastor, or layperson. A very necessary corrective to some contemporary muddled thinking on the doctrine of the Holy Spirit. Reformed.

*Graham, Billy. *The Holy Spirit*. Waco: Warner Books, 1978.

> A popular exposition of the ministry of the Holy Spirit in the life of the believer. Reissued in 2000 by Thomas Nelson.

*Lloyd-Jones, Martyn. Edited by Christopher Catherwood. *Joy Unspeakable: Power and Renewal in the Holy Spirit*. Wheaton: Howard Shaw, 1984.

> Published posthumously, this book of sermons, by the gifted preacher and evangelical leader who served as the pastor of Westminster Chapel in London for twenty-five years, sounds a clarion call to the church that it is definitely in need of revival by the renewing power of the Holy Spirit. He challenges Christians to examine the teaching of the Scriptures concerning the baptism of the Holy Spirit. Lloyd-Jones is always worth hearing and heeding.

!+*Owen, John. *The Holy Spirit: His Gifts and Power*. Reprint, Grand Rapids: Kregel, 1960.

> A marvelous study by the greatest of the Puritan writers. "One of the outstanding books of all time" (Barber, 202).

Ryrie, Charles Caldwell. *The Holy Spirit*. Chicago: Moody, 1965.

> This brief study is a concise summarization of the major ministries of the Holy Spirit. "A brilliantly written, brief, complete study of pneumatology. Ideal for Bible study" Barber, 202). Dispensational.

!+*Smeaton, George. The Doctrine of the Holy Spirit. Reprint, Edinburgh: Banner of Truth, 1958.

> This volume is reprinted from the 1882 edition. It is a classic study of the doctrine of the Holy Spirit along with a historical survey of that doctrine of the Holy Spirit from the apostolic age. Reformed.

+*Spurgeon, Charles H. *12 Sermons on the Holy Spirit.* Charles H. Spurgeon Library. Reprint, Grand Rapids: Baker, 1973.

> A masterpiece from the great nineteenth century British preacher on the person and work of the Holy Spirit. You will never go wrong reading Spurgeon.

*Walvoord, John F. *The Holy Spirit.* 3rd ed. Findlay, OH: Dunham Publishing, 1965.

> This book, taken from the author's classroom notes at Dallas Theological Seminary, is a comprehensive examination of the doctrine. One of the first theology books I ever read. Dispensational.

GRACE

Grace is a word that has numerous meanings and connotations. However, when we talk about grace in the biblical sense, it has the meaning of "undeserved blessing freely bestowed on man by God" (*Evangelical Dictionary of Theology*, 479). I have always found it helpful when meditating on the word or in teaching its meaning to use the acrostic, GRACE, God's riches at Christ's expense. Hence, its meaning is central to Christian theology and experience. In other words, salvation is not something that can be earned or deserved by us.

Chafer, Lewis Sperry. *Grace.* Philadelphia: The Sunday School Times Company, 1922.

> Examines the distinctions between law and grace, and argues that salvation has always been by grace.

*Ferguson, Sinclair B. *By Grace Alone: How the Grace of God Amazes Me.* Orlando: Reformation Trust, 2010.

> "A Scottish theologian, Dr. Ferguson is a preacher, teacher, author, speaker, and seminary professor. He has pastored churches in both Scotland and the U.S. including the historic First Presbyterian Church in Columbia, SC (ARP). The

inspiration for this book is a beautiful hymn written by African pastor Emmanuel T. Sibomana (1915–75), and translated into English by Rosemary Guillebaud, a missionary in Rwanda. Published in 1946, the hymn, *How the Grace of God Amazes Me,* has seven stanzas, which Ferguson uses as the format for the seven chapters in his book. Concerned that Christians frequently take the grace of God for granted, Ferguson describes *By Grace Alone* as a series of helpful meditations on the wonders of God's grace in Christ. The chapters, titled My Chains Fell Off, Unconditional Love, At God's Expense, A Great Exchange, Guaranteed Security, Delivered from Evil, and True Freedom, all go to the very heart of the gospel. Ferguson's pastoral ability to present profound truth in a clear and concise way makes this a 123 page companion book to his 2007 *In Christ Alone: Living the Gospel Centered Life,* one that brings a sense of joy, freedom, and amazement at the glory and wonder of God's grace" (**VanHook**). Note: Linda VanHook was a student of Dr. Furguson at Reformed Theological Seminary in Orlando.

*Lucado, Max. *Grace: More Than We Deserve, Greater Than We Imagine.* Nashville: Thomas Nelson, 2012.

> The author, a best-selling writer and pastor, explores what it means to be changed by grace. Winner of the ECPA's 2013 Christian Book Award for Nonfiction.

*Sproul, R. C. *Grace Unknown: The Heart of Reformed Theology.* Grand Rapids: Baker, 1997.

> A primer on the tenets of Reformed theology.

*Strobel, Lee. *The Case for Grace: A Journalist Explores the Evidence of Transformed Lives.* Grand Rapids: Zondervan, 2016.

> The author traces his own journey from atheism to faith in Jesus Christ. In this book, the reader will meet numerous vile sinners such as racists, addicts, and murderers, who have experienced the grace of God and have evidenced changed

lives. Winner of the ECPA's 2018 Christian Book Award in the Nonfiction category.

*Yancey, Philip. *What's So Amazing About Grace?* Grand Rapids: Zondervan, 1997.

> Explores the concept of grace as it works itself out in action. How are believers exhibiting grace in the midst of an unbelieving world? Winner of the ECPA's 1998 Jordon Christian Book of the Year.

JUSTIFICATION

Justification is a theological term that signifies the believer's status in the sight of God. It is central to our understanding of salvation. In simple terms, justification is a judicial rendering indicating that God sees the believer, even as he continues to sin on a daily basis, as innocent in the court of Heaven. A helpful and easy way to look at it is to see justification as "just as if I had never sinned."

!*Berkouwer, G. C. *Faith and Justification.* Studies in Dogmatics. Translated by Lewis B. Smedes. Grand Rapids: Eerdmans, 1954.

> This excellent treatment of faith and justification consists of seven sections: (1) Relevance, (2) The Way of Salvation, (3) Confessional Reconnaissance, (4) The Reformation and the Holy Scriptures, (5) Some Objections Considered, (6) Justification from Eternity, and (7) The Value of Faith. A wonderful examination of justification and its historical development in the church.

*Sproul, R. C. *Faith Alone: The Evangelical Doctrine of Justification.* Grand Rapids: Baker, 1995.

> A readable and relevant treatment of the cornerstone truth of the Protestant Reformation, this book reminds readers what the real issue was that prompted the actions of Martin Luther. With the recent trend for Protestants and Roman Catholics to seemingly be moving towards one another in doctrine and

practice, Sproul convincingly demonstrates that the faith/works dilemma is a false one and that true saving faith produces good works, not the other way around. A clear presentation of an important doctrine! Anyone seeking to understand the main issue leading to the Reformation will find a reliable guide in this treatment. Winner of the ECPA's 1996 Gold Medallion Book Award for Theology/Doctrine.

!*Wright, N. T. *Justification: God's Plan & Paul's Vision*. Downers Grove: IVP Academic, 2009.

You may have heard about the "New Perspective on Paul" and wondered what the issues are. One prominent advocate of this new perspective is N. T. Wright, an Anglican New Testament scholar who is currently a senior research fellow at Oxford University. Although an evangelical, Wright has been a controversial figure in this debate. This book is his response to critics who think he has misunderstood Paul's doctrine of justification. If you have questions about the current debate, this is the book for you.

PROPHECY AND THE END TIMES (ESCHATOLOGY)

The word "eschatology" comes from the Greek word *eschatos* (last) and generally refers to the doctrine of the last things. Broadly speaking, the term can include a variety of topics such as death, judgment, resurrection, and the afterlife. Usually, however, it refers to the last days or end times and includes such topics as the second coming of Christ, the tribulation period, and the millennium. There is an old joke among evangelicals that the millennium is 1000 years of peace over which Christians fight.

Some evangelicals obtain their understanding of eschatology from reading books such as the enormously popular sixteen-volume *Left Behind* series or Hal Lindsey's *The Late Great Planet Earth* without giving the matter much deep thought or theological scrutiny. However misguided, the prospect of imminent apocalypse is tremendously exciting and more marketable in book-selling terms than what Scripture actually teaches. With this in mind, those who want to do a bit of intellectual investigation will find the following books to be food for the mind.

!*Archer, Jr., G., P. D. Feinberg, D. J. Moo, and R. R. Reiter. *The Rapture: Pre-, Mid-, or Post-Tribulational? Contemporary Evangelical Perspectives*. Grand Rapids: Zondervan Academie Books, 1984.

> This book examines the question of the timing of the Rapture from three premillennial positions by three evangelical scholars. Feinberg argues for the pretribulational rapture, Archer for the midtribulational position, and Moo for the posttribulational one. Each writer presents his case, which in turn is followed by critical responses by the other two. The quasi-dialogue format allows the reader to understand the distinctive characteristics of each position as well as their strengths and weaknesses.

!*Berkouwer, G. C. *The Return of Christ*. Studies in Dogmatics. Translated by James Van Oosterom. Edited by Marlin J. Van Elderen. Grand Rapids: Eerdmans, 1972.

> A scholarly treatment of the second advent of Christ. Amillennial.

!*Blaising, Craig A., Douglas J. Moo, and Alan Hultberg. *Three Views on The Rapture: Pretribulation, Prewrath, or Posttribulation*. Counterpoints. Second edition. Grand Rapids: Zondervan, 2010.

> This book examines the question of the timing of the Rapture from three premillennial positions by three evangelical scholars. It covers much of the same territory that Archer, Feinberg, and Moo's 1984 book, *The Rapture: Pre-, Mid-, or Post- Tribulational? Contemporary Evangelical Perspectives*, did, but with a fresh appraisal due to the recent prominence of the Pre-Wrath (mid-tribulational) view. The introduction gives a historical overview of the doctrine of the Rapture. The counterpoint format allows for robust clash of contributors allowing readers to understand each position as well as each one's strengths and weaknesses.

!*Clouse, Robert G., ed. *The Meaning of the Millennium: Four Views.* Downers Grove: IVP, 1977.

> This book examines the three major views on the millennium (historic premillennialism, amillennialism, and postmillennialism), as well as dispensational premillennialism, in point and counterpoint format. The format allows for a clear presentation of each view as well as robust debate. Very helpful!

!Feinberg, Charles L. *Millennialism: The Two Major Views.* Third edition. Chicago: Moody, 1980.

> The author, a dispensational premillennialist, examines and compares the Premillennial and Amillennial systems of eschatology. A major weakness of the book is that it does not consider either historic premillennialism or the postmillennial position.

!*Hoekema, Anthony A. *The Bible and the Future.* Grand Rapids: Eerdmans, 1979.

> This is the best work available on the Amillennial position of eschatology. It is scholarly, comprehensive, thorough, and convincing. Hoekema argues that the coming of God's kingdom is both present and future. He structures his book into two major sections: inaugurated eschatology (the "already") and future eschatology (the "not yet"). I have read this book twice and it is to me the best work of this kind on the subject. Highly recommended! "A scholarly reconstruction of the history of eschatology with a deft application of biblical teaching to future events" (Barber). Amillennial.

Hoyt, Herman A. *The End Times.* Chicago: Moody, 1969.

> An older work from a dispensational premillennial perspective.

!*Ladd, George Eldon. *The Blessed Hope: A Biblical Study of the Second Advent and the Rapture*. Grand Rapids: Eerdmans, 1956.

> George Eldon Ladd was one of the foremost evangelical New Testament scholars of the twentieth century. In this user-friendly book, he examines the premillennial position and concludes that the Rapture of the Church will be after the tribulation period. This is a classic apologetic for that position easily accessible to both scholar and layperson.

Pentecost, J. Dwight. *Things to Come: A Study in Biblical Eschatology*. Grand Rapids: Zondervan, 1958.

> A defense of dispensational premillennialism by a distinguished professor emeritus of Bible exposition at Dallas Theological Seminary. "An exhaustive, well-outlined, clear, comprehensive presentation of premillennial eschatology" (Barber, 223).

Walvoord, John F. *The Millennial Kingdom*. Grand Rapids: Zondervan, 1959.

> This book is a defense of the dispensational premillennial view by one of its leading proponents. John F. Walvoord was, until his death, president of Dallas Theological Seminary. "An exceptionally fine, Biblical evaluation of the various schools of thought" (Barber, 226). Premillennial. Dispensational.

Wood, Leon J. *The Bible and Future Events: An Introductory Survey of Last-Day Events*. Grand Rapids: Zondervan Academie Books, 1973.

> As the title indicates, this book is an introductory treatment and is not meant to be comprehensive in its scope. It is helpful in that it surveys the major themes in eschatology from a premillennial perspective. "An overview of God's prophetic program. Significant because it deals with eschatology from the viewpoint of a Semitics scholar. Provides an entirely new perspective on many old, timeworn themes" (Barber). Premillennial.

PROVIDENCE

"Providence" is one of those doctrines, like "The Trinity," for which there is no word occurring in Scripture, but which can be inferred throughout its pages. It may be defined as God's guardianship and care for his creation and creatures.

!*Berkouwer, G. C. *The Providence of God*. Studies in Dogmatics. Grand Rapids: Eerdmans, 1952.

> This volume is a brilliant treatment of the subject. Berkouwer begins with a discussion of the issues surrounding the doctrine up until the middle of the twentieth century. He then discusses his topic in relation to knowledge, sustenance, government, concurrence, history, and miracles. He concludes with a discussion of the problem of theodicy. Reformed.

+*Flavel, John. *The Mystery of Providence*. Reprint, London: Banner of Truth, 1963.

> First published in 1678, this classic Puritan work is the standard treatment of the subject. Like most Puritan writings, reading this book can be tedious, but mining its riches is worth the effort. A real jewel!

REVELATION AND INSPIRATION

There are two types of revelation described in the Bible: general revelation and special revelation. Essentially, revelation means the disclosure of what is unknown. General, or natural, revelation relates what can be understood innately (eg. conscience) or externally through nature. Special revelation, on the other hand, refers to God's disclosure of himself in miraculous ways, primarily through the Bible.

When theologians talk about the inspiration of Scripture, they do not mean that it is inspiring, but that it is "God-breathed" (*theopneustos*, 2 Tim. 3:16). It is a product of the Holy Spirit, not man. The Holy Spirit is the operative power in the creation of Scripture.

!*Berkouwer, G. C. *General Revelation*. Studies in Dogmatics. Grand Rapids: Eerdmans, 1955.

> A seminal study of the extent and meaning of general revelation and what man's responsibility is. Reformed.

!*Blomberg, Craig L. *Can We Still Believe the Bible? An Evangelical Engagement with Contemporary Questions*. Grand Rapids: Brazos Press, 2014.

> This book is a robust defense of the authority of Scripture. Blomberg competently answers the attacks of critics such as Bart Ehrman. He deals with such issues as copies of the text, criteria for selection into the Canon, the reliability of Bible translations, inerrancy, the historicity of biblical narratives, and miracles. Readable and compelling!

Custer, Stewart. *Does Inspiration Demand Inerrancy? A Study of the Biblical Doctrine of Inspiration in the Light of Inerrancy*. Nutley, NJ: The Craig Press, 1968.

> This book is a brief study of the doctrine of inspiration in light of the claims of biblical inerrancy. Particularly helpful for laypersons.

!*Nicole, Roger R., and J. Ramsey Michaels, eds. *Inerrancy and Common Sense*. Grand Rapids: Baker, 1980.

> This book and its contributors are committed to the inerrancy of Scripture as both a biblical doctrine and as the historic view of the Christian church. In addition to the editors, each of whom contributes an article, contributors include John Jefferson Davis, Gordon Fee, Richard Lovelace, James I. Packer, R. C. Sproul, and Douglas Stuart. In this book, the issues are clarified, the battle lines drawn, and the doctrine robustly defended.

SACRAMENTS: BAPTISM

!*Berkouwer, G. C. *The Sacraments.* Studies in Dogmatics. Translated by Hugo Bekker. Grand Rapids: Eerdmans, 1969.

> A brilliant overview of the Sacraments, Baptism and the Lord's Supper, from a Reformed perspective. The author also offers a critique of the Roman Catholic and Lutheran views.

*Bromiley, Geoffrey W. *Children of Promise: The Case for Baptizing Infants.* Grand Rapids: Eerdmans, 1979.

> This helpful volume presents the biblical understanding for infant baptism. A strong apologetic for the practice of infant baptism!

+*Chaney, James M. *William the Baptist.* Reprint, Grand Rapids: Baker, 1982.

> First published in 1877 as an official Southern Presbyterian publication, this helpful volume makes a compelling case in dialogue form for the practice of infant baptism. Excellent for laypersons! Reformed.

!*Jewett, Paul K. *Infant Baptism and the Covenant of Grace.* Grand Rapids: Eerdmans, 1978.

> This volume attempts to demonstrate the logical inconsistency of equating circumcision in the Old Testament with baptism in the New Testament. Jewett rejects the traditional Reformed argument for baptizing infants.

*McKnight, Scot. *It Takes A Church to Baptize: What the Bible Says About Infant Baptism.* Grand Rapids: BrazosPress, 2018.

> In a conversational and easily readable style, the author makes a compelling case for infant baptism. Although he writes from an Anglican perspective, readers from all theological traditions will appreciate his careful arguments, which range from biblical data to historical theology. I thoroughly enjoyed

reading it and wished it had been available forty years prior when I was preparing for Presbyterian ordination.

!+*Murray, John. *Christian Baptism.* Phillipsburg: Presbyterian and Reformed, 1980.

> In this brief volume (ninety pages), Murray presents a brilliant scholarly apologetic for infant baptism and a refutation of immersion as the mode of baptism. Reformed.

*Sartelle, John P. *What Christian Parents Should Know About Infant Baptism.* Phillipsburg: Presbyterian and Reformed, 1985.

> This brief pamphlet is an excellent handout for Reformed pastors to give their congregants. It informs parents in a readable, easy-to-understand format why they should have their infants baptized. Reformed.

!*Schreiner, Thomas R., and Shawn D. Wright, eds. *Believer's Baptism: Sign of the New Covenant in Christ.* New American Commentary Studies in Bible and Theology. Edited by E. Ray Clendenen. Nashville: B & H Academic, 2007.

> The author, a Southern Baptist professor of NT at Southern Baptist Theological Seminary in Louisville, KY, makes a good case for believer's baptism. Schreiner lays a solid biblical and theological foundation for this doctrine. Baptist.

SACRAMENTS: THE LORD'S SUPPER

*Smith, Gordon T., ed. *The Lord's Supper: Five Views.* Downers Grove: IVP Academic, 2008.

> The simple meal that Christ instituted to help unite believers has for centuries left them hopelessly divided. In this helpful and illuminating book, five scholars outline their views on the Lord's Supper with responses from each of the other four scholars. The responses are irenic rather than confrontational.

The views represented are Roman Catholic, Lutheran, Reformed, Baptist, and Pentecostal.

SALVATION

The term "salvation" is a biblical one and describes the saving of people from the power and effects of sin. The technical theological term for the study of salvation is soteriology (from the Greek word *soter*=save). "'Salvation' is the most widely used term in Christian theology to express the provision of God for our human plight" (*New Dictionary of Theology*, 610). The term covers a lot of ground and many topics come under its wide canopy. Theologians often speak of the *ordo salutis* (Latin for "order of salvation") to discuss the different elements of salvation and how they are related to one another. It also seeks to establish a pattern of Christian experience common to all believers. According to the Reformed understanding, the order of salvation (how it is applied), at least according to John Murray (see *Redemption Accomplished and Applied*), is effectual calling, regeneration, faith and repentance, justification, adoption, sanctification, perseverance, union with Christ, and glorification.

!*Edwards, James R. *Is Jesus the Only Savior?* Grand Rapids: Eerdmans, 2005.

> "The author, professor of biblical languages and literature at Whitworth College in Spokane, WA, is an ordained Presbyterian minister who has also served as a contributing editor of *Christianity Today*. In this book, he responds to both scholarly and popular attacks on the Christian doctrine of salvation in and through Jesus Christ alone. Edwards reviews the foundations of this belief, including the historical reliability of the NT witness notwithstanding critics such as the Jesus Seminar. Especially helpful is the discussion of competing first century world views: Jewish Torah, the Roman imperial cult, and Greek mystery religions. Edwards also examines more recent cultural perceptions that the gospel is intolerant and exclusive and therefore cannot be true. Sensitive questions about other religions, including Judaism, are handled fairly and reasonably, and mysteries such as the Incarnation are explored with

intellectual humility. All in all, a stimulating read and valuable resource" (**Brafford**).

Pink, Arthur Walkington. *The Doctrine of Salvation*. Grand Rapids: Baker, 1975.

An easy-to-read exposition of the doctrines of salvation. Reformed.

!*Sproul, R. C. *Willing to Believe: The Controversy over Free Will*. Grand Rapids: Baker, 1997.

This book is a popular examination of the Protestant doctrines of man's total depravity and God's effectual grace from a biblical perspective. Sproul traces the controversy over the doctrine of free will from the Augustine-Pelagius debate to the end of the twentieth century. The author is always engaging and easy to read. Reformed.

SANCTIFICATION

Sanctification is a theological term that indicates the believer's ongoing walk with Jesus Christ in which he continually conforms to his savior. Literally it means "to be set apart" and describes the process of becoming more and more like Christ through the daily ministry of the Holy Spirit. Sanctification begins with justification and ends with glorification.

Baxter, J. Sidlow. *Christian Holiness: Restudied and Restated*. Grand Rapids: Zondervan, 1977.

This volume is a compilation of the author's three earlier books, *A New Call to Holiness, His Deeper Work in Us,* and *Our High Calling,* all published in 1967. It is a careful study of the doctrine of sanctification that is ideal for the layperson. In an engaging and warm style, the author traces and refutes different theories of holiness, and then goes on to offer his own view of sanctification.

!*Berkouwer, G. C. *Faith and Sanctification.* Studies in Dogmatics. Translated by John Vriend. Grand Rapids: Eerdmans, 1952.

> This study is an excellent treatment of the doctrine of sanctification and its relationship to theology and Christian living. Of particular interest is the final chapter, "Sanctification and Law." Reformed.

!*Dieter, Melvin, et. al. *Five Views on Sanctification.* Counterpoints: Bible and Theology. Revised edition. Grand Rapids: Zondervan, 1996.

> Confused by the debate over Calvinism and Arminianism? This helpful volume presents in the popular Counterpoints format five views on this important doctrine. The five contributors and their respective views are: Melvin E. Dieter, "The Wesleyan View"; Anthony A. Hoekema, "The Reformed View"; Stanley M. Horton, "The Pentecostal View"; J. Robertson McQuilkin, "The Keswick View"; and John F. Walvoord, "The Augustinian-Dispensational View."

*Piper, John. *What Jesus Demands from the World.* Wheaton: Crossway, 2006.

> The Christian life does not end with a "decision" for Jesus Christ. Some churches act as if conversion is the "end-all-and-be-all" and then rarely move their converts beyond that stage. While conversion and justification are wonderful theological concepts, the Christian life is much more than that. It is a demand to acknowledge the Lordship of Christ, a clarion call for supreme loyalty to the King of Kings. This book, by the former Pastor for Preaching and Vision at Bethlehem Baptist Church and currently chancellor of Bethlehem College & Seminary both in Minneapolis, demonstrates, in the words of Jesus, just what our Lord expects from believers in everyday life.

*Sproul, R. C. *Pleasing God.* Wheaton, IL: Tyndale, 1988.

> This study is a penetrating look at the doctrine of sanctification written for the layperson. As always, Sproul's prose is engaging and straightforward. Reformed.

SOVEREIGNTY OF GOD

This term is another one, like the Trinity, that does not occur in Scripture, but describes what can clearly be seen on every page of the Bible. It describes the biblical teaching that God is the true sovereign and supreme ruler of the universe. The teaching of the sovereignty of God answers the question of who is in charge on this planet, God or Satan. God is in control of the world from the machinations of nations and empires to the smallest bird falling in the forest.

*Pink, Arthur W. *The Sovereignty of God.* Swengel, PA: I. C. Herendeen, 1930; Reprint, Grand Rapids: Baker, 1984.

> A satisfying and user-friendly guide to a difficult scriptural doctrine. "Handles the intricacies of the doctrine with the skill of an accomplished theologian" (Barber, 204).

Bibliography

Barber, Cyril J. *The Minister's Library*. Grand Rapids, MI: Baker, 1974.
_____. *The Minister's Library: Periodic Supplement #1*. Grand Rapids: Baker, 1976.
_____. *The Minister's Library: Periodic Supplement #2*. Grand Rapids: Baker, 1978.
_____. *The Minister's Library: Periodic Supplement #3*. Grand Rapids: Baker, 1980.
Bauer, David R. *Essential Bible Study Tools for Ministry*. Nashville: Abingdon Press, 2014.
Branson, Mark Lau. *The Reader's Guide to the Best Evangelical Books*. San Francisco: Harper & Row, 1982.
Carson, D. A. *New Testament Commentary Survey*. Seventh edition. Grand Rapids: Baker Academic, 2013.
Danker, Frederick W. *Multipurpose Tools for Bible Study*. Third edition. St. Louis: Concordia, 1970.
Elwell, Walter A., Editor. *Evangelical Dictionary of Theology*. Grand Rapids: Baker Book House, 1984.
Evans, John F. *A Guide to Biblical Commentaries and Reference Works*. 10th edition. Grand Rapids: Zondervan, 2016.
Ferguson, Sinclair B., and David F. Wright, eds. *New Dictionary of Theology*. Downers Grove: IVP, 1988.
Glynn, John. *Commentary & Reference Survey: A Comprehensive Guide to Biblical and Theological Resources*. Tenth edition. Grand Rapids: Kregel Academic & Professional, 2007.
Longman III, Tremper. *Old Testament Commentary Survey*. Fifth edition. Grand Rapids: Baker Academic, 2013.
Petersen, William J., and Randy Petersen. *100 Christian Books That Changed the Century*. Grand Rapids: Fleming H. Revell, 2000.
Rosscup, James. *Commentaries for Biblical Expositors*. Sun Valley, CA: Grace Books International, 2004.
Spurgeon, C. H. *Commenting & Commentaries*. London: Banner of Truth, 1876; Reprint ed., London: Banner of Truth, 1969.
Wiersbe, Warren W. *Listening to the Giants*. Grand Rapids: Baker, 1980.
_____. *Walking with the Giants*. Grand Rapids: Baker, 1976.
Yost, Robert A. *The Pastor's Library: An Annotated Bibliography of Biblical and Theological Resources for Ministry*. Eugene, OR: Wipf & Stock, 2017.

Author Index

Adamson, James B., 135
Adeney, Walter F., 70, 71
Aharoni, Yohanan, 13
Akin, Daniel L., 141
Alden, Robert L., 77
Alexander, David, 20
Alexander, Pat, 20
Alexander, T. Desmond, 90, 91
Andersen, Francis I., 73
Andrews, Samuel J., 264
Arana, Nikki, 169
Archer, G. Jr., 273
Arnold, Bill T., 27, 66
Arnold, Clinton E., 97
Arp, Claudia, 204
Arp, Dave, 204
Arthur, Kay, 205
Atkinson, David, 65
Augustine, Aurelius, 155, 261
Avi-Yonah, Michael, 13

Bacon, Ernest W., 155
Baillie, John, 218
Bainton, Roland, 5, 156
Baker, David W., 51, 89, 90, 91, 92, 93, 94
Baldwin, Joyce G., 66, 72, 85, 93, 94
Balswick, Jack O., 205
Balswick, Judith K., 205
Barber, Cyril, 3, 8, 65
Barclay, William, 95
Barker, Kenneth L., 34, 50

Barna, George, 201
Barnhouse, Donald Grey, 110, 236
Barton, Ruth Haley, 229
Battles, Ford Lewis, 248
Bauer, David R., 8
Baxter, J. Sidlow, 281
Beale, G. K., 126
Beck, John A., 13
Beilby, James K., 259
Beitzel, Barry J., 13
Benner, David, 223
Bennett, Kyle David, 229
Bergen, Robert D., 66
Berkouwer, G. C., 264, 265, 271, 273, 276, 277, 278, 282
Berry, William S., 218
Bickersteth, Edward Henry, 262
Blackwood, Andrew W., 189
Blaikie, W. Garden, 66, 67, 149, 150
Blaising, Craig A., 273
Block, Daniel I., 61
Bloem, Steve, 197
Bloesch, Donald G., 255
Blomberg, Craig L., 97, 98, 114, 277
Blum, Ed, 35
Boa, Kenneth D., 201, 223
Bock, Darrell, 102
Boda, Mark J., 93, 94
Boettner, Loraine, 255
Boice, James Montgomery, 110, 121, 141, 150, 250
Bonar, Andrew, 60

AUTHOR INDEX

Bonhoeffer, Dietrich, 198
Bounds, Edward McKendrie, 218
Bowman, Robert M., 201
Bradbury, Ray, 1
Brand, Chad, 18
Brandt, Henry R, 205
Branson, Mark Lau, 8
Breneman, Mervin, 70, 71, 72
Bright, John, 27
Brisco, Thomas V., 14
Broadus, John A., 190
Bromiley, Geoffrey W., 278
Brooks, Geraldine, 169
Brooks, Phillips, 190
Brown, John, 117, 132, 138
Brown, Sharon Garlough, 169
Brown, Walt, 54
Bruce, A. B., 198
Bruce, F. F., 10, 28, 103, 106, 108, 111, 122, 133
Bruckner, James K., 91, 92, 93
Bullock, C. Hassell, 73, 81
Bunyan, John, 169
Burge, Gary M., 104, 141
Butler, Alban, 156

Calvin, John, 47, 120, 248
Campbell, Constantine R., 142
Campbell, Donald K., 71
Carey, George, 256
Carey, Phillip, 231
Carr, G. Lloyd, 80,
Carson, D. A., 3, 8, 34, 96, 104, 195
Carson, Herbert M., 232
Chafer, Lewis Sperry, 250, 269
Chambers, Oswald, 195, 229
Chan, Sam, 202
Chaney, James M., 278
Chapman, Gary D., 206
Chappell, Bryan, 129, 232
Charnock, Stephen, 263
Chaucer, Geoffrey, 23
Chesterton, G. K., 170
Chisholm, Robert B., 67
Ciampa, Roy E., 114
Clarke, Adam, 47
Clendenen, E. Ray, 49
Cloud, Henry, 207

Clouse, Robert G., 274
Clowney, Edmund P., 58, 138
Cockerill, Gareth Lee, 133
Cohen, Gary G., 145
Cohick, Lynn H., 122
Cole, R. Alan, 57, 60, 100, 117
Coleman, Robert, 199
Collins, Gary R., 184
Collins, Francis S., 237
Colson, Charles, 156
Colson, Christine A., 184
Conway, Jim, 207
Coppes, Leonard J., 248
Cowman, L. B., 195
Crabb, Larry, 223
Craigie, Peter C., 86
Crouch, Andy, 207
Cruden, Alexander, 15
Cundall, Arthur E., 64, 65
Custer, Stewart, 277

Dalimore, Arnold A., 156
Danker, Frederick W., 8
Dante, Alighieri, 171
Davids, Peter H., 138, 140, 143
Davidman, Joy, 58
Davis, John Jefferson, 53, 57, 63, 64, 65, 67, 68, 257
DeHaan, Richard W., 78, 236
Dearman, J. Andrew, 88
Demarest, Bruce, 224
DeSilva, David A., 118
Dewey, David, 24
DeYoung, Kevin, 58
Dickason, C. Fred, 236
Dickson, David, 75
Dieter, Melvin, 282
Dobson, James, 207
Dobson, Kent, 33
Dongell, Joseph R., 249
Dorr, Lawrence, 171
Dostoevsky, Fyodor, 171, 172,
Douglas, J. D., 18, 253
Douglas, Lloyd C., 172
Downs, Tim, 202
Duguid, Iain, 83
Dunning, H. Ray, 248
Duthrie, Alan S., 24,

Duvall, J. Scott, 20

Eareckson, Joni, 157
Early, Joseph Jr., 253
Eaton, Michael A., 78
Eddy, Paul Rhodes, 259
Edersheim, Alfred, 150
Edwards, James R., 100, 102, 280
Edwards, Jonathan, 157
Eggerichs, Emerson, 208
Eims, LeRoy, 199
Eldredge, John, 219
Elliot, Elisabeth, 215
Elwell, Walter A., 253
Endicott, Irene, 208
English, E. Schuyler, 133
Enns, Peter E., 57
Erdman, Charles R., 102, 104, 106
Erickson, Millard J., 262, 265
Estes, Daniel J., 79
Evans, C. Stephen, 238
Evans, John F., 3, 8
Evans, Tony, 267

Fabry, Chris, 172
Fairbairn, Patrick, 84, 91
Farrar, Frederic W., 265
Fee, Gordon D., 114, 122, 126, 243
Feinberg, Charles Lee, 84, 87, 274
Feinberg, P. D., 273
Fensham, F. Charles, 70, 71
Ferguson, Sinclair B., 267, 269
Fernando, Ajith, 106
Flavel, John, 276
Fleming, Bill Owen Jr., 219
Forbush, William Byron, 254
Ford, Paul F., 224
Foster, Richard J., 219, 220, 229, 230
Foster, Rupert Clinton, 265
France, Richard T., 98
Fredericks, Daniel C., 79, 80
Freedman, David Noel, 18
Friessen, Gary, 231
Fung, Ronald Y. K., 118

Gaebelein, Frank E., 90, 91, 92, 93
Gane, Roy, 60, 61

Garland, David E., 47, 101, 116, 125, 131
Garrett, Duane A., 77, 79, 80, 88, 89
Geiger, Eric, 200
Geisler, Norman, 11, 238
George, Timothy, 118
Getz, Gene A., 122, 128, 150
Gibson, Shimon, 11
Gill, David W., 150
Gish, Duane T., 54
Glickman, S. Craig, 80
Glynn, John, 8
Goldingay, John, 245
Graham, Billy, 157, 236, 268
Graham, Franklin, 158
Greathouse, William M., 248
Green, Gene, 127
Green, Joel B., 102
Gromacki, Robert G., 118
Grubbs, F. Michael, 184
Grudem, Wayne, 139, 259, 260
Guiness, Os, 185
Gurnall, William, 236,
Guthrie, Donald, 129
Guthrie, George, 134

Hafemann, Scott J., 116
Haig, Matt, 197
Hailey, Homer, 87
Halley, Henry H., 20
Hamilton, James, 151
Hamilton, Victor P., 62
Hannah, John D., 254
Harmon, Rebecca Lamar, 158
Harper, Steve, 249
Harrison, Everett F., 106, 125
Harrison, R. K., 19, 50, 51, 60, 82, 83, 258
Hassey, Janette, 259
Hays, Daniel, 20
Hedlund, Jody, 172
Henderson, E. Harold, 92
Hendriksen, William, 96, 102, 119
Henry, Matthew, 48
Hewitt, Thomas, 134
Hiebert, D. Edmond, 97, 101, 108, 127, 132, 136, 139
Hill, Andrew E., 69

AUTHOR INDEX

Hill, Jonathan, 254
Hillenbrand, Laura, 158
Hoekema, Anthony A., 274
Holden, Joseph M., 11
Holmes, Michael W., 127
House, H. Wayne, 12
House, Paul, 68
Howard, David M. Jr., 62, 63
Howard, Jeremy Royal, 35
Hoyt, Herman A., 274
Hubbard, David Allan, 88, 89, 90
Hubbard, R. L., 51, 63
Hudson, Trevor, 224
Hughes, Philip Edgcumbe, 11
Hughes, R. Kent, 129
Hugo, Victor, 173
Hunt, Dave, 249
Hurnard, Hannah, 173
Huxley, Aldous, 1
Hybels, Bill, 208
Hybels, Lynne, 208

Issler, Klaus, 166

Jacobs, Alan, 159
James, Katherine, 173
James, Steven, 173
Jeremiah, David, 220, 232
Jewett, Paul K., 278
Jobes, Karen, 72, 132
Johns, Loren L., 45
Johnstone, Robert, 123
Jones, E. Stanley, 215
Josephus, Flavius, 28

Kaiser, Walter C. Jr., 28, 32
Karon, Jan, 173, 174
Keener, Craig S., 32, 145
Keller, Timothy, 119, 209, 238, 239
Kelly, William, 103
Kelso, Don, 76
Kempis, Thomas á, 166
Kennedy, D. James, 202, 251
Kent, Homer A. Jr., 120, 129, 134
Kenyon, Kathleen M., 11
Kessler, Jay, 209
Kidd, Reggie, 233
Kidner, Derek, 53, 71, 75, 77

Kimmel, Tim, 209
Kingsbury, Karen, 174
Kirk, Thomas, 151
Kistemaker, Simon, 96, 106, 115, 139, 140, 143, 145
Kohlenberger, John III, 15, 17, 50
Konkel, August H., 68
Köstenberger, Andreas J., 259
Kruse, Colin, 111, 116, 142
Kuiper, R. B., 242

Ladd, George Eldon, 275
Laetsch, Theo, 87
LaHaye, Beverly, 209
LaHaye, Tim, 209
Lalleman, Hetty, 83
Lammerts, Walter E., 55
Lane, Anthony N. S., 249
Lane, William L., 101
Larimore, Walt, 203
Lawrence, Brother, 225
Lawrence, Paul, 14
Lawson, Steven J., 74
Lee, Tosca, 174
L'Engle, Madeleine, 174
Lennox, John C., 55
Lewis, C. S., 175, 239
Liefeld, Walter L., 129, 261
Lindsell, Harold, 185
Littell, Franklin H., 14
Little, Paul, 202, 239
Lloyd-Jones, D. Martyn, 99, 140, 190, 197, 268
Lockyer, Herbert, 151
Long, Kathryn, 216
Longenecker, Bruce W., 109
Longman, Tremper III, 3, 8, 18, 47, 49, 77, 79, 80, 85
Lucado, Max, 270
Lucas, R. C., 125, 131
Luther, Martin, 190

MacArthur, John, 32, 96, 143, 151, 152, 233
MacDonald, Gordon, 225
MacDuff, John Ross, 153
Machen, John Gresham, 265
Maclaren, Alexander, 191

Manton, Thomas, 144
Marshall, Catherine, 159, 176
Marshall, I. Howard, 107, 142
Marshall, Michael, 159
Marshall, Peter, 191
Martin, Charles, 176
Martin, D. Michael, 127
Martin, Hugh, 91
Martin, Ralph P., 123
Martin, Walter R., 256
Mather, George A., 256
Matthews, Victor H., 21
Mazzarella, Nicole, 176
McConnell, Douglas, 216
McCracken, Brett, 185
McDowell, Josh, 210, 239, 240
McDowell, Sean, 239
McGee, J. Vernon, 50
McGrath, Alister, 159
McKnight, Scot, 49, 99, 119, 131, 136, 243, 278
McMinn, Mark R., 186
McQuilkin, Robertson, 244
Mears, Henrietta, 20
Mehl, Ron, 210
Meissner, Susan, 176
Melick, Richard R., 123, 125, 131
Merrill, Eugene H., 62
Meyer, F. B., 57, 153, 192
Michaels, J. Ramsey, 277
Miller, Douglas B., 45
Miller, Keith, 166
Miller, Walter M. Jr., 177
Milton, John, 177
Mitchell, Eric, 18
Mohler, R. Albert Jr., 59
Moo, Douglas, 111, 112, 125, 131, 136, 141, 144, 273
Moore, Russell, 210
Moore, Thomas V., 94
Moore, Waylon B., 203
Moreau, A. Scott, 216
Morgan, G. Campbell, 88, 103, 107, 115, 192, 266
Morison, Frank, 240
Morris, Henry M., 55
Morris, Leon, 64, 98, 103, 105, 127, 128

Morris, Michael, 177
Motyer, J. A., 46, 81, 89, 137
Moule, H. C. G., 120, 124, 125, 129
Mounce, Robert, 146
Mounce, William D., 16, 29
Muck, Terry, 49
Murray, Andrew, 220, 221
Murray, John, 112, 242, 278
Murray, Kitti, 199
Musser, Joe, 157

Negev, Avraham, 11
Newell, William R., 146
Newton, John, 160
Nicole, Roger R., 277
Nichols, Larry A., 256
Nichols, Linda, 177
Notley, R. Steven, 13
Nystrom, David P., 137

O'Brien, Peter T., 121, 135
Ortberg, John, 186
Ortlund, Ray, 210
Orwell, George, 1
Oswalt, John N., 82
Owen, J. Glyn, 153
Owen, John, 262, 266, 268
Owens, Virginia Stem, 186

Packer, J. I., 59, 186, 203, 225, 263
Palmer, Earl F., 100, 103
Parrish, Christa, 178
Patterson, Paige, 146
Payne, J. Barton, 246
Peel, William Carr, 203
Penner, Clifford, 211
Penner, Joyce, 211
Pentecost, J. Dwight, 275
Peretti, Frank, 178
Petersen, J. Allan, 211
Peterson, David G., 107
Peterson, Eugene, 25, 186, 226
Petterson, Anthony R., 93, 94
Pfeiffer, Charles F., 14, 50
Phillips, John, 146
Pink, Arthur Walkington, 58, 63, 153, 154, 226, 262, 263, 281, 283
Piper, John, 187, 196, 199, 260, 282

Pippert. Rebecca Manley, 204
Pocock, Michael, 216
Pohill, John B., 107
Pollock, John, 160
Poole, Matthew, 48
Pope, Randy, 199
Pratt, Richard L. Jr., 221,
Price, Randall, 11, 12
Prior, David, 115
Provan, Iain, 79, 80

Rainey, Anson F., 13
Rainer, Thomas, 200
Rainey, Barbara, 211
Rainey, Dennis, 211
Ramsay, William M., 109, 147
Redpath, Alan, 115, 154
Reeves, Michael, 262
Reiter, R. R., 273
Rhodes, Ron, 256
Rice, Anne, 178
Ridenour, Fritz, 257
Rivers, Francine, 178
Robertson, Archibald Thomas, 30, 124
Robertson, O. Palmer, 246
Robinson, Marilynne, 178
Roe, Earl O., 160
Rosberg, Barb, 212
Rosberg, Gary, 212
Rosenberg, Joel, 179
Rosner, Brian S., 114
Rosscup, James, 3, 8
Rydelnik, Michael, 48
Ryken, Philip Graham, 59
Ryrie, Charles, 31, 226, 260, 268

Safrai, Ze'ev, 13
Samson, Lisa, 179
Sartelle, John P., 279
Sayers, Dorothy, 179
Scazzero, Peter, 226
Schaap, James Calvin, 179
Schaeffer, Edith, 161. 187, 212
Schaeffer, Francis A., 227, 251
Schmidt, Alvin J., 256
Schnabel, Eckhard, 97, 101
Scholer, David M., 8

Schreiner, Thomas R., 109, 139, 141, 144, 246, 259, 279
Scroggie, W. Graham, 76, 98
Seifrid, Mark A., 117
Selderhuis, Herman, 162
Selman, Martin J., 69
Shakespeare, William, 23
Shannon, Ellen C., 4, 251
Sheldon, Charles, 179
Shelley, Bruce L., 254
Shepard, Valerie, 162
Shirer, Priscilla, 221
Short, Robert L., 187
Sider, Ronald J., 187
Silva, Moises, 18
Singer, Randy, 180
Skinner, Kerry L., 205
Smalley, Gary, 212
Smeaton, George, 268
Smith, Gary V., 88, 90, 91
Smith, Gordon T., 279
Smith, J. B., 147
Smith, James K., 227
Smither, Edward, 216
Smucker, Shawn, 180
Snodgrass, Klyne, 121
Solganick, Harvey, 162
Solzhenitsyn, Aleksandr, 162
Sprinkle, Preston, 260, 261
Sproul, R. C., 112, 180, 213, 221, 244, 258, 264, 270, 271, 281, 282
Spurgeon, Charles H., 3, 7, 76, 192, 196, 269
Stalker, James, 110, 266
Stanley, Charles F., 32, 163
Stearns, Amy, 217
Stearns, Bill, 217
Stedman, Ray C., 73
Stein, Robert H., 244
Stern, David H., 95
Stewart, James S., 193
Stier, Rudolf, 137
Stifler, James M., 112
Still, Todd D., 109
Stott, John R. W., 46, 100, 121, 128, 130, 143, 147, 266
Strauss, Mark L., 50
Strawn, Brent A., 27

Strobel, Lee, 204, 240, 270
Strong, James, 16
Stuart, Douglas K., 58, 243
Sunquist, Scott W., 217
Sweeting, George, 167
Swindoll, Charles R., 72, 154, 167, 187, 213, 227, 251

Tasker, R. V. G., 137
Tatford, Frederick Albert, 87
Taylor, Daniel, 180
Taylor, Frederick Howard, 217
Taylor, G., 217
Taylor, John B., 84
Taylor, Kenneth, 25
Taylor, Thomas, 130
Ten Boom, Corrie, 163
Ten Elshof, Gregg A., 188
Tenney, Merrill C., 18, 119
Thielman, Frank, 124, 246
Thiselton, Anthony C., 252
Thoene, Bodie, 180, 181
Thoene, Brock, 181
Thomas, Gar, 227
Thomas, W. H. Griffith, 113, 135
Thompson, J. A., 12, 69, 83
Tolkien, J. R. R., 181, 182
Torrey, R. A., 221
Towner, Phillip H., 130
Tozer, A. W., 193, 228, 233, 264
Treat, Jeremy R., 243
Treier, Daniel J., 253
Trent, John, 212
Tripp, Paul David, 213
Tucker, Ruth A., 261,
Turner, Jamie Langston, 183
Tuttle, Robert G., 249

Unger, Merrill F., 12, 19, 21, 237

Vanauken, Sheldon, 164
Vanlaningham, Michael, 48
Van Rheenen, Gailyn, 216
Vine, W. E., 19, 30
Virkler, Henry A., 244
Vos, Howard F., 255

Wacker, Grant, 164

Wallace, J. Warner, 240, 241
Walls, Jerry L., 249
Waltke, Bruce K., 78, 90, 91, 247
Walton, John H., 32, 50, 52, 53, 56, 74
Walvoord, John F., 85, 148, 267, 269, 275
Wangerin, Walter Jr., 183
Wardlaw, Ralph, 79
Ware, Bruce A., 263
Ware, James P., 110
Warren, Rick, 204
Warren, Tish Harrison, 228
Waterhouse, Steven, 213
Watson, Thomas, 59
Webb, Barry G., 82
Webber, Robert, 233
Wegner, Paul D., 28
Wenham, Gordon J., 51, 61
Westfall, Cynthia Long, 261
Whitcomb, John C., 68, 70
White, James, 249
White, Jerry, 214
White, John, 188, 198, 200, 222
White, Mary, 214
White, William Jr., 19
Whitefield, George, 194
Whitney, Donald S., 230
Whyte, Alexander, 5, 154, 222, 267
Wiersbe, Warren W., 46, 54, 58, 60, 61, 62, 64, 66, 68, 69, 70, 71, 72, 73, 74, 76, 78, 80, 82, 83, 84, 86, 89, 90, 92, 94, 99, 101, 103, 104, 105, 108, 113, 116, 117, 119, 121, 124, 126, 128, 130, 131, 135, 138, 140, 141, 143, 144, 148, 194, 196
Wigger, John, 164
Wight, Fred H., 22
Wilkerson, David, 164
Wilkins, Michael J., 99
Willard, Dallas, 5, 200, 201, 228, 230, 232
Wilson, Bill, 240
Wilson, Douglas, 183
Wilson, Jonathan R., 234
Winner, Lauren, 165, 189
Wiseman, D. J., 52
Witherington, Ben III, 241,

Wolf, Herbert, 52
Wolfe, Suzanne M., 184
Wood, Leon J., 29, 64, 81, 86, 270
Woods, Edward J., 62
Woychuk, N. A., 131
Wright, Christopher J. H., 83, 84
Wright, H. Norman, 198, 214
Wright, N. T., 126, 131, 272
Wright, Shawn D. 279
Wright, Vinita Hampton, 184

Yancey, Philip, 189, 222, 270

Yates, John, 215
Yates, Susan, 215
Young, Davis A., 56,
Young, Robert, 16
Young, Sarah, 197
Youngblood, Ronald F., 19
Younger, K. Lawson, 65

Zaleski, Carol, 165
Zaleski, Philip, 165
Zuck, Roy B, 244, 247

www.ingramcontent.com/pod-product-compliance
Lightning Source LLC
Chambersburg PA
CBHW061429300426
44114CB00014B/1604